PRAISE FOR
MODERN POLITICAL CAMPAIGNS:
HOW PROFESSIONALISM, TECHNOLOGY, AND SPEED HAVE
REVOLUTIONIZED ELECTIONS

"Dr. Cohen has long brought his enthusia̲ ̲gns into
board rooms and classrooms alike. This b̲ ̲:dom he
has garnered both as a practitioner and fr̲c ̲·ly
engages to advance the field."

ᴗcıı Berkowitz,
Founder and CEO, Delve DC

"This book is an incredible opportunity and must read for anyone who is interested in how
to run a campaign in the Twenty-First Century. Dr. Cohen is a master at intuitively
explaining all facets of how to run a professional winning campaign."

Garrison Coward,
Former Candidate for Virginia House of Representatives

"There is no better person to address technology and professionalism in campaigns than
Michael Cohen. Michael provides great insight into modern campaigning and this book
will quickly become a must read for political professionals and public policy students
alike. It's a fresh look at a timeless art—winning elections."

Aaron Evans,
Partner, CEO, WRS

"As both an academic researcher and a political professional Michael Cohen effectively
bridges theory and practice. *Modern Political Campaigns* is an important contribution to
the literature on contemporary political strategy."

Shaun P. Herness, Ph.D.,
GOP Political Consultant

"In *Modern Political Campaigns*, Michael Cohen combines his wealth of experience as
both an academic and practitioner to the evolution and future of campaigns. His insights
and examples provide aspiring professionals with a comprehensive understand of how
campaigning has evolved and the future of campaigns. I have witnessed his ability to do
this as a guest lecturer in several of my courses over the years examining the intersection
of entrepreneurship and politics."

Steve Malter,Ph.D.,
Senior Associate Dean of Experimental Learning & Strategic Programs
and Senior Lecturer in Management, Washington University in St. Louis

"For anyone who is looking to work in political campaigns or understand how it really
works, *Modern Political Campaigns* by Michael Cohen is the book to read right now."

Rory McShane,
Principal, McShane, LLC

"Michael Cohen has written a book that is rare in politics. It is both practical and aspira-
tional, concluding that technology innovations are both the cause of division and our
potential salvation. It's a must-read for all political professionals who work to elect candidates and help them move the nation forward once in office."

Bruce Mehlman,
Founder, Mehlman, Castagnetti, Rosen, & Thomas

MORE PRAISE FOR
MODERN POLITICAL CAMPAIGNS: HOW PROFESSIONALISM, TECHNOLOGY, AND SPEED HAVE REVOLUTIONIZED ELECTIONS

"The Obama campaign opting out of public funding in 2008 supercharged the professionalization of politics through the democratization of participation and activation. The combination of more resources and the inability of the traditional gatekeepers to stay current with the world around them, has fundamentally changed how campaigns are waged and won, and a new generation of decision makers has emerged. Dr. Michael Cohen has managed to capture just how much professionalism, technology, and speed have revolutionized elections and the potential implications going forward."

Zac Moffatt,
CEO, Targeted Victory

"'Voters live online . . .' says Michael D. Cohen in *Modern Political Campaigns*. Cohen has written a perceptive, lucid and entertaining account of how political campaigns actually operate, and gives the reader a much more realistic framework for viewing contemporary politics than can be gained from most academic analyses or the conventional wisdom narratives many in the media rely on. Most usefully, he provides an insightful examination of the modern transition from persuasion to turnout strategies in political campaigns, and its impact on the health of our Republic."

Alan Rosenblatt, Ph.D.,
Partner, Unfiltered.Media and Turner4D

"Most books about money in politics take a cynical view that is wrong and makes the system worse. Michael Cohen's refreshingly candid *Modern Political Campaigns* shows the practical side of political fundraising. He demonstrates that it is good business and good politics for fundraisers to retain their ethics while working to provide campaigns the resources they need to compete and win."

Lisa Spies,
President, The LS Group

"A fantastic read to understanding the intricacies of contemporary campaigns. Dr. Cohen's work leaves no stone unturned in tackling the subject with plenty of pragmatic examples, taking readers on a journey of exploration behind the curtain of twenty-first-century campaigns."

Frank Terraferma,
Director of House Campaigns, Republican Party of Florida

"Mike is a 'Mad Political Scientist', his book perfectly captures the never-ending campaign in this digital era."

Jesse Thomas,
CEO & Founder, JESS3

Modern Political Campaigns

How Professionalism, Technology, and Speed Have Revolutionized Elections

Michael D. Cohen

ROWMAN & LITTLEFIELD
Lanham • Boulder • New York • London

Published by Rowman & Littlefield
An imprint of The Rowman & Littlefield Publishing Group, Inc.
4501 Forbes Boulevard, Suite 200, Lanham, Maryland 20706
www.rowman.com

British Library Cataloguing in Publication Information Available

Library of Congress Cataloging-in-Publication Data

Names: Cohen, Michael D., 1970- author.
Title: Modern political campaigns : how professionalism, technology, and speed have revolutionized elections / Michael D. Cohen.
Description: Lanham, Maryland : Rowman & Littlefield, 2021. | Includes bibliographical references and index. | Summary: "Michael D. Cohen, a 20+ year veteran of working on, teaching, and writing about political campaigns, takes readers through how campaigns are organized, the state-of-the-art tools of the trade, and how some of the most interesting people in politics got their big breaks"-- Provided by publisher.
Identifiers: LCCN 2021014383 (print) | LCCN 2021014384 (ebook) | ISBN 9781538153802 (cloth) | ISBN 9781538153796 (paperback) | ISBN 9781538153819 (epub)
Subjects: LCSH: Political campaigns--United States. | Political campaigns--Technological innova-tions--United States. | Campaign management--United States. | Campaign management--Techno-logical innovations--United States.
Classification: LCC JK2281 .C65 2021 (print) | LCC JK2281 (ebook) | DDC 324.70973--dc23
LC record available at https://lccn.loc.gov/2021014383
LC ebook record available at https://lccn.loc.gov/2021014384

To my dear friend H. Christopher Tompkins, II, who should have been the 45th Governor of Florida and the 46th President of the United States of America. He died campaigning for the Florida House of Representatives in 2004, which would have been his first big step along that path.

A portion of the proceeds of this book will be donated in his name to the political campaigning program at the University of Florida, our alma mater, beginning in Spring 2021.

Go Gators, Spud.

Contents

Preface

Most political science programs do not prepare students for modern political campaigns. I should know—I was one of them. In 1988, I began as a political science student at the University of Maryland, where well-intentioned professors took us on a long and winding path through various competing theories of government and politics. Nothing taught me about how political campaigns work or how to win elections. Frustrated, I switched schools and majors, settling on mass communication.

During my time at the University of Florida, I got involved on campus. I ran for office, served in student government, and met incredible people who would go on after graduation to be political leaders and leaders in a host of other endeavors, from education to business. We learned on the job, made mistakes, and got involved in political campaigns while we were students.

As it turns out, that is exactly how the best in the business learned: on campus, then locally, a chance meeting, then a breakthrough. Mine came as a volunteer for a congressional candidate in Gainesville. Within a short period of time he hired me as his communications director. My first candidate, Dave Gentry, won a three-way race for the nomination but lost in the general election because he couldn't raise enough money to compete. But it was an amazing experience: clumsy, goofy, raw, and exhilarating.

Our opponent was Karen Thurman, a well-known, well-liked incumbent, who did just enough to stay out of trouble of being unseated by Republicans and connected enough to the community to get reelected. Gentry was the publisher of a local magazine that took rather questionable ads on—and I'll clean this up a bit—"anatomy enlargement." My first bit of paid consulting: cancel the ads, find every single copy of the magazine I could, and destroy them. Thankfully, neither our primary opponents' teams nor Thurman's found any. It's one thing to lose; it's quite another to be embarrassed. (That would come another time, in a different race, and I'll wait to tell that story a bit later.)

No one taught me how to be a communications director or, a bit later, how to run campaigns. In that first race, I winged it. I wish there were more formal education in the practice of politics and more books like the one you are about to read, detailing how political campaigns are actually run rather than studying and analyzing them in the aggregate. The program I graduated from at the University of Florida had elements of it in a great course by Bill Hamilton, a Democratic pollster considered a founding father of professional campaigning. He told us what it was really like, gave us relevant readings and assignments, and put us in campaign simulations that were fantastic.

During the last year of my doctorate, in 1996, I had the opportunity to work for the Republican Party of Florida while my dissertation was stuck in the black hole of editing, quarantined by my adviser, Dr. Stephen Craig, who could not understand why I wanted to graduate so quickly. We both hated my dissertation: I, because it was in my way of moving on; he, because he thought it was an A idea but a C execution.

I think it was better than that, but it didn't really matter to me anymore. I had already moved on. One of my candidates was a shoo-in incumbent and another was a smart fraternity brother who vouched for me for the job; yet another, Nancy Argenziano, in my mind, had a real shot at upsetting well-liked incumbent Helen Spivey for the Florida House of Representatives. Argenziano won, giving Republicans control of the lower legislative chamber for the first time since Reconstruction. They haven't lost it since.

But she almost killed me. Late in the campaign, after I'd endlessly lobbied my boss, Frank Terraferma, about her, the party paid for a series of campaign ads through the National Republican Senatorial Committee's independent expenditure program. Radio ads ran on all of the major stations around Halloween, and I'll never forget them. To the tune of the theme song to *The Addams Family*, the jingle went, "Her name is Helen Spivey, she's raising all your taxes, less money for your family, she's Hellen, Spiiiiiii-vee," followed by the inescapable earworm, "Dah, dah, dah, dum (snap snap); dah, dah, dah, dum (snap snap)."

I'm sure there were other verses, but that one stuck, and it *really* pissed off Argenziano. She was hearing it from voters—too negative! So she let me have it. I called Frank, and he pulled the polling from the Tarrance Group: Argenziano was closing in on Spivey, and if I could just calm her down, we were going to win. I called her back, first getting her frazzled campaign manager and then her, making the case that no, we were *not* going to pull the ads. They were funny and they were working. They still are and they did.

From there, my wife and I moved to Washington, DC, where I worked for the Gallup Organization, mainly on government contracts, healthcare, and media research. I got to write for the Gallup Poll and worked on a project with George Gallup Jr., which was a treat. After 9/11, I moved on to work with past Bob Dole and future Donald Trump pollster Tony Fabrizio, who taught me so much more about campaigns than I learned in college. While Trump wasn't my guy in 2016, I'm happy for my mentor that he was able to win the big one.

In 2004, I opened my own firm with Fabrizio's permission and support. That year my wife and I also moved from Maryland to Virginia, and our son was born. During this time, I met with Rowman & Littlefield, who bought the rights to my first book. I had a good idea about updating the literature on the permanent campaign, and with a book contract and a vast underestimation of the undertaking, I was set to write. It was also during this period that Chris Tompkins died. I was devastated by the loss. It was obvious that the book would have to wait. I wasn't ready to write it.

In the meantime, I bookended service as the interim director of the political management master's program at George Washington University with stints as in-house pollster at Microsoft under the tutelage of Mark Penn and as chief strategy officer at WPA Intelligence, an innovative polling, data science, and digital firm.

I kept one foot in academia but taught from a professional perspective, like Bill Hamilton did. I designed and taught a course in digital political campaigns for the graduate program in communications at Johns Hopkins University and another course called Modern Political Campaigns for students from the University of California system interning Washington, DC. I didn't know it at the time, but the seeds of my book were being planted in the lectures, guest speakers, and readings I brought to my students.

Over the years, every time I looked at the dedication, writer's block locked me down. After a while, I thought that I'd never get back to this, and then the COVID-19 pandemic locked us all down. In late March I took another shot at it, but from a different perspective. So much has changed in the world of campaigns over the past twenty-five years, especially in the last fifteen with the maturing of the profession, the explosion of technology in daily life, and the speed of politics. This book pulls all of this experience altogether. It is something I couldn't have possibly written a decade and a half ago. Apologies for the delay. I hope you enjoy it.

In addition to the extreme patience of my publisher, I am especially thankful to the campaign professionals from all points on the political spectrum who are named and who shared their stories on the condition I would not use their names. Please note that this book is not an exposé or a tale of settling scores. That's for other books. What you'll hear from them here are stories about what goes into modern political campaigns, why they've changed in the past three decades, and how to launch a career in political consulting. If you are thinking of a career in this field, I hope this helps you along that path. If you are simply interested in politics, I hope that hearing from professionals gives you greater insight into how we now choose our leaders.

Extensions of this book are available at http: //modernpoliticalcampaigns.com, and you can follow @MPCampaigns on Facebook, Twitter, and YouTube for additional content as well as interviews with many of the people I spoke with in writing this book.

Finally, while many people were involved in producing this book, I am responsible for any and all errors. If you see something that needs to be corrected, let me know. Thanks in advance. If you'd like to chat about campaigns, I'm always game.

Michael D. Cohen, PhD

Cohen Research Group

Spring 2020

Introduction

Modern political campaigns are more professional, technologically advanced, and responsive to changing conditions than ever before in American history. All aspects of running for office—the initial decision to enter a race, understanding the voters and the opposition, organizing a team of volunteers, developing a message and communicating it, and getting out the vote—have improved over the past fifty years with better decision making, deeper access to useful information, and greater speed to react to changes in real time.

Campaigns used to be run by friends of a candidate, usually well-intentioned and well-connected amateurs, and in some races that remains true. People will always like to work with people they trust. However, campaign work has become more professionalized in the past fifty years, led by the founding of the American Association of Political Consultants in 1969, which gave the practice of politics a trade association and a forum to share best practices. Fifty years ago, political science was primarily theoretical, focusing on classic studies of theory and systems. The modern study of politics has added a more practical approach, measuring the impact of various campaign approaches with comparative testing and field experiments, leading to a more professional set of tools to use in election campaigns.

Campaign technology has advanced dramatically in the past fifty years in terms of readily accessible information. The sheer amount of background available on prospective candidates and voters is both astounding and unnerving at the same time. Much of the initial vetting and opposition research is conducted online, not on the ground. Modern voter files now contain not only name and address but also patterns of voting, which can be connected to a host of other commercial and opinion data to better understand how voters think and how we might be motivated to support one candidate over another.

The quality of the media we consume has increased dramatically, where dead-tree editions of newspapers and magazines are just as likely now to be read online or using an app. Radio still persists, but we are just as likely to listen to audio programming on streaming apps or podcasts. Television has developed from grainy black-and-white images watched on heavy boxes to streamed 4K on-demand programming viewed on mobile devices. How we connect to each other has changed, too. We are more likely to connect with each other on social media and in messages than to dial a phone number we no longer need to memorize.

These advances in professionalism and technology have met the defining characteristic of modern lifestyles: speed. Candidates need to decide to run earlier, run smarter, and run faster. Campaigns that are able to understand the political environment and move quickly when it shifts are winning elections. Voters live online and are available anytime, so when an issue rises or an opposing campaign hits another, the response can't wait for the next morning's strategy meeting. It has to happen right away or it will be too late.

HOW THIS BOOK IS ORGANIZED

This book is constructed as if you were taking my Modern Political Campaigns course. Each chapter represents a week in the course, and my goals for each are the same:

1. To give background about how we got here
2. To highlight what has changed in the field
3. To provide an understanding of the state-of-the-art techniques
4. To incorporate interesting and relevant stories
5. To help you identify whether this is a career path you would like to pursue
6. To assign scenarios for you to test your understanding
7. To provide resources for additional learning

Let's break down what this book covers.

Chapter 1 — Parties and Elections

We begin with an overview of how political parties and elections have changed over the past few decades. It will show how parties have become less central to deciding who will run for public office and yet remain essential to how self-starter candidates win races. This chapter covers shifts in party affiliation, voter polarization, expansion of voter access, and how important it is to understand the changing rules governing elections in your area.

Chapter 2 — Planning and Management

With that background, we move on to putting together a political campaign, starting with the most important question, which is why the candidate is running, and how that focuses all of the campaign's major decisions. This chapter will walk you through the components of a campaign plan from understanding the political landscape to setting specific goals on how many votes are needed to win, how the campaign will be organized, and what tools will be essential to get you there within an achievable budget.

Chapter 3 — Fund-raising

This chapter will highlight the *Citizens United* case and other changes, which opened up and complicated the financing of elections. Within the realm of what a campaign can control, we will focus on low-dollar donors, fueled by the maturing of Internet platforms and the speed of SMS. This chapter will also cover the development of high-dollar donors, now better managed with improved data and tracking systems.

Chapter 4 — Independent Groups

This chapter will demonstrate how the campaign plan is impacted by uncontrollable forces unleashed by *Citizens United* and subsequent case law. The shifts in money and the ability to communicate have fueled political action committees (PACs), super PACs, and various educational committees as campaign adjuncts and opponents. Developing relationships with independent groups is no longer optional; it is central to winning modern political campaigns.

Chapter 5 — Vulnerability and Opposition Research

In a world where everything is available online or remotely, the premium in modern political campaigns is on the analysis and deployment of the information. This chapter will cover techniques in both Internet and field research with an emphasis on why professional analysis and storytelling are more important than the speed of available information.

Chapter 6 — Data and Analytics

One of the most significant shifts in the past ten years is in data and analytics. The sheer amount of political and commercial information available on voters has led campaigns toward greater understanding and targeting. The growth in the use of statistical modeling techniques has moved our thinking about voters from self-reports to behavior-driven tendencies.

Chapter 7 — Focus Groups and Polling

The growth of the Internet and mobile technology both destroyed traditional research and saved it. Voter lists and online panels have replaced sampling voters by phone book or random-digit dials, while advances in e-mail, web-based surveys, and SMS have given pollsters many different ways to reach a representative sample of voters who are screening or avoiding phone calls. As I write this in spring 2020, focus groups have moved online, where more voters can join safely, and survey response rates have rebounded because they have more time to participate.

Chapter 8 — Earned Media

The art of getting attention for a candidate without paying directly for it is called earned media. While advertising still drives the bulk of campaign spending, earned media can be very powerful. During the 2016 race for the Republican nomination, Donald Trump spent only $10 million but earned $1.9 billion in free media. His primary opponent Jeb Bush spent $82 million and earned only $215 million. Not every candidate is Trump or Bush, but the growth of political media now provides greater opportunities.

Chapter 9 — Paid Media

The shifts in paid media from newspaper, radio, and television to paid search, social media, and over-the-top ads have allowed modern political campaigns to leverage everything mentioned above to targeted audiences. Just as important is the ability small campaigns now have to place ads themselves rather than through a broker, using their own data to create look-alikes for voters who are not on their lists.

Chapter 10 — Social Media

Earned and paid media have converged on social media platforms and are pervasive enough in our lives and on political campaigns that they merit their own chapter. Social media is a blend of owned media, a campaign's set of accounts, and paid advertising. Twitter, Facebook, Instagram, and YouTube are the main platforms we will discuss, and each is used very differently by political communicators. All offer ad platforms, but post-2016 it is less-than-clear whether they want to be in the paid political media business at all.

Chapter 11 — Field Operations

Grassroots volunteer and get-out-the-vote (GOTV) operations have greater tools to feed information back into the campaign and to better leverage what the campaign wants to communicate. Mobile data entry systems have transformed door-to-door voter contact into one-on-one data collection opportunities. The growth of social pressure field experimentation has changed how GOTV is approached in the mailbox, in person, and online.

Chapter 12 — The New Permanent Campaign

All of these changes in professionalism, technology, and speed add up to what I call the new permanent campaign. A pervasive belief among modern political consultants is that election contests have become "base dominant." As the electorate has become seemingly more polarized, it is more difficult to persuade. It is easier to reflect voters' values and mobilize. I close with an argument for a return to "base-plus," a more inclusive campaign strategy that uses all the tools of the modern political campaign to help lead voters to a better future, not simply represent them where they are.

As you go through the book, it's natural to gravitate toward one aspect of campaigns over another, so don't feel like if you don't get it all, you can't do this. You can. Remember that most campaigns are teams of specialists and you (eventually, if you're good) get to decide what you'd like to do. Even those who have the title of campaign manager started somewhere, usually in media strategy and increasingly in digital media strategy, but sometimes in other areas.

So let's begin with the basics: How are our elections set up, how did we get here, and why do we run our political campaigns this way?

ONE

Parties and Elections

"Given a room full of people I wouldn't automatically say that the people with experience are the better ones. There are some amazing really young people out there."
—Sue Zoldak, Republican political strategist

Modern political campaigns in the United States are influenced by how they are structured, formally with elections and informally with political parties. This chapter will cover some of the components of elections as they're held today and the roles parties now play. How elections have evolved, and the roles of how political parties might play in them, are very different from how the Founders envisioned them.

Increasing political professionalism, technology, and speed have created a set of unintended consequences that drive today's parties and elections. As Sue Zoldak foreshadows above, campaigns have shifted from being party focused toward more talent-driven, candidate-centered campaigns. The parties still retain a behind-the-scenes role, and that's where it gets interesting.

THE CHANGING ROLE OF THE POLITICAL PARTY

Throughout the American experience, political parties have had both central and peripheral roles in campaigns and elections. American history has seen political parties appear during John Adams's presidency and through urbanization. Their influence fell after World War II and the growth of suburbs. More recently, political parties have risen again with their ability to become supportive consultants to self-recruited candidates for public office.

Founding Era

Political parties are not in our founding documents, but they were certainly on the minds of the authors. In the spirit of defeating the dominant world power, Americans were initially in no mood for division, and the Articles of Confederation, insufficient to hold the nation together, were a reflection of a "leave us alone" ethos. The Constitution was sold to weary veterans and their families as a way to unify under common cause, rallying around their unassailable leader, George Washington.

Viewed within this context and in light of the bloody French Revolution, James Madison argued in Federalist No. 10 that the best way forward was a republican form of government where power was diffused as well as shared. This empowered the ability of factions to raise important issues but mitigate the potential threats to liberty and safety. Madison saw political parties as inevitable and the best they could do was to protect the nation by managing the side effects of democracy.

It didn't take long. While no one would challenge George Washington outright, factions immediately surfaced, resulting in the well-documented split between Federalists John Adams and Alexander Hamilton and Republicans Thomas Jefferson and James Madison. In addition to personality conflicts, the policy disagreements were real, primarily over the role of government, which would divide Americans throughout our history. The first president would be the last nonpartisan one.

Growth and Recession

The parties would grow in influence over much of the next century, professionalizing American politics at the local level. By 1890 most cities were ruled by political bosses and their machines, serving to help integrate waves of immigrants. Bosses helped organize communities and balance ethnic and religious rivalries, blurring divisive issues to win elections. In addition, local party leaders, elected and unelected, knew how to hand out the right jobs to the right people so they could gain or protect their influence. This public-private partnership also screened candidates and made sure that supporters got what they needed to remain in the tent.

Over time, the political spoils system of hiring party supporters eroded. At the federal level, it took to acts separated by almost one hundred years, the 1883 Pendleton Civil Service Reform Act, and the 1978 Civil Service Reform Act, to dislodge most jobs from party decision makers. In the states and cities, these machines began to die out during the post–World War II suburbanization and economic boom of the 1950s. Education played a role as well, moving not only voters to lucrative jobs in the private sector, but the bosses as well.

Meanwhile, the professional ecosystem around campaigns was exploding, reducing the primacy of political parties. News went from print to radio to video within a relatively small period. When radio was invented in 1920, candidates could now carry their message without the need for the political parties to shepherd it. Seven years later, television's invention made politics even more personal, and now everyone could see a candidate for themselves, not just take the local party's support for granted. Political polling reinforced that individuals, not just parties, mattered, and in 1948 George Gallup, the founder of the Gallup Poll, was on the cover of the widely read *Time* magazine. Moreover, the World Wide Web went online in 1991 and grew to carry political messages and writing directly to and from individuals, bypassing party leadership.

Partisan Press

The first outside entity to involve itself in elections was the press, but it began as an unofficial arm of the political parties. The first printed materials in the United States advocating for one party or another were openly partisan yet ghostwritten by those already in the arena including Thomas Jefferson ("a correspondent in Virginia"), James Madison ("Helvidius"), and Alexander Hamilton ("Phocion"). These publications were owned by partisans, and those who purchased them knew it.

Objectivity in press coverage evolved through changes in individual technology with the invention of the telegraph in 1843 and the advent of telephone subscriptions in 1879. Political news and analysis could be carried by voters without the party involved, sparking a rise in objective journalism that continued to evolve through the 1950s. The fourth estate (legislative, executive, and judicial being the first three) began viewing itself as a check on parties and elected officials rather than an instrument of it. As the nation's consumerism increased, the reliance on nonpartisan advertising drove the industry toward political independence.

But the expansion of radio, television, and the internet into daily life blew up that business model, as the need for mass marketing was reduced and advertising revenue followed. Instead of a few voices in a media market, there were now several, some of which better conformed to existing partisan leanings than others. In the 1980s and 1990s, cable television networks were founded, providing left- (MSNBC) and right-leaning (Fox News) homes for parties and their voters. The end of the Fairness Doctrine in 1987 was a win for Republicans first, offering conservative radio listeners Rush Limbaugh and other alternatives to the mainstream media. Democrats would also find their homes on all three platforms.

This narrowcasting of party ears and eyeballs has had a price. Early 2018 polling from my former colleagues at Gallup shows that most Americans now cannot name a neutral news source in part because

Americans have been conditioned over the past 20 years to believe that reporting that challenges their assumptions and beliefs must be "biased" and the natural reaction of the news industry to serve and reinforce these increasingly politically polarized audiences. In the same year, daily newspaper circulation was at its lowest level in almost sixty years. Ad revenue was down more than 60 percent from 2008. As I am writing, during the 2020 COVID-19 pandemic, many newspapers are struggling just to get an edition out, and many businesses are setting aside ad budgets for salaries, spending between 20 and 30 percent less compared with 2019, according to FTI Consulting. Quite a few may not be able to survive. Instead, ads are moving online, where Americans have retreated back to their partisan leanings.

VOTER AFFILIATION

The changing role of parties and the press has complicated how Americans identify themselves politically. In his seminal work on political parties in 1957, Anthony Downs argued that political parties formulate policy as a means of gaining votes. Parties are pushed to the political center because they seek to maximize the number of votes they will receive. This purely economic view of politics (the name of the book was *An Economic Theory of Democracy*, not of campaigns) predates this revolution in campaigns away from rational parties and toward candidates, who are more than just the sum of their policy positions or party affiliations. But it also misses the regeneration of the parties as placeholders for values and opinions, which have hardened recently, not just whether the economy is performing well or poorly.

Studies show that while we have become more polarized along party lines, the issues that used to define them have become muddled. President Donald Trump, for example, was not a traditional Republican. He was unconcerned about the growth of federal spending and was more restrictive than any Republican in recent memory on trade issues and immigration policy. However, he was also highly popular with people identifying as Republicans, peaking at more than 90% support in public polling. Conversely, he was highly unpopular with Democrats. Still, evidence over the past thirty years shows that party identification shifts not just before and after elections but during elections, meaning that these labels are not as important as the candidates who carry them. In a sense, we're fluidly polarized around candidates.

But party affiliation goes beyond the most visible candidates. One real-world consequence is a lack of split-ticket voting. As FiveThirtyEight found, split-ticket voting hit a new low in 2018, down from more than 20 percent in 1990 to close to 10 percent in 2018. In 2019, Pew Research Center published compelling data showing that self-reported independents who say they hold no party affiliation actually do hold a weak connection, which results in their voting for a party most of the time. Pew reported that in 2018 only 7 percent of voters were truly independent, meaning they didn't lean one way or another, while 30 percent leaned toward the Republicans or Democrats. As someone who has worked in and around campaigns for more than twenty years, I'll say this: You always count the leaners.

PARTIES AS CAMPAIGN ADJUNCT ORGANIZATIONS

With changes in technology allowing voters to more directly identify with candidates, the parties needed to adjust their strategic position to maintain relevance in modern political campaigns. Instead of exclusively identifying or choosing among primary candidates, they now play a more supportive role, not unlike parenting a rising teenager. When your kids are young, you can make most decisions for them. But as they get older, you play a more supportive role, nudging here, coaching there, but only in the rarest of cases putting your foot down. Modern political parties are rarely in a position to tell candidates what exactly to do.

The role of parties as centralizing political institutions began to break down when technology allowed candidates to communicate with groups beyond the reach of their natural voices. Radio allowed Franklin Delano Roosevelt to hold together a nation at war. Televised debates catapulted a young senator in John F. Kennedy to the presidency over an experienced vice president in Richard Nixon. The internet opened up windows of opportunity for candidates at all levels to reach voters directly. Social media propelled one candidate to the presidency who never served in government or the military: Donald J. Trump. The lessons were learned down ballot as well: You no longer needed party permission; you could grab it on your own.

Political parties have become adjunct organizations to the core of modern campaigns: the candidates themselves. Instead of paying their dues, literally and figuratively, any American of age can wake up one day and simply decide to run for office; no conversation with the party is necessary, although it is generally a wise move. Candidates launch campaigns they lead, in their voice, with money raised and spent in their names. Donald Trump and Alexandria Ocasio-Cortez did not ask to run for their parties' nominations. They ran against their parties and ultimately won them over as adjunct supporters. Their core coalitions came together outside the party structures, not from within them.

As this relationship has shifted, the parties have become focused on helping defend incumbents and supercharging its nominees. As we will see later in the book, parties not only have some of the best tools, including voter and donor lists, but serve as clearinghouses for choosing teams and consultants. For first-time candidates, parties organize campaign schools as well, on-the-job training in how to win elections.

DEMOCRATIZATION OF VOTING

While the Declaration of Independence asserted that "all men are created equal" voting rights under the Constitution were restricted to white men who owned property, which, incredibly, was about 6 percent of the population. As I write this today, women have had the right to vote for only one hundred years, let alone non-whites, non–property holders, or people who could not pay a poll tax or pass a test designed for low-income minorities to fail. Within my lifetime, adults aged eighteen to twenty-one were granted the right to vote by the 26th Amendment to the Constitution, and deployed military were ensured their right to vote. More than half of states now allow convicted felons to vote.

In every state except for North Dakota, adults eighteen years old on or before Election Day need to register to vote. Registration is handled differently across the nation, so the best bet is to check with your state's local election office. The U.S. Vote Foundation provides a clearinghouse for voter registration information by state, county, and city, outlining upcoming election dates and deadlines, eligibility and identification requirements, and provide the ability to double-check to see if you're already registered. This is good not only for individuals but for campaigns to be able to help register new voters, if the campaign is relying on growing the number of voters to win.

While we have come a long way toward universal suffrage, obstacles to voting remain. Election Day is not a national holiday, ensuring that some workers who cannot take time off are unable to vote. The rules governing absentee ballots vary widely, resulting in fifty-one different sets of rules and regulations, which can be a lot for our highly mobile population. Moreover, each state has different laws regarding what is required to be presented at the polling location, again making it difficult for some Americans to vote if they do not have current documentation.

As I write this, during the COVID-19 pandemic, states' responses to holding elections are varied. Some states have moved their primaries and elections, while others, like Wisconsin, held theirs as usual, eliminating those who are sick with the virus from the pool of eligible voters because they could not vote remotely. Those caring for people with the virus could not vote either, as they had immediate life-and-death concerns. This has exposed the underbelly of modern elections: In a pinch, we do not have a backup plan that can handle the speed of a catastrophe like COVID-19. So elections officials have improvised, leading to a confusing set of changes that varied by state and localities, and opening the door to chaos and legal challenges of unfair partisan advantage, fraud, and even outlandish international conspiracy theories.

ELECTIONS

At their most basic, there are three types of elections: primaries or conventions, general elections, and special elections. Members of a political party decide who their nominee will be, either in primaries that are available to the public or at conventions where members convene over one or more days. Primaries are held by political parties, sometimes with, but often without, public assistance. These can be open to all voters, closed to only party members, or somewhere in between, based on state law. Primary candidates generally produce general election candidates who have broader appeal to the electorate because they are run much like general elections, as public-facing efforts with fully modern campaigns.

Alternatively, some parties choose their candidate at nominating conventions, which usually attract only the most hardened activists and produce more polarizing candidates, making winning the general election more challenging in competitive races. Convention campaigns are a misnomer; they are more about relationship building and leverage than message and media. Party activists are the audience, not the public or even the slice of the electorate who identify as party members. While not perfect corollaries, conventions resemble old-style smoke-filled rooms (with less smoke): General public be damned; we're going to choose who we want to represent the party.

Most modern general elections feature the nominees of the Democratic and Republican parties, the chosen candidates of other minor parties, and sometimes independents and write-ins. While most campaigns are won between the two leading parties, there are upsets such as Senator Lisa Murkowski of Alaska, who lost her bid for the Republican nomination in 2010 but won a write-in campaign. Helping her effort was that she had already served twice and that her father, who has the same last name, had held the seat and then served as governor, appointing her to his seat. Prior to serving in Washington, she was the Majority Leader of the Alaska House of Representatives.

Special elections are the trickiest of the trio. Governors have wide latitude to call special elections, which are generally held outside of the normal election cycle. Practical and political considerations play sometimes competing roles. Optimally, governors prefer that the candidate chosen to serve were a member of their own party. If an election is unlikely to result in that outcome, governors can delay until the next election or appoint someone to hold it temporarily until the next election. If there is enough time, that strategy is often the best as it gives the appointee some gifts of incumbency—with some of the downsides as well. An example of this is Kelly Loeffler, who was appointed to serve in the US Senate but is now under public scrutiny for the sale of stocks after learning of the scale of the COVID-19 pandemic. Loeffler would go on to lose her seat in the January 2021 runoff election.

Even in the modern era of campaigning, special elections are challenging. Usually, the window to stand up a campaign is compressed, so the need to hire professionals, get the right technology online, and move forward with speed favors those with experience and/or available cash. This is entirely predictable and intentional, and it favors those with connections to the party or self-funders who can launch a start-up on a moment's notice. The best consultants know immediately who the party is backing and who will have enough money, so it is rare that someone from out of nowhere wins a special election. Two caveats: (1) if the special election is announced early enough the field could open up a bit and an underdog would emerge, and (2) the voter universe will change, meaning the actual number and which specific voters will cast ballots will be different than during a regularly scheduled primary or general election.

RULES

The rules and timelines for running for a party's nomination vary quite a bit, so you'll want to check with your state party as well as the state and local boards of elections. Aside from Googling it directly—which you could do, of course—USA.gov has an excellent page (https://www.usa.gov/election-office) that will get you to the right site. For example, Virginia's Department of Elections offers a section on candidate information (https://www.elections.virginia.gov/candidatepac-info/), which walks you through the process of becoming a candidate, including campaign finance and political committees.

State departments of elections also give you the opportunity to purchase data from them directly, which can include the registered voters list, who is new to the voter rolls, voter history, and who prefers to vote absentee. Again, this official information varies quite a bit by state, so your state parties and best general consultants will know the ins and outs of the rules.

Get ready: there is a lot of paperwork. In addition to basic contact information, you'll be asked quite a few questions about your candidate and who is on the team, including who is set to handle the finances. Websites, telephone numbers, e-mail and physical addresses are all basic to the forms, so if you haven't figured out where the campaign will be run, get that together first. Disclosure requirements can vary quite a bit from state to state as well as for different races. For federal races, you can start at the Federal Election Commission guide page (https://

www.fec.gov/help-candidates-and-committees/guides/), which helps you register and shows you how to handle donations and disbursements as well as loans, debts, and advances. There is advice for how to keep records and filing candidate reports and how to wind down the campaign if you lose.

During the 2020 election, state governments struggled with COVID-19 and its potential impact on elections. Most states moved their primaries and runoff elections to the late spring or summer of 2020. Many state legislatures and governors amended their rules to file candidate petitions electronically and expand the rules to allow for greater access to absentee ballots and mail-in voting. For example, Iowa mailed all registered voters' absentee ballots and extend voting to forty days. Georgia sent absentee ballot *applications* to active voters for the upcoming primary. Quite a few states relaxed the rules by which absentee ballots were allowed to be issued, including concerns about COVID-19 as an acceptable excuse. The result was that mail-in voting soared to 46 percent from less than 25 percent, according to the U.S. Census Survey of the Performance of American Elections. This placed a significant strain on the ability of states to certify their elections because there were so many more votes that needed to be processed, slowing down final reporting and leading to partisan clashes over the "Election Day" and mail-in ballots.

Which party or candidates these changing rules benefits is up for debate. I have seen both Democrats and Republicans say that mail-in benefits them. Democrats believe their highly mobile (although less so currently) voters need options to participate. While President Trump announced his opposition to mail-in ballots, based on cheating and corruption concerns, California held a special election with them, sent to registered voters without requiring voters to request them. The Republican won by a landslide. In reality, the move to mail-in voting is more a technical issue than a political one: How can you get your people to request ballots, if necessary, and mail them in on time? We will cover this question more in chapter 11.

CAREERS

Jobs at political parties, especially in the run-up to an election, provide a great way to get involved at the ground level. My second job in politics (but my first full-time one) was with the Republican Party of Florida as a field representative. The pay was low, and the days were long, but the experience was amazing. I worked with Frank Terraferma, the longtime head of state House elections for the party, and learned a great deal. We remain friends to this day, and I'm still in contact with my former candidates. Jobs like these offer a way to work in politics for a finite amount of time and decide if it is right for you or if it is just a crazy experience from which you need a vacation.

Professionally, what you gain from these jobs is the ability to—and expectation that you will—fail. You don't realize it at the time, but it is a fairly unique situation. The longer you work in politics, the more the wins matter. Candidates like to hire people who win. But at this stage, working for the party, it is the organization that wins, not you, even if you play a big part in it. While you are learning, make sure that you leverage all of the experience around you, from the consultants to the party lifers who hired you. There is just a great wealth of information and fantastic stories to learn from. Some of the best stories are ones of utter failure, and I'll share a few of these later in the book. Political professionals like to talk about their victories, but they love to talk about their defeats and why they happened.

While most people will cycle out of party jobs, there are opportunities to grow within the state or national organizations. The best field reps get offered jobs at the party or other kinds of starter jobs that might be more in line with what you envision your career. Everyone begins by stuffing envelopes and knocking on doors (at least they did before COVID-19), but everyone also expects to move on from those jobs, and the constant party churn of people provides openings for those who would like to stay a while and contribute a little more of their career to their party. Within the party's network there are additional ways to grow, such as joining special campaign committees or semi-affiliated nonprofits and PACs. No matter where your career takes you, starting it with the party is time well spent.

As a former colleague once told me, starting with the party not only served as the bridge between campus politics and professional politics, it introduced him to a group of friends and future clients. For some, working at the political party is something of a finishing school for aspiring pros, a place to learn practical skills to build on the theoretical ones learned in college and to meet the top people in the field as well as bond with those on the way up. In my time as the interim director of the political management master's degree program at George Washington University we did a lot of good in the classroom, but what made it all real was the work our master's candidates did in DC, and much of it was within the party's extended networks.

THE FUTURE

Party-centered campaigns are defined by leaders or committees recruiting some candidates and blocking others. The party designs strategies, deploys talent, and funds large parts of the campaign budgets. To a certain extent, this remains the case at lower levels of government, where

parties are active and cohesive. However, now most races are character-
ized by candidate-centered campaigns in which individuals choose to
run on their own, hire their own experts and field teams, and raise the
vast majority of their money outside of the party. Once the nominations
are won, the parties engage.

It is more likely than not that this trend will accelerate down the ballot
as campaigns become more professional. Fund-raising and communication costs have come down to the point that relying on the party alone is
unnecessary and counterproductive. Due to the widening of available
campaign finance options, PACs and ad-hoc independent expenditure
groups complicate party activities, including the ability to raise money
and spend it on behalf of their preferred candidates. Quite a bit more on
this will be discussed in chapter 4.

Parties will also need to double down on investments in political professionalism. In most cases, as noted above, party employees are less
experienced than professional consultants, which means that if you were
putting your life in public view, you would listen to the pros who had
party experience rather than the junior staffers who were just starting
their careers. The best role parties can play is to train their staff so they
can seed the ecosystem of professionals that have some affinity for and
ties to the party. Many of the best people I've worked with in politics, on
both sides, at some point worked for their party, either directly or in the
field, and used it as a career launching pad.

Beyond supporting the professionalism of campaigns, parties can do
far more to seed the political ecosystem with better technology. As you
will see later in this book, party commitment to this space has been spo-
radic and uneven. Innovation has largely come from vendors, who have
then been hired by the parties. Democrats were ahead in some respects,
such as online fund-raising, but behind Republicans in others, such as
voter list sharing. If the parties are to succeed, meaning candidates will
be more likely to listen to them than to ignore them, technological carrots
are an important factor. The parties would be wise to run mini start-ups
within their headquarters to be able to offer more to candidates than a
line on the ballot and support after they win the nomination.

Eric Wilson, who heads up Startup Caucus, dedicated to growing the
ecosystem of political technology for Republican candidates, argues that
the next wave of advances should be partisan. Despite the move to
candidate-centered campaigns, parties remain the center of political grav-
ity in that their networks are built on common goals, trust, and consistent
markets that need these services.

All of this is to say that parties need to continue find innovative ways
to connect with voters directly. Parties used to be broadcasters; now they
help campaigns narrowcast messages by directing data and technology
solutions toward meeting voters where they are.

ASSIGNMENT

Congratulations—you have decided to run for the state senate! Let's make a list of things you need to do to register as a candidate, including official documents in your state as well as any additional requirements for your state party. Does your state party have a track record, reported or rumored, of handpicking candidates, is that left up to local party organizations, or is there an individualist streak in who runs successfully for public office there? Who is the head of your party's state senate candidates division? Who is the head of the local party? Locally, is there a partisan media outlet, online or offline, that makes sense to engage early? Are there already other candidates running and if so, when did they file? Have they run before this cycle? Would you like to reconsider?

SOURCES AND ADDITIONAL READING

Adgate, Brad. "Newspaper Revenue Drops as Local News Interest Rises Amid Coronavirus." *Forbes*, April 13, 2020. https://www.forbes.com/sites/bradadgate/2020/04/13/newspapers-are-struggling-with-coronavirus/#7e014cc239ef.

Annenberg Classroom. "Voting Rights." Retrieved April 16, 2020, from https://www.annenbergclassroom.org/resource/voting-rights/.

Baughman, James L. "The Fall and Rise of Partisan Journalism." Center for Journalism Ethics, School of Journalism and Mass Communication, University of Wisconsin-Madison, April 20, 2011. https://ethics.journalism.wisc.edu/2011/04/20/the-fall-and-rise-of-partisan-journalism/.

Bowden, Mark. "'Idiot,' 'Yahoo,' 'Original Gorilla': How Lincoln Was Dissed in His Day." *Atlantic*, June 2003. https://www.theatlantic.com/magazine/archive/2013/06/abraham-lincoln-is-an-idiot/309304/.

Brady, Henry, Richard Johnston, and John Sides. "The Study of Political Campaigns." In *Capturing Campaign Effects*, 1–26. Ann Arbor: University of Michigan Press, 2006.

C-SPAN. "Presidential Historians Survey." 2017. https://www.c-span.org/president-survey2017/?page=overall

Downs, Anthony. *An Economic Theory of Democracy*. New York: Harper, 1957.

Ellis, Joseph P. *Founding Brothers*. New York: Random House, 2000.

Federal Elections Commission. "Candidates and Their Authorized Committees." Retrieved April 16, 2020, from https://www.fec.gov/help-candidates-and-committees/guides/.

Franklin, Charles. "Trends in Party ID, 2004–2018." Medium, February 11, 2018. https://medium.com/@PollsAndVotes/trends-in-party-id-2004-2018-143a7fddde58.

Glass, Andrew. "Alexander Hamilton Attacks Thomas Jefferson under a Pseudonym, Oct. 20, 1796." *Politico*, October 19, 2010. https://www.politico.com/story/2010/10/alexander-hamilton-attacks-thomas-jefferson-under-a-pseudonym-oct-20-1796-043776.

Hesse, Jonas, and Vishal P. Baloria. "Research: The Rise of Partisan Media Changed How Companies Make Decisions." *Harvard Business Review*, October 30, 2017. https://hbr.org/2017/10/research-the-rise-of-partisan-media-changed-how-companies-make-decisions.

History. "Morse Code and the Telegraph." Retrieved May 15, 2020, from https://www.history.com/topics/inventions/telegraph.

Kuypers, Jim A. *Partisan Journalism*. Lanham, MD: Rowman & Littlefield. 2013.

Jones, Jeffrey M., and Zacc Ritter. "Americans See More News Bias; Most Can't Name Neutral Source." Gallup, January 17, 2018. https://news.gallup.com/poll/225755/americans-news-bias-name-neutral-source.aspx.

Martinez, Antonio Garcia. "Journalism Isn't Dying. It's Returning to Its Roots." *Wired*, February 10, 2019. https://www.wired.com/story/journalism-isnt-dying-its-returning-its-roots/.

Morris, Jason. "History of the Telephone." Independent Telecommunications Pioneer Association. Retrieved May 15, 2020, from https://www.nationalitpa.com/history-of-telephone.

National Archives. "Expansion of Rights and Liberties—The Right of Suffrage." Retrieved April 16, 2020, from https://web.archive.org/web/20160706144856/http:/www.archives.gov/exhibits/charters/charters_of_freedom_13.html.

National Conference of State Legislatures. "COVID-19 and Elections." Retrieved April 24, 2020, https://www.ncsl.org/research/elections-and-campaigns/state-action-on-covid-19-and-elections.aspx.

Pew Research Center, "Political Independents: Who They Are, What They Think." March 2019. https://www.people-press.org/wp-content/uploads/sites/4/2019/03/Independents-Report.pdf.

Phillip, Abby. "Republican Victory in California Special Election Undercuts Trump's Unfounded Claims about Mail-in Voting." CNN, May 14, 2020, https://www.cnn.com/2020/05/14/politics/vote-by-mail-trump-california/index.html.

Rakich, Nathaniel and Jasmine Mithani. "What Absentee Voting Looked Like in All 50 States." FiveThirtyEight. February 9, 2021. https://fivethirtyeight.com/features/what-absentee-voting-like-in-all-50-states/.

Rothman, Lily. "How One Many Used Opinion Polling to Change American Politics." *Time*, November 17, 2016. https://time.com/4568359/george-gallup-polling-history/.

Shannon, William V. "The Political Machine: Rise and Fall of the Age of the Bosses." *American Heritage* 20, no. 4 (June 1969). https://www.americanheritage.com/political-machine-i-rise-and-fall-age-bosses.

Skelley, Geoffrey. "Split-Ticket Voting Hit a New Low in 2018 Senate and Governor Races." FiveThirtyEight, November 18, 2018. https://fivethirtyeight.com/features/split-ticket-voting-hit-a-new-low-in-2018-senate-and-governor-races/.

George Washington's Mount Vernon Library. "Pacificus/Helvidius Letters." Center for Digital History. Retrieved May 15, 2020, from https://www.mountvernon.org/library/digitalhistory/digital-encyclopedia/article/pacificus-helvidius-letters/.

Thomas Jefferson Foundation. "Pseudonyms." Retrieved May 15, 2020, https://www.monticello.org/site/research-and-collections/pseudonyms.

Virginia Department of Elections. "Candidate Information." Retrieved April 16, 2020, from https://www.elections.virginia.gov/candidatepac-info/.

USA.gov. "Find My State or Local Election Office Website." Retrieved April 16, 2020, from https://www.usa.gov/election-office.

———. "Who Can and Can't Vote in U.S. Elections?" Retrieved April 16, 2020, from https://www.usa.gov/who-can-vote.

U.S. Vote Foundation. "Election Official Directory & State Voting Requirements & Information." Retrieved April 30, 2020, https://www.usvotefoundation.org/vote/eoddomestic.htm.

Wilson, Eric. "Why Campaign Technology Must Be Partisan." Startup Caucus. Retrieved May 16, 2020, from https://startupcaucus.com/why-campaign-technology-must-be-partisan/.

TWO
Planning and Management

"You don't get a reputation by winning the races you should win. You get a reputation by winning the races people think you shouldn't win."
— Tony Fabrizio, Republican strategist and Trump pollster

Political campaigns are a collection of well-intentioned bad personal choices, beginning with the decision to run for public office in the first place. Managing them is a close second. Both candidate and campaign manager are all-encompassing jobs, and you give up a lot to be in the arena. The more challenging the race, the more important it is to plan and manage what you can along the way.

In *What It Takes: The Way to the White House*, the consensus best book of all time on running for president, Ben Cramer recounts a discussion that Joe Biden's kitchen cabinet had with him: "You give up everything . . . give up your life. It's gone. Home, friends, you're not there. And you're all alone. Completely alone. Your relationship with your wife, your whole family, is going to suffer. . . . You know why? Because you're going to want this worse than anything, and it's going to take over."

The idea that you could open up your imperfect life to public scrutiny and get through it intact is self-delusional. Most candidates lose, and many have lost parts of themselves on the way to victory. People who run for public office should get more respect from the rest of us because we, as voters, are so demanding. We're not perfect but we expect those who run to be exactly that. The bar is so high that most people quite rationally decide that running for office is not worth the hassle. Therefore, planning and managing a modern political campaign should first answer a simple question: Why?

START WITH WHY

The reason to begin here is because it helps answer everything that follows, including what the message will be, who will be on the team, and how the campaign will find a way to win. All modern campaigning flows from asking this question, because it focuses the process of getting there around the answers through planning and management. The why needs to be focused on two things: the candidate and the agenda. In modern campaigns the voter connects with the agenda through the candidate, not the other way around. The why needs to be viewed as authentic and voter-focused or it will be viewed as just an effort in self-aggrandizement.

The best explanation of how starting with this question works is from Simon Sinek, whose relatively low-tech TED Talk titled "Start with Why" details how leaders reach us. The talk has been viewed more than 50 million times online and the book was a best-seller. As many candidates come from the private sector and have likely run across this concept, it is a great way to connect with them and to get them to open up about why they are running and the best strategy to create a bond with voters.

Sinek's vision is a golden circle comprising three rings. The outer circle is focused on "what," sparking the brain's neocortex, which is responsible for facts, figures, benefits, and language. This is where the details of issues and proposals live for voters, and these are not the core reason for their choices. It is also what candidates see in terms of a campaign. Most candidates know they want to run but not necessarily how they do it. The outer circle is where the planning and management begin: What needs to be done?

Moving inward, "how" describes the process by which these ideas might become a reality. Again, voters do not get caught up too much in process unless it does not seem like what the candidate is proposing is possible. On the candidate side, this is the next step in campaign planning, the road map for how to enter a race and win it. Candidates will react the same way voters will if a plan is not realistic or seems too difficult to manage given their personal and professional lives.

Finally and most crucially is the "why," accessing our brain's limbic region, which holds our feelings and our gut instincts. Great candidates know how to move people and recognize that the why is far more important than the what or the how. This is where connections are made with voters that allow them to see past negative information or specific issues on which they do not agree with the candidate. It is also important for candidates themselves. The commitment involved in running for office is heavy and the lack of a core emotional understanding of why they're doing it will undermine a candidate's ability to be all in when the campaign overwhelms other aspects of their lives.

Let's take an example from the 2020 Democratic nomination race: Senator Elizabeth Warren of Massachusetts. Warren rose in the polls early on the strength of detailed policies (the what). But as the campaign moved along, it became apparent that her Medicaid for All plan was going to be too expensive and she did not have a great answer for how to pay for it beyond a tax on the wealthy, which did not seem to add up. In short order, once her full plan to pay for Medicare for All went live, her campaign slipped. While one could blame the how, the real problem is that it was a question of why—one that her opponent had solved in 2016.

Bernie Sanders saw the inequities in the United States decades ago and his plans, which Warren largely adopted, were the core of his candidacy. The why was that Americans were getting screwed by the wealthy and corporations who didn't care about them. Sanders did, and that was his why. So when Warren's Medicare for All plan faltered and attention turned back to Sanders, he was able to avoid collateral damage to his campaign because his core voters felt, in their gut, that he would do his best for them. Warren's core appeal wasn't her humanity, it was her plans. Once they were compromised, her candidacy was as well. The whys in a campaign are more resilient than the what and how because they access our emotions.

Let's look at Donald Trump's 2016 why for a moment. The unifying theme of "Make America Great Again" has been derided by critics as a backward-looking argument. But to voters who felt the American Dream was now elusive compared with years past, this was a reason why they chose Trump. Despite his signature bravado—and the word "great" comes off as authentic because of it—the focus on why voters chose him over Hillary Clinton matters.

Clinton's theme "I'm With Her" was self-aggrandizing and "Stronger Together" too amorphous. It was reported that when her Brooklyn-based team asked the basic question of why she was running, her reply was that answering the question was the team's job, not hers. That's completely wrong, and voters, in my experience, can sense that kind of inauthenticity. In the modern era of campaigning, where candidates are visible and available, it's even more obvious. There are many things a campaign team can and should do, but defining why the candidate is running is not one of them.

Warren, Sanders, and Trump knew in their hearts why they were running. They were internally driven to go through the process, regardless of the outcome. They weather attacks that most of us would have wilted under and the reason was they found a place inside themselves—a why—to hold onto and persevere through the campaign. Clinton didn't have that center, and it was obvious not only to her team, but to the nation she was seeking to lead.

PLANNING

Once the personal choice to run is made, or seriously considered, the question to be answered is what to do next. How do you win when it's obvious that running is a crazy decision in the first place? You give up all of the natural rhythms of your work-life balance. You give up your privacy. You give up your right to have ever made a mistake or changed your mind. Above all, you're asked to be an authentic human while operating at the meta-human level. This stuff is hard, and anyone who thinks it's going to be easy needs more help than you can provide. You need a plan and a structure to get there.

For decades, political scientists taught a minimal-effects model of campaigns, which argued that party affiliation, incumbent approval ratings, and the state of the economy were the driving forces in determining who won elections. Incumbency and the political environment both influence whether a candidate can win a specific office in a specific area at a specific time. What the ivory tower models fail to account for is that quality candidates make decisions about whether to run based on myriad factors (which impacts who actually runs) and the outcomes of the academic models that say campaigns don't matter.

Party affiliation, demographics, and gerrymandering effect are incumbency factors that impact fund-raising and the ability to assemble a winning team. The state of the economy and an incumbent's approval ratings are varying environmental factors that the campaign must operate within and influence. Challengers cannot directly influence these factors, but they help frame how to approach the race and which provide opportunities to engage. The bottom line for political scientists is that campaigns have only minimal ability to set the priorities of the race for voters and move the other factors in this complex equation.

But modern campaigns have more influence because of their greater ability to communicate. Campaigns effect elections through priming, emphasizing some issues over others and determining what is salient for voters to consider. Campaign plans also move voters through informing and educating voters on the candidates and their issues and proposals. The most difficult aspect of running a campaign is persuasion, where campaigns attempt to change voters' minds about who to support and why. Finally, the endgame of a campaign is mobilizing, which means moving the public to be active in the campaign and show up on Election Day. All of these are core aspects of campaign planning and management.

CAN YOU WIN?

While I respect citizens who run for public office to draw attention to their ideas or to ensure that voters have a choice, the serious ones do it to win. Modern political campaigns are long, brutal, and revealing, and if you are not in it to win it, I question your sanity if not your guts. So, as a professional, the second most important factor behind why is how. How do we win this thing? Can we do it? Is this the right place at the right time, and is our candidate the right person?

The mechanics of modern campaigning allow you to make this a much more data-driven decision than relying on pols who *just know*. The decision basically comes down to this: Is the office competitive? Over the past three cycles, is the margin of victory under 10 percent, meaning that the incumbent won with no more than 55 percent of the vote? Even better, is the office now open because the incumbent retired or found a bit of trouble and needed to find other, less public employment? Open seats are the most competitive and draw the most money, media attention, and party support.

Voting history is important as well. Do the voters have a consistent pattern of voting for one party or the other? If you're in that party, great. If you're not, is it trending in your direction? Finally, have the lines been redrawn lately so that the electorate that voted in the past three elections is not the same as currently exists? If so, the rules have been changed on you and you need to consider the electorate that exists now not what happened in previous elections.

From there, it's time to put a number on it. What is the exact number of votes you'll need to get on ballots to win the race? This puts the planning into focus. The goal isn't to get one more vote than the other candidate. That's a meta-goal. The real goal, which you can plan and manage around, is how many living humans, registered to vote, you need to win the election.

You can determine this by looking at how many votes have been cast in previous elections and extrapolating trends. Alternatively, you can view these patterns as rubrics and then, with research and modeling, project what the universe of voters will be this time around due to a variety of factors. We will spend a great deal of time on this subject in chapter 11.

PLAN DESIGN

In reviewing dozens of campaign plans over the years, there are several common elements, such as an overview of the political landscape, goals, strategy, message, tactics, organization, and budget. Other plans take a more functional approach, including specific proposals for targeting voters, communications options, and specific choices on research, policy, technology, scheduling, operations, and finance. Regardless of form, plans usually begin with voters and end with money, meaning this is a proposal document and subject to the evaluation by the candidate and the most trusted advisers.

Once a proposal is presented, there is quite a bit of negotiation between the consultants and the candidate's team. Not everyone will agree on different parts of the plan and usually it is wrapped too tightly into a calendar that does not allow for bubble time, as things always take longer to execute than anticipated, and contingencies for when the opponent hits you with something unexpected. Moreover, it is important to have unwritten rules for the campaign, such as who is authorized to speak for it and the pecking order of volunteers, consultants, and paid staff. If any of these components break down, so does the campaign, and it could have a real impact on who wins the race.

While this book is organized around campaign functions, here let's look more broadly at the themes that must be covered in the campaign plan, beginning with the overview of the political landscape, as each race operates in a unique environment. There are four basic areas that need up-front attention: the basic election rules, known characteristics of the race and the voters, the history of similar elections in the area, and the current environment within which the campaign will operate.

POLITICAL LANDSCAPE

Breaking election rules can prematurely shut down a campaign at the starting line. Campaigns need to know how to file for the election, which may involve paying a fee to get on the ballot or delivering a certain number of signatures by registered voters on specific documents to a government agency before a hard deadline. Residency rules for candidates vary, meaning you may have to live in a certain area for a particular period of time, which may be shorter or longer depending on the office. Age is often a factor—while you can vote at age eighteen, you cannot run for president of the United States, for example. Partisanship is a factor as well, as some races are run without party labels while others allow two candidates from the same party to face off in a general election if they got the most votes. Finally, know whether you simply need to win more votes than anyone else or if you need to win a majority, which might result a runoff? All of these variables factor into campaign plans.

While who will vote on Election Day is something we can only estimate, the universe of voters and where they live is knowable, with a little help from the voter file available through the state elections office or one curated and analyzed by a consultant. In our modern gerrymandered districts, this information is widely available because the data used to make these political decisions is what makes many districts so challenging to win. Therefore, we know not only who voted but also many of the demographic characteristics we can use to target them in future elections as well as any trends over time. We'll get more into that later, but for now it is important to understand that we do not start from zero. Does the area where the campaign will be waged stretch across a wide area of land and overlapping media markets or is it distinct enough where you can focus more on a few important members of the press and local leadership?

Historical electoral patterns are also readily available, providing the team insight into how easy or difficult the race will be this time, especially if the district has not been—or could not be, because it is statewide— reconfigured after redistricting. If the race is against an incumbent, has it been tracking closer over the past few cycles? Does the opponent appear to have a ceiling, or could their previous win percentages be explained by other factors? If it is an open seat, some of these patterns will be interesting but not determinative as those in their first race, even if their party has been favored over time there. As you will see later, large donors and political action committees spend heavily in those races because the power of incumbency is so strong that it is exceedingly difficult to pull an upset.

The current political environment is more difficult to estimate, but there are some components that are knowable, usually from the beginning. We have a sense of what regional and national issues will be interesting and important to voters, which party is ascendant, how the economy is performing, and how crowded will the ballot be. All of these will influence how to plan, manage, and run the race. Finally and most crucially is the question of how our candidate stacks up against opponents. We will get more into the weeds on this in chapter 5, but before our candidate declares, it is important to understand there are basic strengths and weaknesses that are known to all in terms of personal and professional biography, and how they compare.

GOALS

The most important component of the plan is the vote goal because every strategy and tactic that follows takes you toward this objective. If this number is off, then everything the campaign does is in service of the wrong goal. The good news is that the overall number of votes needed to win is a knowable figure based on the voter file and a look at recent elections for the same office and at key demographic patterns, which might suggest turnout rates.

One important consideration in getting to a vote goal is whether the campaign will focus on enlarging the electorate, which means an effort at voter registration in addition to communicating with registered voters. This is an expensive undertaking but could pay off in races where there are more members of the opposing party than of your candidate's.

The nuts and bolts of getting to the win total include working with the voter file, which is usually in various levels of disarray, based on my experience. Ensuring what's in the voter file is accurate, which includes telephone numbers, email and physical addresses, and other data, is crucial to not only estimating the win total but making sure you can get there with communication and mobilization. Cleaning the voter file can be done in various ways, including low-cost robocalls to check to see if phone numbers are live, having volunteers make calls to gather data, and simply handing it over to a vendor or consultant, who will check what is there and update it for voter modeling purposes.

Additional data you can match includes voter trends: how often people have voted in the past and whether or not they are registered to a party. This will help in modeling turnout scores in conjunction with commercial data, polling, and door-to-door engagement. The goal is to ascertain enough information to determine a score modeling the probability that voters will support your candidate and what patterns emerge in terms of demographics and the ability to persuade enough voters to win.

STRATEGY

With a clean voter file, all is possible. Identifying and targeting voter groups by their demographics, their voting behavior, and their current opinions is both an art and a science. Understanding which communities will help the candidate win is the strategic component of the plan, answering the question of who will support your candidate if you do the right things such as registering voters, getting infrequent voters, encouraging voters who can be persuaded to choose the candidate, and energizing the natural base of supporters.

Beyond scoring the voter file for turnout, you need support and persuasion scores, which are separate. Support scores help identify who are most likely to support your candidate, which focuses initial outreach to the public. Contacting those with high supporter scores is relatively high value and low cost because the bar for asking for the vote is lower as they are already inclined to help. In a perfect world, a campaign would have scores for all registered voters, and volunteers would work through the list through outreach including texts, phone calls, and knocking on doors.

Persuasion is the most difficult thing a campaign attempts to do. Strategically, your campaign should focus on the voters who are most persuadable and have the highest likelihood to vote in order to maximize the time and money it takes to move these voters to support your candidate. Trying to convince *every* voter in *every* region of a geographic area is wasteful. Given our polarized politics and gerrymandered districts, the slice of the electorate that is persuadable is small, so you must have solid, current data here to maximize the campaign plan.

MESSAGE

Most voters will never meet the candidate, so it is crucial to communicate the core why of the campaign along with the what and how messages. This section of the plan might not detail all of this initially, unless both your candidate and their team have a clear sense of what works where you are running. But even if you can answer these questions, a process will need to be in place to identify the best way to deliver the campaign messages, prioritizing which will work in *this* campaign and which delivery systems will be best to optimize the budget.

Even—and especially—the most substantive candidates need focus. With strategic polling, the campaign can identify issues to highlight, matching the mood and needs of the electorate, boosting the strengths of the candidate and hitting the weaknesses of the opponents. Issue selection should reflect not only the candidate's interests but the moment in which the campaign exists. While a candidate might want to talk about taxes and spending, it needed to be done differently in 2016 compared with 2020, in which everything had to be discussed in terms of COVID-19 because that was the top issue.

TACTICS

This section of the plan focuses on how to hit the vote total through voter identification and registration, issue education and persuasion, early voting organization, and getting out the vote on Election Day. This is the "how to win" section of the plan, and it could get very complex and expensive, depending on the race. There are three main areas of tactics the plan will execute, which include voter registration, communications, and mobilization.

Voter registration involves identifying people who are eligible to vote but have not taken the step of filling out the right forms with the local agencies to have the ability to vote. Current registration data provides a starting point that needs to be evaluated in terms of who has not opted into the voter pool. In some cases, the underserved communities will be identifiable in terms of demographics or geography, and depending upon the voter history, support, and persuasion scores of those already registered, this will help the campaign identify opportunities for growth. While registering voters is a public good, it only helps the campaign if potential voters are identifiable and are likely to support the candidate.

The communications section of the plan needs to list the media markets as well as the leading programming voters consume. This will help plan where the campaign content will be purchased, earned, or socialized through social media. Paid media advertising should be presented in detail, with a rationale for each station or outlet as well as the number of people who can be reached, the likelihood of a match to the voters the campaign needs to target, and the relative cost of grabbing that attention. The paid media plan needs to have a timeline, working backward from Election Day; this will impact fund-raising because in many cases ads need to be paid several weeks or months in advance to get the best pricing and availability.

An earned media plan should complement the paid version in that the same voter targets are reached and the messages are reinforced. Examples include live events such as rallies, town halls, and meetings, as well as press-centric outreach such as op-eds, press conferences, and interviews with local journalists and other programming. All of these opportunities provide less control than paid advertising but can be more powerful because the media itself is behind them and the audience is already there.

If paid or earned media does well, it could have a secondary audience on social media platforms. While campaigns can buy ads on social media, the potential network effects are what make them special. An ad on social media can be shared with like-minded users and find an audience that was not targeted or purchased. The same is true with an earned media opportunity—if it resonates with voters, they can help extend the message for free. Therefore, a coordinated effort at sharing the best content a campaign has on social media should be featured in the plan.

The cliché that "it all comes down to turnout" is somewhat overstated. Voter mobilization is like the free throws at the end of a tight basketball game—they can help in the final minute, but you wouldn't be there if it were not for how you competed in the first forty-seven. A lot can be done early. Depending on the rules of your state, you may be able to bank votes early through absentee ballots, early in-person voting, or voting by mail. Some states even let you register to vote on the same day as the election.

Identifying these patterns and mobilizing infrequent, busy, or elderly voters to avoid lines on Election Day could make a big difference in a tight race. Moreover, a get-out-the-vote operation should include all kinds of communication activities from volunteers by text, e-mail, or phone as well as in-person. In addition, there should be a specific plan for Election Day that includes voter transportation and supporters at polling stations to hand out literature and monitor the process.

TECHNOLOGY

While traditional political campaigns were run with people and money, they are now fueled by technology. Modern campaign plans often include a separate section for technology because, in some respects, these decisions need to be made early so technology can work throughout the race and on Election Day. The collections of available platforms to run campaigns are growing. You can now execute a campaign plan in much the same way a company uses Salesforce.com, where donations and expenditures are managed, teams are organized, and information is shared.

Much of what is decided at this stage has to do with what the general consultant, campaign manager, and candidate are comfortable with and what they envision needing for the race. Technology is a cost center, but it can also be a way to bring in donations. Still, the costs of technology are today and the promise of donations is tomorrow.

Beyond campaign management, most campaigns will spend money on technology for voter contact and communication tools. These could include hardware and software as well as payments for enhanced voter lists, complementary commercial databases, website and e-mail platforms, and voter contact software, which has become increasingly mobile. The hardest part of all this is getting the computers and apps to work together across platforms, on desktops, notebooks, and mobile devices.

While it is great that "there's an app for that" to cover these needs, the best way to go for an underfunded campaign is a web-driven service that handles most of these tasks. The part that you cannot control when you go this way, however, is security. If someone gets the password and passes it off to another campaign or organization, all of your data is compromised. Still, we are a long way from pen and paper, and factoring in leaky electronic data is a price of doing business in politics.

ORGANIZATION

Virtually every candidate believes they are going to be carried into office on a wave of grassroots support, but it takes a team of paid consultants and professionals to win. By law, every campaign needs at least one member—a treasurer—who is responsible for the donations and expenditures and signs the official reporting documents for the state or federal governments. This is not optional, and I'd counsel you to get someone who knows these requirements, not a family member (unless they're a pro), so you can avoid making costly mistakes. Beyond that, there are a lot of roles up for grabs, and depending on the size of the campaign, they can be bundled together to involve fewer people.

Here is a partial list of official roles:

- *Campaign manager.* The titular head of the campaign, this person's responsibility is to the candidate for executing the plan. Campaign managers should have some experience working on campaigns before they run one. The best ones are entrepreneurial, organized, and loyal.
- *Counsel.* The election law expert, this individual might also serve as the treasurer. Most campaigns do not need a full-time counsel, but it is helpful to know who to contact in a pinch.
- *Finance director.* The head of fund-raising, the finance director is the person charged with raising enough money for the campaign to execute the plan. The best heads of finance are excellent salespeople and connectors, people who always know someone you should meet.
- *Advance.* This person handles the planning and coordination of public events, including all the logistics of the traveling road show that is a political campaign: reserving space, managing what the stage will look like, and determining how the event will be covered by the news media and on social media.
- *Scheduler.* This is the one person who has ability to put a meeting or event on the candidate's calendar. This helps keep the candidate on-track and moving the plan forward.
- *Volunteer coordinator.* This person is in charge of organizing, encouraging, and deploying supporters to do everything from walk door-to-door, phone bank, text voters, show up to events and bring others, and provide feedback of all of this information to the team. Effective volunteer coordinators are motivators: organized, friendly, and inclusive.
- *Press secretary.* This person should have an intuitive sense for what the press will cover and have great relationships with them. The press secretary should be someone who does not need to be the focus of attention but is viewed as positive, credible, and helpful.
- *Digital director.* This person should be someone who cannot put their smartphone down. They should know what will work on the hot social media platforms as well as what people will pay attention to online. Generally, this person is young, quick, smart, and snarky.
- *Precinct directors.* These are local leaders who are responsible for specific geographic areas of a campaign. The best ones have lived in the area for a long time and know local issues as well as potential supporters and folks who will never vote for your candidate. They will help organize local events and voter contact efforts. In some races, precinct directors will report to a campaign's political director who has close relationships with local party leaders and groups.
- *Consultants.* This is the category I've lived in most often throughout my career. Consultants are the adjuncts to the campaign, bringing

in expertise when needed. Pollsters, advertising, and fund-raising teams are the most common, but other consultants and vendors specialize in media training, event planning, and campaign merchandise.

Unofficial roles are just as important, if not more. These include:

- *Significant other/spouse.* The significant other (SO) in the candidate's life is the most important person on the campaign without a title. Chances are that the candidate's SO/spouse had (and might retain) veto power over running or the overall message of the campaign. Win or lose, the campaign team gets paid and moves on to the next race. The SO/spouse will need to help the candidate if they win and pick up the pieces if they lose.
- *Kitchen cabinet.* This is the unofficial group of family, distant relatives, friends, and colleagues the candidate listens to or calls upon for advice. They know the candidate separate from the campaign, either personally or professionally, and if you do not know them, you should. Over the course of a campaign, especially when times get challenging, the candidate will reach out beyond their official team for gut checks. This is where they will go.
- *Outside advisers.* These are people with varying degrees of expertise who the candidate listens to on various policy areas. Most people cannot upend their lives to serve on a campaign, and successful people tend to be busy. Therefore, be on the lookout for people outside the campaign the candidate references in discussions. They have the candidate's ear, and it is important to make sure they are integrated into the campaign or they will find ways around the official structure and may create potential problems when opinions do not align.

BUDGET

The budget is where the campaign plan becomes a proposal, often the scariest part for a candidate. The idea of a political campaign becomes real when there is a price tag attached to it. This section of the plan includes everything that will cost money and how that money can be raised. Most of a campaign's money goes toward communication by way of earned and paid media, as both cost money to execute. Research, voter contact, and salaries are all accounted for in this section. In my experience, once candidates see this part of the campaign plan you know for sure whether or not they are going to run. Candidates who can envision raising this kind of money are ready to go, and those who hedge either drop out early or should have passed altogether.

Expenses

What do campaign expenses look like? I'd say they go into four categories: operations, research, voter contact, and fund-raising. Operations includes everything from salaries to gas for the campaign vehicle to office space, bank fees, and office supplies. This is the business side of the campaign, money that supports the team and does not move a single voter. Therefore, it's important to keep the budget down on these expenses, around 10–15 percent if possible.

My bias as a pollster shows a bit here with a separate category for research. Some will put this in the operations category, but I combine voter files the campaign can purchase and other database development with candidate and opposition research, focus groups, and polling. This is a bloc of money, in my view, because it adds up to basic intelligence about voters and the candidates, which sets up everything for voter contact and fund-raising. This should be about 20 to 25 percent of the overall budget.

Voter contact is where the majority of the campaign budget should be spent. Traditionally, campaigns have had separate lines for printed materials ranging from palm cards handed out to voters to yard signs, road signs and billboards, and direct mail. Standard media production and placement costs for local newspaper, radio, and television should be separated out as well, once there is a greater understanding of the local media consumption of targeted voters. The voter contact budget also includes community meeting and event expenses.

Canvassing door-to-door and other volunteer-related expenses are standard budget lines. Modern campaigns are increasingly using software platforms like Ecanvasser, which helps to manage field activities through mobile mapping and real-time volunteer tracking as well as the ability record information from personal interactions. Expenses directly related to absentee ballot support and getting out the vote on Election Day should also be separated from these high-touch voter experiences.

The shift in voter contact for modern political campaigns is to e-mail, paid search, SMS, and digital advertising as well as alternative channels for audio and video content. Some of the budgets I've seen combine these into digital advertising, but they're really separate efforts and, based on what is learned about the electorate, should get their own line items. Media buying firms have become more sophisticated in being able to take enhanced voter files and targeting them to build a media mix that maximizes this portion of the budget. An example of this for video is Cross Screen Media, a platform that dynamically analyzes cost and screen preference for audiences within each market for traditional television, cable, over-the-top services like Hulu, and social media video.

Fund-raising

It takes money to raise money. Events and donation cards, printing, postage, letterhead, and envelopes are all traditional line items for fund-raising. Here is where the lines get blurred because modern campaigns use digital advertising to drive not only voter contact and message but fund-raising as well. You can attempt to separate out percentages of digital budgets for voter contact, message, and fund-raising, but they will invariably overlap. Strive to set aside 25 percent of the digital budget strictly for fund-raising and fund-raising-adjacent activities. Moreover, well-funded campaigns hire outside consultants or firms to handle fund-raising, which could drive the cost of raising money higher.

Revenue

What goes on the revenue side of a campaign plan? Campaign budgets are based on the ability to execute a fund-raising plan, which includes an overall goal to raise as well as a detailed breakdown of who the candidate knows and can ask for money as well as anticipated challenges to overcome. Off-budget but just as important is understanding how much it takes in expenses and candidate time to raise money for the campaign. A tracking system of time spent raising money is useful to understanding the return on investment on the most valuable commodity in campaigns: time.

A structure for raising money includes donors at various levels, targeted communities based on network opportunities, the right messages, and potential surrogates. In addition, it will include a list of outside groups, including political parties and political action committees, the team can approach and the candidate can lobby for support. Each of these will have a dollar amount attached to show the candidate how it all adds up to the revenue budget.

There are alternatives to raising money directly. In some areas public funding programs are available that might include small donor matching, clean election grants or citizen-funded programs, or local tax credits for donors to participate. Finally, a portion of the revenue side of the budget should be set aside for in-kind donations, services like transportation, printing, equipment, or event space.

CONSULTANT STORY

Terry Sullivan ran hundreds of Republican campaigns at all levels for twenty years, culminating in his leadership of the Marco Rubio for President team in 2016. Perhaps his best story was about which level he liked most: He loved state house campaigns, which allowed him to be involved in every aspect of the race, from finance, where he started, to communications, which he now does for public affairs clients, choosing to pass on campaigns after "losing to a reality television star."

What is not told often is the story of how grueling campaigns can be and the high cost to your life. Sullivan recounted for me the nights he slept with his laptop open after working until 2:00 a.m., only to be awakened by an alarm to get ready for his 5:00 a.m. campaign principals meeting. As one might imagine, that is not sustainable, and it is a big reason why the burnout rate among campaign managers is high and why, as Sullivan found when he researched it, no one has ever run a winning presidential campaign twice. It is not for a lack of demand; it is just too physically demanding to do more than once.

My conversation with Rory McShane, a leading Republican campaign consultant, reinforced this point. Managing campaigns is a grind, and the traditional path of spending two or more cycles running candidates before moving up has become shorter. McShane said that it has become harder to keep the bullpen of campaign managers full as they move on to other pursuits and become general consultants faster because of their ability to leverage technology.

Both Democratic and Republican consultants agree that another growing trend is the increasing number of women willing to run for public office. Several told me they found that women work harder than men and are more demanding and more committed to planning the campaign. As political science has chronicled, more than one hundred years after getting the right to vote, it remains more difficult for women to run for office because the expectations from voters are higher. In turn, women are more reluctant to enter the arena. Women who get in are more clear-eyed about what they're up against and therefore work harder and demand more from their campaign leadership.

Finally, there were stories about boundaries. Campaigns are hotbeds for hot tempers. One consultant told me that he came in to help save a US Senate campaign, which was several points down at the time. This happens more often than you'd think and resembles sports, where you can't fire the star player but you can fire the manager. In politics, the one person who cannot be fired is the candidate, but campaign managers are replaceable.

In this case, the candidate was a yeller, always upset about something related to the management of the campaign. When you're losing, there's always something wrong. After weeks of abuse, the candidate was told that if this kept happening the consultant would hang up, every single time. What hit home for the consultant was when a child overheard the conversation and asked why they put up with it. There was no good answer. If there had been more time left in the campaign, the consultant might have quit after that, but there were only a couple of weeks left and they stuck it out. The consultant no longer returns the senator's phone calls.

CAREERS

All of this planning comes together with the leadership of a general consultant (GC) or campaign manager (CM). As mentioned above, the vast majority of the campaign budget comes from communications, so often GCs and CMs come from that field. As the keepers of the campaign message, they are in the best position to pull together the rest of the team, such as consultants in research and teams of volunteers and paid staff. Most often, they have gone through the party campaign schools, so they have strong relationships with leadership or at least enough familiarity to know who the good people are, whether they're available, and what it will take to form a winning team.

Beyond expertise in communications, the most important asset general consultants and campaign managers bring to the table is these relationships. In most campaigns, general consultants act as the gatekeepers to candidates, so vendors act as subcontractors to the overall campaign. Typically, there is a financial relationship as well, where consultants might pay a GC a finder's fee for a project or may have ongoing referral relationship that candidates may not see unless they ask, which I'd suggest they do. The better the referral fee, the more likely the GC will be to suggest a specific consultant or campaign manager, so it is important to ask the right questions in evaluating the plan.

Those who have run campaigns say that the best way to become a campaign manager is to volunteer on campaigns first and while you are there, start building the relationships that will help build a winning team. If you are not given the opportunity to learn, volunteer, as you will be ultimately responsible for all aspects of a campaign as its manager. Chances are, as most consultants have told me over the years, if you're competent and committed, you'll be given a lot to do, and that will help launch you toward leadership. Everyone I interviewed for this book said that what they learned on their first campaign was valuable and helped them grow into leaders in their field. Don't discount anything.

There are enough elections that moving up and running one is not as difficult as one might think. Most of the people I spoke with for this book served in leadership roles on campaigns at a relatively young age. Several were able to parlay college leadership positions in or activity in the Young Democrats or Young Republicans into opportunities to run a county commission race or a campaign for the state legislature. A general theme of successful campaign leaders is that they do whatever it takes to get the job done and figure it out along the way. People in politics are problem solvers by nature.

Working on lower-level campaigns builds your résumé for greater challenges. By nature, people who work in campaigns are highly networked, meaning that if you do a good job or win a tough race, you get noticed. Just as important, if you stay in the game, you'll get additional opportunities at the state and federal levels. Relationships matter, and those you helped win at one level will take you with them when they are ready to move up.

A great example of this is Terry Sullivan. In my interview with him, Sullivan said a national race was never something he chased, but it came to him through his long-standing relationship with Rubio. Sullivan actually put together a 101-slide PowerPoint for Rubio's kitchen cabinet, his most trusted personal advisers, on what it would take to win at the highest level. Their response was: Great, you run it. Sullivan couldn't turn it down.

Perhaps the best advice I've gotten over the years was from my mentor Tony Fabrizio, a Republican strategist and pollster for Donald Trump's presidential campaign. His point of view is that you need to make an important decision early in your career: Are you going to try to run the favored races or the underdogs? Running the favored races requires building relationships with the national and state parties to become their preferred hire. More likely than not, you will end up with a better winning percentage. But, as he told me, you really make history—and a reputation—in winning upsets.

All of this is to say there is no one sure path to running campaigns. Some will start in media and grow into it over time, while others will find themselves with the top job relatively early due to relationships or circumstances beyond their control. While modern campaigns post jobs on websites (see the end of this chapter for a list), the top job is usually not posted because that remains a personal choice, often by candidates themselves or someone close to them. The best way to land the big job is to know the right person, at the right time, when a race can be won.

The organization to join is the American Association of Political Consultants (AAPC), a very well-funded and well-run trade association for politics. Founded in 1969, it is the umbrella group for political campaign consultants and managers, public affairs pros, and communications specialists. It sponsors dozens of events, webinars, and regional conferences each year focusing on every aspect of campaigning you didn't learn in political science courses. It is a great organization for professional development. Each year, it hosts the Pollie Awards, which, ironically, does not have separate categories for polling (a gripe of mine, to be sure). The AAPC also offers a "40 Under 40" award recognizing industry leaders under forty years of age, as well as its own Hall of Fame, which reads like a who's who in the history of political campaigns.

Membership benefits include a wide array of services and discounts, including a membership directory and a job board, both of which are very helpful in landing jobs and clients. Student memberships are available for $60 and party or campaign staffers as well as young professionals aged thirty and under can get full membership for $100. The AAPC is a bipartisan organization and can be found online at https://theaapc.org.

Finally, Rory McShane offers up a specific suggestion on what someone should learn before diving into managing campaigns: Microsoft Excel. While this might seem elementary, I can confirm that Excel is the one app that hits many different parts of the campaign, from planning, to research, to media and grassroots. "They should know how to sort sheets, filter, vertical lookups, dedupe, pivot tables—all of that. It will save them and the campaign countless hours," McShane counseled. One highly rated way to learn Excel is through Coursera, which is free to audit if you don't want to get officially certified. You can also go the direct route through Microsoft and get certified for $100. In my experience, if you can do the things McShane references, there is no gatekeeping reason for the certification.

THE FUTURE

While federal races generally get this level of professionalism, technology, and speed in plan development, it is increasingly becoming standardized down ballot. Relatively low-budget campaigns should now expect a full plan including these elements from a general consultant or campaign manager. All of the upfront elements are readily available, so they cost much less than they did decades ago. The level of professionalism and the technology to analyze the data has increased and the price has dropped, bringing these insights to virtually all campaigns. The speed at assembling a plan and a team will improve on the state and local levels as hard costs for consultants continue to decrease, making these campaigns worthwhile for them financially.

What we will begin to see going forward, however, is specialization. The outline of a campaign plan presented here will not fit all campaigns, especially those with relatively low budgets. But as more of the components we will see later in this book improve and become more affordable due to technology at the same time as fund-raising increases due to the same forces, local campaign plans will find themselves with highly sophisticated, customized plans for how to win elections.

Overall, the planning and execution of political campaigns in the modern era will be more directed at leveraging understanding the variability of voters within larger, reachable groups. As future campaigns get better tools to reach, inspire, and persuade individuals, voter contact will become more relevant and personal, which will drive up turnout.

ASSIGNMENT

Review the Michelle Nunn for Senate campaign memo (available at https://cdn.factcheck.org/UploadedFiles/235287519-2014-Michelle-Nunn-Campaign-Memo.pdf) and reflect on how it was organized and what you would adapt for your campaign. What information is available to you before the team is assembled, what data would need to be gathered, and what should be ignored? What assumptions by the plan did not turn out to be correct, and how would you avoid making the same mistakes for your campaign? Given that the plan was released to the public without consent of the team, what might you hold back so it would not be embarrassing? (In other words, while it is better to write down the plan, which is what all the experts say you should do, what should be off the books? (Finally, choose one specific part of the plan in a subject matter area where you are most interested and break down the Nunn campaign's execution versus the opponent's. Why did Nunn lose, and was it avoidable?

SOURCES AND ADDITIONAL READING

American Association of Political Consultants. Retrieved May 5, 2020, from https://theaapc.org/.

Beach, Michael. "State of the Screens." Cross Screen Media. Retrieved May 19, 2020, from https://stateofthescreens.com/author/stateofthescreens/.

Brady, Henry E., and Richard Johnson. "Introduction: The Study of Political Campaigns" in *Capturing Campaign Effects*. Ann Arbor, MI: University of Michigan Press, 2006.

Breyer, Yvonne. "Excel Skills for Business Specialization." Coursera. Retrieved May 21, 2020, from https://www.coursera.org/specializations/excel.

CallHub. "Creating a Political Campaign Budget." Retrieved May 19, 2020, from https://callhub.io/creating-a-political-campaign-budget/.

Cramer, Ben. *What It Takes: The Way to the White House*. New York: Random House, 1992.

King, Josh. *Off Script: An Advance Man's Guide to White House Stagecraft, Campaign Spectacle, and Political Suicide*. New York: St. Martin's Press, 2016.

McShane, Rory. Interview with the author. May 18, 2020.

Microsoft. "Excel Video Training." Retrieved May 21, 2020, from https://support.office.com/en-us/article/excel-for-windows-training-9bc05390-e94c-46af-a5b3-d7c22f6990bb.

Michelle Nunn for Senate. "The Campaign Plan." 2014. Retrieved April 21, 2020, from https://cdn.factcheck.org/UploadedFiles/235287519-2014-Michelle-Nunn-Campaign-Memo.pdf.

Microsoft. "Exam 77–727: Excel 2016: Core Data Analysis, Manipulation, and Presentation." Retrieved May 21, 2020, from https://docs.microsoft.com/en-us/learn/certifications/exams/77-727.

National Democratic Institute for International Affairs (NDI). *Campaign Planning Manual.* 2009. https://www.ndi.org/sites/default/files/Political_Campaign_Planning_Manual_Malaysia_0.pdf

Sinek, Simon. "How Great Leaders Inspire Action." TEDx Puget Sound, September 2009. Retrieved January 15, 2021, from https://www.ted.com/talks/simon_sinek_how_great_leaders_inspire_action?language=en.

———. *Start with Why*. New York: Penguin, 2011.

Starrett, J. R. "The Secret to Building a Volunteer Juggernaut." *Campaigns and Elections*, March 10, 2015. https://www.campaignsandelections.com/campaign-insider/the-secret-to-building-a-volunteer-juggernaut

Sullivan, Terry. Interview with the author via Zoom. April 30, 2020.

Wellstone. "The Campaign Plan." Retrieved April 22, 2020, from https://www.wellstone.org/sites/default/files/attachments/The-Campaign-Plan_1.pdf.

THREE

Fund-raising

"A lot of people think it's just event-driven, and you just show up and have a good time. A lot of it, what's hard about it, and why few people do it versus other things, is you're asking people for money. You're not giving them anything tangible. They're giving you money because they believe in something."

— Lisa Spies, Republican fund-raiser

The lifeblood of modern political campaigns is fund-raising. Virtually everything you want to do will cost money, usually more than the team anticipates, even with a plan and a budget, as the latter is a moving target based on donations. From the decision to run, fund-raising precedes polling as an indicator of how the talent you can help execute the campaign plan.

Conversely, if planning falls apart at any one place in a campaign, it is fund-raising. Without it, collateral can't be made, ads can't be placed, and consultants can't be paid. This surprised me after I moved from Gallup to working in politics directly. Candidates don't . . . pay? My colleagues looked at me like I had just realized that elections were held in November every two and four years. Yes, Mike, sometimes candidates can't raise enough money to pay the bills. Even worse, the winners sometimes take a *long* time to pay.

More than a few great candidates in recent years, Republican and Democrat, have been undone by lagging fund-raising. Martha McSally in Arizona comes to mind in her 2020 attempt to fill the late John McCain's seat. Also in 2020, Cory Booker was conspicuously unable to raise presidential-level dollars to keep his campaign moving. Beyond the campaigns, in some races the candidate isn't even the biggest fund-raiser— it's a super PAC, a labor union, a corporation, or a wealthy individual. But if a campaign shuts down, the candidate may find others to join.

Mike Bloomberg's 2020 campaign shut down and he immediately began to seed other campaigns with the money he intended to spend on his own.

One alternative to this web of fundraising is public financing, which would outlaw private donations to political campaigns in favor of a system that's funded by taxes. A deep dive into polling on campaign finance from 1972 to 2000 by the Campaign Finance Institute, which has a horse in this race, showed that the public supported public financing but when neutral questions refer to "using taxpayer dollars to pay for political campaigns" versus "public financing" or "voluntary taxpayer designations of funds that do not increase their personal taxes," support for programs is very low, under 20 percent. Recent polling from the National Opinion Research Center (NORC) confirms this.

This is exactly how opponents would attack public financing and telegraphs why this has gone nowhere in twenty years since the research concluded. Moreover, public financing would limit how much candidates could raise and create an unintended consequence of unnecessary incumbent protection. Elected officials have already developed networks of fund-raising, whereas new candidates have to build them from scratch. Moreover, with the advantage of name identification alone, the cost is actually higher to run as a challenger than an incumbent, making it harder to win and keeping those in power safe.

Therefore, let's set aside this as an alternative campaign universe and focus on what the current environment is instead. The modern system of campaign funding is a very complicated web of money, technology, and relationships. Money arrives to a campaign through one of two funnels: a virtual one, mainly through e-mail, SMS, digital, and online sources; and a highly personal one, through donor research and deep relationships. This chapter will look at how both work and how they direct campaign playbooks. First, we need to look at the universe of voters who give money to campaigns and understand why they do it.

WHO DONATES TO CAMPAIGNS?

According to the Center for Responsive Politics (CRP), a "tiny elite" of Americans (0.47 percent) contributes more than $200 to candidates, parties, or PACs and even fewer (0.07 percent) contribute the current maximum of $2,800. This is why fund-raising lists are so highly sought-after—the universe of relatively high-dollar donors is small but crucial to running an effective campaign.

Several of the top contributors in the 2018 cycle are household names, including Las Vegas Sands/Adelson Clinic owners Sheldon and Miriam Adelson, who gave $123,744,400 to Republicans and conservative causes. Ahead of his presidential campaign, former New York City mayor Michael Bloomberg gave close to $94 million to Democrats and liberal causes, followed by Tom Steyer, also ahead of his candidacy, who donated more than $73 million.

Bloomberg and Adelson also contributed through their organizations. Bloomberg, LP contributed close to $96 million, while Las Vegas Sands contributed more than $62 million and the Adelson Clinic for Drug Abuse Treatment & Research contributed almost as much, about $61 million.

Interestingly, the top PAC contributors in 2018 were the National Association of Realtors, who split their money almost evenly among Democrats (51 percent) and Republicans (48 percent), followed by the National Beer Wholesalers Association, skewing a bit toward Republicans (52 percent versus 48 percent), and AT&T, which also leaned Republican (60 percent versus 40 percent).

Beyond the top donors, how many Americans overall participate in giving to candidates or political causes? Since the Federal Election Commission (FEC) only requires the names of people who give more than $200, most donations are nonassignable, so we have no idea beyond polling, which probably inflates the numbers. Still, the best polling available is from the Pew Research Center, which found that more Americans were donating to campaigns, doubling from 6 percent in 1992 to 12 percent in 2016. Donations to parties were up from 4 percent to 9 percent in the same period, while the share of Americans who say they gave to a group that supported candidates was within the margin of error from 6 percent to 5 percent over that period. Overall, 55 percent of those who said they gave money to a candidate or group donated less than $100.

Beyond the top line, those who are most likely to donate share several characteristics that could be targeted by campaigns. Most obvious is those who are politically engaged and follow what is going on in government and public affairs; they were four times as likely to say they donated than those who follow these developments less often (28 percent versus 7 percent). An artifact of the 2016 election was that Democrats were at least twice as likely as Republicans to donate (22 percent versus 10 percent), but generally there is no statistical difference just based on party identification. What this tells us is that a highly polarizing candidate or set of candidates can move some who don't normally donate to chip in to a campaign.

Demographically, higher-income, more educated, and older Americans were more likely to donate to campaigns, all of which match up with the political science literature and what we've learned in the field. As all three groups are more likely to vote, anyway, they overlap with those who are more likely to be politically engaged. They're also more likely to have money to donate.

Again, no matter whether you're looking at large or small donors, most voters do not donate anything to campaigns or political causes. This means that the data you have on potential donors must be solid or you will waste resources—spending too much time and money to make money.

CONSULTANT CORNER

This chapter owes a great debt to two people. The first is Lisa Spies, a fundraiser who specializes in high-dollar donors for Republican candidates including Mitt Romney, Jeb Bush, and several others. She gives a great, off-the-record (sorry) guest lecture for my course and is the one who surprises students the most, as my students tend to be more liberal than conservative. A great fund-raiser like Lisa lives for people, loves to help others make valuable connections, and is absolutely fearless. One of the best pieces of advice she gives to my students is to volunteer for everything—be the person who will do the grunt work with a smile, and you'll go far. It worked for Lisa in fund-raising, and it is great advice more broadly in campaigns.

The second person is a former George Washington University student of mine who is a Democrat and whose specialty is online fund-raising: Tyler Giles. His work tends to be more experimental and analytical in nature and he is always looking for ways to get you to open an e-mail, pay attention to an online ad, and convert your eyeballs into the movement of your hand to your pocket to get that CVV number off your credit card for a political donation. Tyler is all about people as well, but more along the lines of what will motivate us to do something rather than spending extended periods of time with us. His work is all about scale, and that requires constant movement.

With apologies to Bloomberg, who spent close to a *billion* of his own dollars only to drop out before Super Tuesday in 2020, most modern campaigns need OPM: Other People's Money. Most campaigns need both the high-dollar donors Lisa curates and the relatively low-dollar online donors Tyler targets to be successful. Think of the high-dollar donors as angel investors, who are looking to pledge a great deal to a cause: yours. Low-dollar donors are more like paying customers who show the world how much reach your campaign has and what it can accomplish.

BASIC RULES

Let's take a step back for a moment and clarify some of the basic ground rules for raising money for political campaigns. As mentioned above, the maximum an individual can give to a candidate committee is $2,800 per election cycle, but there are other opportunities to give beyond that. That same individual can give up to $5,000 per year to a PAC; $10,000 per year each to a state, district, or local party committee (a maximum of $30,000 to all three); $35,500 per year to the national party; and up to 105,500 to additional national party committee accounts, which can include the presidential nominating convention, election recounts and other legal support, and helping to fund national party headquarters buildings.

The committees, then, can give that money to candidates directly in larger sums, effectively bundling smaller donations to make a bigger impact. For example, a candidate committee can give $2,000 per election to another candidate committee, $5,000 to a PAC, and unlimited transfers to party committees at all levels. This money not only helps others, but it reinforces the status of the candidate donating or regifting donor money elsewhere. Most candidates who do this are in some position of leadership, and this kind of behavior is expected. Still, it is another loophole through which dollar limits are circumvented.

Super PACs, which are independent of all of these organizations, may accept unlimited contributions from individuals, including from labor organizations and corporations, effectively blowing up the campaign finance limits. Why give hard money, which is limited and reportable, when you can donate anonymously and at higher levels?

This is how Jeb Bush was able to fuel his early candidacy with a relatively small campaign team and donation pool, while his super PAC raised most of the money ahead of his announcing his candidacy. This is why "forming an exploratory committee" is such a farce, because once potential candidates make this technical statement, it signals to friends and close colleagues that they're in and opens the door for others to raise substantial money on their behalf, to be folded into the tent once the circus opens.

I'd like to highlight two additional notes: in-kind contributions and postcampaign funds. Nonmonetary contributions need to be assigned a fair market value so they can be counted as well. This ensures that the use of an office donated by a potential constituent results in a reportable donation and is disclosed to the public. Print shops, restaurants—just about anything of value a campaign accepts needs to be tallied. After a campaign, the money needs to either be returned or remain in the campaign account, which can be used to fund a race for another office. This is how Senator Elizabeth Warren of Massachusetts seeded her presidential campaign—with money intended to help her Senate race. This is a common occurrence and completely legal under current campaign laws.

This can go badly, of course. One of my favorite stories is the tale of Aaron Schock, who was a thirty-seven-year-old rising star in the Republican party, a member of Congress who used campaign funds to decorate his office in the style of *Downtown Abbey*. Schock was a superstar fundraiser who raised $2.7 million for his 2014 race and had a final cash-on-hand of $3.2 million. What's a few thousand to redecorate a congressional office? It was enough to force his resignation in disgrace on March 31, 2015, and a plea deal to avoid jail time. As one might imagine, the purchase of office furniture with campaign donations is against federal law in addition to just being unethical.

HIGH-DOLLAR FUND-RAISING

In most races, the people who have the most money to invest in your campaign is relatively obvious. Successful local businesspeople, high-profile locals, and organizations that want certain policy outcomes are the first cut in high-dollar fund-raising. Hiring someone like Lisa Spies right away is crucial so you can create runway money from which to build the campaign you planned in chapter 2.

Your Lisa (if it's not her) will put together a list of people with whom to organize small, intimate meetings where the candidate can make the pitch. These potential donors want to know that the candidate wants to do, and they push the candidate very hard during these conversations. Anyone who is as good as Lisa will help prep you for those conversations and give tips on how to handle difficult situations where you do not agree 100 percent with the donor. But most donors and bundlers are strategic enough to understand, and respect, that 75 percent is quite enough to support the campaign.

For top donors and those with the individual networks to bundle donations, these conversations are intimate, including only the candidate, the consultant, and the donor. This is about as personal as it gets, and donors get to ask all kinds of questions, some of which test the candidate's knowledge, but most of which test the plan and ability to win, because the very best high-dollar fund-raisers know these people so well that they will not waste their time putting together a meeting where the probability of success is low. Everyone's time is valuable, especially the donors at this level, so it is critical that fund-raising matchmaking is effective before the meetup.

If all of this seems very traditional, to a certain extent it is. The modern twist on this is that information about how much each donor has spent in the past is readily available, so political matchmaking is much more efficient. This makes for much more informed conversations, as a candidate or a campaign teammate would not ask for $1,000 from someone who hadn't given one dime to a candidate in three cycles. Moreover, the web of contacts is much easily woven and maintained with software packages that range from spreadsheets and electronic address books to full-blown Salesforce.com-like solutions, tracking every text, e-mail, call, or meeting at all stages of fund-raising.

Deployment of that network is crucial to growing the base of high-dollar donors beyond the obvious suspects. Each of these donors has the ability to introduce your campaign to others who might join, so the best high-dollar fund-raisers know how to use the tools available to make more effective introductions and connections, which result in opportunities.

LOW-DOLLAR FUND-RAISING

In contrast with relationship-driven high-dollar fund-raising, inspiring people to give $1, $5, $10, $50, or $100 multiple times is more message-driven. Unlike with high-dollar donors, most low-dollar donors will never get time with the candidate and will only respond to engaging appeals, increasingly via text and social media. If you've ever donated to a campaign before, you'll find that you'll be tagged by future campaigns in every subsequent cycle unless you opt out. As we will discuss in chapter 6, the amount of data on each of us is both incredible and more than a bit creepy. We've all left digital footprints through our behavior, and this allows fund-raising to scale at this low donation point.

The wording and visuals in all electronic asks are tested dozens, if not hundreds, of times in well-funded campaigns. If the campaign launches with or has raised enough start-up investment, it then has the opportunity to utilize national donor files to target individuals who are not only in your campaign's area but outside of it, allowing for someone who was a bartender to defeat a future Speaker of the House in New York's Seventeenth Congressional District (yes, AOC).

ONLINE PLATFORMS

Before Senator Bernie Sanders fueled his presidential campaign with online fund-raising, another Vermonter, a longtime governor, pioneered small-dollar online fund-raising. Like Sanders, Howard Dean caught nationwide appeal with his opposition to the Iraq War, and the money boosted his prospects to the front of a crowded field in 2004. Also like Sanders, Dean was unable to capture the Democratic nomination, but his committed following translated into a reliable source of fund-raising for the party, something he helped build as the chairman of the Democratic National Convention.

The parties couldn't go at this alone, however, which led to the founding of organizations like ActBlue and WinRed, which could leverage what was learned in the campaigns and create platforms for fundraising without endorsing individual candidates. ActBlue was first, founded in 2004 by Benjamin Rahn and Matt DeBergalis, two computer scientists who sought to make fund-raising affordable for candidates and available for small donors. In a profile of the team, they say they wanted to make "campaign fund-raising really easy, as easy as ordering a book online," reflecting the early success of Amazon.com, which began as an online bookseller. As of 2020, ActBlue has raised more than $4.7 *billion* for Democratic candidates and aligned organizations and is the party's unofficial default fund-raising platform for online donations.

Other than being first to market, why does ActBlue stay relevant in an era where competitors are offering suites of services? The platform takes a relatively small processing fee of 3.95 percent on donations, which provides the dominant share of the cash for campaigns and organizations. ActBlue rigorously tests its contribution forms on all platforms, so whether you are on a desktop, notebook, tablet, or smartphone, you'll get a form that will look right and take secure payments correctly. But beyond the tech, it is its commitment to providing the same tools for school board and presidential candidates alike. Its commitment to keeping credit card information secure is about as good as you'll find in any industry, and it has a support staff to help teams get going.

On the Republican side, WinRed is attempting to narrow the gap in online fund-raising, without the benefit of ActBlue's long head start but with strong support from the party, which ActBlue did not have initially. Launched in 2019, far behind ActBlue, the site is sparse in comparison, but under the hood the platform looks familiar. WinRed charges 3.8 percent plus $0.30 per transaction, making it potentially slightly less expensive than ActBlue. Donations split among multiple candidates incur the transaction fee only once, which enhances donor goodwill.

WinRed raised $30 million in its first three months, during Trump's first impeachment battle, proving that online fund-raising knows no party bounds. According to the FEC and as reported by Fox News, WinRed's start was better than what ActBlue raised in its first three and a half years. The difference? President Trump endorsed the platform and all the party committees and Republican candidates in the top targeted races used it. Additionally, the party has taken active steps to shut down any competition to WinRed.

Fueling both ActBlue and WinRed is cross-fund-raising opportunities. Each platform offers donors the ability to donate to like-minded candidates beyond the one they were there to support, like you would see if you were purchasing something from Amazon.com: *People who bought the thing you want also bought this other thing you might like.* The modern political campaign equivalent is: *People like you who donated to this candidate also support this one or this cause. Want to add another $5/$10/$20 . . . ?* Also like Amazon.com, you've already entered your credit card number, so there is no fumbling around to try to donate.

As mentioned in chapter 1, ActBlue and WinRed are quasi adjuncts to the political parties, vendors the parties endorse but do not own outright. In a sense, these spinoffs are the grassroots fund-raising operations the parties once had in-house but, because they could not innovate, ended up being run outside their respective tents. This allows for competition among vendors as well as less responsibility from the parties themselves to get the platforms right and support them, all of which is very expensive. However, this means that the parties are also less relevant in one of the core aspects of a campaign and leads to unintended consequences like Dean/Sanders-like candidates who are running against the party.

Both online platforms make it easy to get started, and for most down ballot campaigns this will be part of the job function of the fund-raising director. Therefore, it is crucial to hire someone who can not only raise money from big donors and might have the right kinds of relationships but can also work with technology-driven platforms like these. As we have seen in previous chapters, the definition of who might be the right person to lead a part of a campaign has changed, and in fund-raising if you do not have someone fluent with ActBlue or WinRed, you're likely going to leave money on the table that you'll need to defeat your opponent.

There is an art to getting the most out of these platforms. ActBlue offers a lot of customizable features, including the ability to embed single-click payments in e-mails, branding, targeting, and A/B testing to maximize conversion rates. ActBlue also offers Eventbrite-like ticketing and tracking for events, which helps coordinate donations, and integrates with campaign suite platforms so that you can track donors and manage compliance. WinRed's website is less transparent in what it offers, but in an interview with its president, Gerrit Lansing, I was assured that anything ActBlue can do, WinRed can do or will be able to do soon.

CAREERS

There is a big difference between a career in primarily high-dollar fund-raising and one that is more focused on mass fund-raising. High-dollar fund-raisers live for and on relationships. They are connectors, people who know hundreds if not thousands of people. They love to spend time with people and would prefer to meet with them in person as opposed to remotely. COVID-19 has been awful for them, but they remain in touch, as well all do, through texts, calls, and videoconferencing through platforms like FaceTime and Zoom. Mass fund-raisers, who live on low-dollar contributions, tend to be more technical and enjoy writing short-form appeals. They are comfortable with the analytics discussed above and understand what it takes to move the needle. Both are important to campaigns.

Breaking into high-dollar fund-raising involves building relationships through working on campaigns. While you might be setting up a room for a meeting or event, future high-dollar fund-raisers will spend their time working the room and understanding who the movers and shakers are and making connections with them. High-dollar donors appreciate the personal touch, so while a phone call or a text is nice, a written notecard or something from the candidate is better.

Working on campaigns also provides an ancillary benefit in building high-dollar donor relationships: the ability to tell political stories. If you've lived it, you can tell it. Being around charismatic political people leads to great tales, generally of close losses, as everyone in politics knows that's where you learn the most and where commitments are tested. Being in the room where it happens is not just a lyric: It's the real thing.

Breaking into mass low-dollar fund-raising is less onerous. By the time you're ready to enter politics as a profession or even to try it out, you've sent e-mails, written posts for social media, and know intuitively what you respond to and what might move someone else to action. There are a lot of great tools available, as discussed in this chapter, and it does not take much to put together a fund-raising appeal and test it on e-mail and social platforms. What you learn in addition on a team at a political party or a fund-raising agency that focuses on low-dollar donations is how to break through the noise and optimize the messaging based on data.

One way to break in is to join the National Association of Political Fundraisers. For $300 you get a basic membership, which opens the doors to network with some of the best in the field, become certified by the organization as a professional fund-raiser, and opt in to getting requests for proposals. The organization is bipartisan and can be found online at https: //www.napf.us.

THE FUTURE

What I expect to see in this space is a doubling down on the professionalism necessary to raise money and cultivate donors, artificial-intelligence-driven technology that will anticipate your interest in candidates or causes, and increasing speed of start-up to delivery of asks directly to your smartphone. Again using the Amazon.com metaphor, individual candidates may be able to leverage the platform, but those who succeed will be able to design the tweaks that maximize ActBlue's or WinRed's databases to target the right people at the right time. Fund-raising pros adept at designing short, impactful, messages will be in high demand as donor texting becomes more the norm, rather than social media or cultivated e-mail lists.

The only things that can hold back these developments in modern political campaigns is regulation and security. One can envision a backlash of smartphone owners petitioning government agencies for relief from political fund-raising via text as too invasive, much in the same way that surveys are now outlawed if they are autodialed, meaning if they're done automatically and without human interaction. This would effectively slow down the pace of electronic fund-raising and require more volunteers to text to donors.

Transaction and data security are other aspects that cannot be ignored here. If ActBlue or WinRed were to be hacked and user data leaked, platform confidence might erode, causing disruptions in campaigns and perhaps leading to the parties opening up the space to competitors or taking it in-house. Alternatively, one can also see that if they were hacked, as many of our other accounts have been, donors would simply change their passwords and methods of payment because of the convenience the platforms offer.

It's not outside the realm of possibility that components of these platforms could be offered open source, which would provide tech-savvy campaigns a way to skip the processing fees altogether, lowering the cost of raising money and shrinking platform dominance. Again, this is less likely, as these tools are highly proprietary and supported strongly by the parties, but if it were to happen, campaigns who hire the right professionals could save important dollars here.

The future of high-dollar fund-raising is data driven. High-dollar fund-raisers are already seeing the dividends in their ability to shorten the time spent doing background research on a donor before making the appeal. As voter data becomes more readily available, we will see races up and down the ballot being more efficient in who they approach, as they will be able to determine not only previous donation patterns but preferences on candidates, issues, and personal interests.

The most productive time with donors is spent getting to know them, and the very best high-dollar fund-raisers ask for money only after spending a lot of time with them. What if you didn't have to ask basic questions or questions that might make someone feel uncomfortable, and could better tailor how you approach someone as an individual, not just a random person who gives money to candidates? That would lead to better fund-raising success and, frankly, better relationships. This is why websites like Match.com are so successful: The more you know about someone before you meet, the better the interaction is for the both of you when you do. It is the same for high-dollar fund-raising—and all levels of fund-raising.

Initially, the effect of COVID-19 on political fund-raising was significant. As the virus hit, the official unemployment rate rose sharply to almost 15 percent and the actual figure closer to 20 percent, within range of the rate during the Great Depression. With so many people out of work, I've heard anecdotally that many campaigns have dialed down their fund-raising activities or are finding less interest from donors.

Still, there are signs that fundraising has resisted the virus on the macro level. As reported by *Politico*'s Zach Montellaro, ActBlue saw relatively healthy fund-raising in April 2020, which was the first full month of the pandemic. The $141 million collected on the platform was up 24 percent from March. On the Republican side, WinRed said it raised $129 million in the first quarter of 2020, which exceeded the $70 million raised in the fourth quarter of 2020. (Remember, WinRed's first full quarter of fund-raising was the third quarter of 2019 so there was no yearly trending available at this point.) By the end of the cycle, despite the pandemic, fund-raising had rebounded and eclipsed previous records.

ASSIGNMENT

Outline a draft finance plan for your candidate. Based on your analysis of previous races in your area, how much money will you need to raise to be competitive? Who will be the top donors and groups that will contribute to the campaign? Make a list of people you might know or contact to make pitches to each donor and group. Will you be able to afford a full-time fund-raiser or hire a consultant or firm? What events do you envision setting up for high-dollar donors? What is your low-dollar donor strategy? What technology will you need to invest in and which platforms will be most likely to pay off in terms of fund-raising? Finally, is the candidate in a position to lend the campaign money? Then, wrap all of this up on the revenue side of the planning spreadsheet from chapter 1 and see if you have enough money to run this campaign, comparing what you can raise to what candidates won with previously.

SOURCES

Ad Age. "Ad Age Agency Family Trees 2020." Retrieved May 11, 2020, https://ad-age.com/datacenter/agencyfamilytrees2020#549.

Andrews, Joe. "Majority of Americans Say They Won't Donate to 2020 Presidential Campaigns." CNBC, July 1, 2019. https://www.cnbc.com/2019/06/28/majority-of-americans-wont-donate-to-2020-presidential-campaigns.html

Center for Responsive Politics. "Aaron Schock—Illinois District 18." Retrieved May 10, 2020, from https://www.opensecrets.org/members-of-congress/summary?cid=N00029273.

———. "Donor Demographics, 2018." Retrieved May 10, 2020, from https://www.opensecrets.org/overview/donordemographics.php.

———. "Top Organization Contributors, 2018." Retrieved May 10, 2020, https://www.opensecrets.org/overview/toporgs.php.

———. "Top PACs, 2018." Retrieved May 10, 2020, https://www.opensecrets.org/overview/toppacs.php?cycle=2018.

Evers-Hillstrom, Karl. "Most Expensive Ever. 2020 Election Cost $14.4 Billion." Center for Responsive Politics. February 11, 2021. https://www.opensecrets.org/news/2021/02/2020-cycle-cost-14p4-billion-doubling-16/.

Federal Election Commission. "Contribution Limits." Retrieved May 10, 2020, https://www.fec.gov/help-candidates-and-committees/candidate-taking-receipts/contribution-limits/.

Greenwood, Max. "GOP Online Fundraising Platform Raises Nearly $130 Million for Republicans in First Quarter." *The Hill*, April 1, 2020. https://thehill.com/homenews/campaign/490560-gop-online-fundraising-platform-raises-nearly-130-million-for-republicans.

Hughes, Adam. "Five Facts about U.S. Political Donations." Pew Research Center. May 17, 2017. https://www.pewresearch.org/fact-tank/2017/05/17/5-facts-about-u-s-political-donations/. Topline results from the September 27-October 10, 2016 survey retrieved on May 19, 2020.

Iacurci, Greg. "Unemployment Is Nearing Great Depression Levels. Here's How the Eras Are Similar—and Different." CNBC, May 19, 2020. https://www.cnbc.com/2020/05/19/unemployment-today-vs-the-great-depression-how-do-the-eras-compare.html.

Isenstadt, Alex. "GOP Shuts Down Fundraising Rival." *Politico*, July 17, 2019. https://www.politico.com/story/2019/07/17/gop-fundraising-rival-1418073

Markay, Lachlan. "The Republican Party's Big New Online Donor Portal Is Off to a Bumpy Start." *Daily Beast*, August 6, 2019. https://www.thedailybeast.com/winred-the-republican-partys-big-new-online-donor-portal-is-off-to-a-bumpy-start.

Montellaro, Zach. "Morning Score." *Politico*, May 20, 2020. https://www.politico.com/newsletters/morning-score/2020/05/20/quorum-restored-at-the-fec-787764.

National Opinion Research Center (NORC) at the University of Chicago. "Americans' Views on Money in Politics." Conducted November 12–17, 2015. http://www.apnorc.org/PDFs/PoliticsMoney/November_Omnibus_Topline_FINAL.pdf.

Pappas, Alex. "WinRed, New GOP Donor Platform, Reaps Impeachment Windfall, Rakes in Millions Since Probe Launch." Fox News, October 1, 2019. https://www.foxnews.com/politics/winred-impeachment-republican-donor-platform-windfall

Schwartz, Brian. "Republican Firm Ramps Up Digital Fundraising for Push to Take Back the House in 2020." CNBC, June 11, 2019. https://www.cnbc.com/2019/06/11/gop-firm-ramps-up-digital-fundraising-in-2020-house-election-push.html.

Sparks, Grace. "Very Few Americans Are Satisfied with Campaign Finance Laws but Most Don't Know a Lot About Them." CNN, April 4, 2019. https://www.cnn.com/2019/04/04/politics/campaign-finance-polling/index.html.

Wayne, Leslie. "A Fund-raising Rainmaker Arises Online." *New York Times*, November 29, 2007. https://www.nytimes.com/2007/11/29/us/politics/29actblue.html.

Weissman, Stephen R., and Ruth A. Hassan. "Public Opinion Polls Concerning Public Financing of Federal Elections 1972–2000." Campaign Finance Institute. 2005. http://www.cfinst.org/president/pdf/PublicFunding_Surveys.pdf.

Wired. "How the Internet Invented Howard Dean." January 1, 2004. https://www.wired.com/2004/01/dean/

FOUR

Independent Groups

"If you only look at what is happening that's driven by the candidate, you're only looking at about 1 to 3 percent of the entire buzz about that candidate at the presidential level. The percentages will go up as you go further down the ticket."
—Dr. Alan Rosenblatt, Democratic digital strategist

The most significant change in how political campaigns are waged is the increase in the number and activity of independent groups and their increasing control of modern races. As we have seen, we have moved from an era where political parties ruled who appeared on a ballot and how campaigns were run into an era of candidate-centered campaigns, where self-starters launched their campaigns sometimes with, and often without, the party's blessing or support. With the recent shifts in campaign finance law and policy, outside groups have gained influence, at times with tacit support from candidates and the parties, but often without it.

As a historical aside, the Founders would be horrified. If they were concerned about political parties, though Jefferson came around to the idea, the proliferation of well-funded independent groups brings us closer to their nightmares of mini mobs influencing government. In Federalist 10, James Madison argued, "The influence of factious leaders may kindle a flame within their particular States, but will be unable to spread a general conflagration through the other States." The problem in the modern era of political campaigning is that they have burned brightly and spread nationally.

LOSS OF CONTROL

By law, the ecosystem of independent groups we will discuss later in this chapter cannot coordinate with political campaigns directly. In reality, it is not uncommon for intermediaries to share their best information and strategies behind the scenes among people who know and support each other well. However, there are groups that occasionally operate completely independent of candidates and at times execute strategies that run against the campaigns.

Overall, this has made planning and executing a campaign much more difficult and akin to multidimensional chess: the campaign, the opponent, both parties, the media, and now rogue independent groups. This chapter will cover some of the ways we got here and how this has changed the strategies and tactics used by campaigns to try to keep a handle on the race. In short, it's much harder now to manage a campaign with all of the outside groups involved.

Making this even more complicated is that unlike campaigns, which have a shelf-life that expires on Election Day, independent groups have no such limits, meaning they have more time to raise money, organize, communicate, and, when it is time, engage the public without the written and unwritten constraints on candidates. For example, independent groups can be much more aggressive in attacking opponents than candidates can on their own, because if the message boomerangs, the candidate can simply disavow the tactic. Conversely, independent groups also serve to draw candidates closer to their purity tests on issues, while competitive general election campaigns would rather keep things a bit squishier.

Well-funded independent groups usually have elite-level staff, long-term access to the latest platforms, and enough run time to be speedy in a pinch. A mature independent group can do everything a start-up candidate-centered campaign can do, sometimes even better. Independent groups answer the question: What would happen if you didn't have to stop campaigning on Election Day?

Madison could not predict the ability of a faction to reach the entire country given the state of eighteenth-century campaigns. While our trio professionalism, technology, and speed dissolved the traditional level of control campaigns had, the prerequisite for this is the change in how groups are funded. For that, we turn back to the most important court case in modern elections, *Citizens United v. Federal Election Commission*, decided in 2010.

CHANGE IN MONEY FLOW

As most contentious decisions in American history go, it was close. By a 5–4 decision of United States Supreme Court, the federal Bipartisan Campaign Reform Act of 2002 (BCRA), also known commonly as the McCain-Feingold Act, was struck down. The act had prohibited advertising in support of a candidate in any context within thirty days of a primary or sixty days of a general election. Citizens United had sought to advertise *Hillary: The Movie* on television within thirty days of the 2008 Democratic primaries. The movie, produced by Citizens United, amounted to a feature-length hit piece on the former first lady and United States senator, in a sense a ninety-minute negative ad.

The court could have simply said that the ads for the documentary could not be aired or that the movie could not be run because it was made by a nonprofit 501(c)(4) organization, which limits election activity, but it went in the opposite direction entirely, overturning the BRCA completely and allowing not only nonprofits like Citizens United but also corporations and unions to make expenditures for "electioneering communications" independent of campaigns. This effectively opened the floodgates for contributions to all three, even if the court upheld requirements for disclosing who sponsored the ads themselves. That turned out to be a clerical sideshow, not a limit.

In a follow-up decision that same year, *SpeechNow.org v. Federal Election Commission*, the FEC lost again when the Federal Court of Appeals for the DC Circuit held that political action committees could accept unlimited individual donations as long as they did not directly give that money to candidates, parties, or other political action committees. This became the loophole for super PACs, which could raise money to spend independent of campaigns with an important caveat: The donors could contribute *unlimited* sums of money.

In both cases, the courts sided with free speech, albeit paid free speech. However, the practical effect of eliminating direct-to-candidate limits through super PACs was to drive huge amounts of money to these organizations for political activity. With money comes professionals and the ability to invest in the latest technology advances as well as rapidly deploy them. This is why super PACs are so powerful and how they can leverage all of that money to influence elections and complicate campaigns, even those of candidates they might support.

TYPES OF INDEPENDENT GROUPS

This case law created new kinds of political action committees, so let's make sure we get our definitions right (with the help of the FEC). The jargon can be confusing, so I'll include a couple examples of each one below.

- *Separate segregated funds (SSFs)* are political committees that are connected to corporations, unions, membership organizations, or trade associations. These PACs can solicit contributions only from people working for or associated with the main group. In the real world, this means that a major corporation like Microsoft could also have its own political action committee—which, in fact, it does (https://www.microsoft.com/en-us/corporate-responsibility/public-policy-engagement). Lest I be viewed as picking on a successful corporation, and one that I worked for and enjoyed, recall that the Congress of Industrial Organizations, the CIO in AFL-CIO, organized the very first political action committee in 1943.
- *Nonconnected committees* are political committees without the above strings attached. These are not restricted to soliciting only from the groups to which they are connected; they can raise money from the general public. Emily's List and the Club for Growth are two groups that fall into this category. They are independent organizations that are not connected to a specific company, labor group, membership, or trade association.
- *Super PACs* are political committees that have even fewer restrictions, which is why they have grown so dramatically over the past decade. They can receive any amount from individuals, corporations, labor unions, and other PACs as long as they act independently. In addition to super PACs that have an interest in policy, we have seen a growth of extraordinarily well-funded, semialigned—but *unofficially* so—presidential super PACs. Jeb Bush's super PAC, Right to Rise, raised more than $114 million through July 2015 and helped him dominate the early part of the race for the Republican nomination for president that cycle. Still, they weren't always in sync, as some of Right to Rise's sharper attacks on rivals were disavowed by Bush himself.
- *Hybrid PACs* are political committees that seem more complicated than they're worth. A year after *Citizens United* and *SpeechNow.org*, *Carey v. Federal Election Commission* held that nonconnected campaign committees could keep separate bank accounts, one that solicits and accepts unlimited contributions for independent expenditures and another that can contribute to candidates, if it followed the federal limits. The court, in effect, said, "Fine," so hybrid PACs are also known as Carey Committees. Ready for Hillary was an example of this kind of PAC, which, like Jeb Bush's Right to Rise PAC, preceded (and seeded) the campaign before it went official.
- *Leadership PACs* are political committees set up by members of Congress and other leaders to regift money to other candidates. This is

a standard practice at all levels of campaigns, and you'll find that most of the money raised by many leaders in state legislatures is given to other committees. This kind of PAC allows them to directly raise money for others and keep campaign funds for their own races separate. This helps leaders engender goodwill within their caucuses as well as gain or retain leadership power. For example, both Speaker of the House Nancy Pelosi and Minority Leader Kevin McCarthy both have leadership PACs and are, shall we say, rather generous with their colleagues.

• *Foreign-connected PACs* are PACs formed by foreign companies, which is legal if they have a division in the United States and as long as only their American workers contribute to it. No foreign nationals may contribute to this kind of PAC, and disbursements are allowed only to American candidates and PACs. Some foreign-owned companies that have such PACs might surprise you, as they did me; they include seemingly American institutions such as 7-Eleven, owned by Seven & I Holdings in Japan; Anheuser-Busch, owned by InBev in Belgium; international consulting company Accenture, which is based in Ireland; and T-Mobile USA, which is owned by Germany-based Deutche Telekom.

The following groups are considered nonprofits but cannot explicitly call for the election of a candidate. They can provide certain educational activities, such as public forums and voter education guides, but must do so in a nonpartisan manner. Mind you, this is political participation as long as they do not cross the line of saying, "Vote for Candidate X" or, "Do not vote for Candidate Y."

• *501(c)(3) organizations* are groups whose purpose is organized around activities such as charitable, religious, scientific, or literary pursuits; testing for public safety; fostering national or international amateur sports competition; or preventing cruelty to children or animals.
• *501(c)(4) organizations* are groups that are considered civic leagues, social welfare organizations, and local associations of employees.

EXPANSION OF PACS

In 1975, only 722 political action committees were registered, split among 139 corporate and 226 labor committees. By 1985, this had grown to more than 4,000, with significant growth among nonconnected PACs, and this number plateaued at under 4,500 until 2007. In the run-up to the twin FEC decisions, 359 additional groups were added, but just two years later, after the cases were concluded, the number exploded to 6,331, continuing to grow to 7,548 in 2014 before dropping off slightly in 2015, an off-year election for virtually all federal campaigns. The result was more groups, more spending from relatively fewer donors, and far more influence on elections outside of the parties and campaigns.

With the legalization of super PACs, where wealthy donors could contribute unlimited money, that number grew to 2,276 and close to $3.5 billion, with total independent expenditures of more than $2.1 billion for the 2019-20 election cycle.

For perspective, in 2012, the first election after *Citizens United* and *SpeechNow.org*, super PAC spending in presidential elections alone was $600 million dollars. Four years later it was $1.1 billion dollars. It is even more striking during the midterms. In 2010, super PAC spending was less than $100 million, which grew to more than $350 million in 2014 and more than $800 million in 2018. As the final 2019-20 figures show, this is what happens when you give donors a venue for unlimited contributions—a great deal of the political money goes there.

INDEPENDENT EXPENDITURE

So far, I've focused more on the donation side, but what about the expenditures themselves? How do these groups spend their money? In short, just like a campaign. They commission opposition research and polling, engage media consultants, place ads, and hire field staff. In fact, most consulting firms, no matter what their expertise is, gladly work with the independent expenditure (IE) campaign, instead of the candidate's campaign, as sometimes they are better funded and organized. It is widely known who these groups support and oppose. Moreover, they are empowered with the tacit approval of the party and an unofficial wink and nod from the campaign.

The most powerful independent expenditure tool is advertising, and super PACs spend much of their unlimited donations on ads. According to the Center for Responsive Politics, super PACs raised more than $3.4 billion during the 2020 political cycle and spent more than $2.1 billion, accounting for 63 percent of all outside campaign spending. If you want to spend unlimited money on advertising to communicate with voters, the biggest chunk of it is going through super PACs.

DONATIONS TO CANDIDATES

Political action committees also donate quite a bit to candidates and likeminded groups. PACs may contribute to candidates directly, but these donations must be reported to the FEC and therefore are in full public view, quarterly. The limits on these donations are also far stricter:

- $5,000 to a candidate or candidate committee during the primary and another $5,000 during the general election
- $5,000 to a separate political action committee
- $15,000 to a political party each year

As one might expect, incumbents are overwhelmingly more likely than challengers to get PAC spending. This reinforces the incumbent advantage, which usually gives them about a 9 in 10 chance of winning reelection. Business groups are much more likely to give virtually all of their money to incumbents, while labor and ideological groups are more likely to spread their money around to challengers and to candidates running in open seats, of which there are relatively few. For perspective, based on the 2018 cycle, defense and communications and electronics businesses gave more than 95 percent of their money to incumbents. Ideological groups, by contrast, gave about 58 percent to incumbents, while they gave 23 percent to challengers and 19 percent to candidates running in open seat races.

Remember that indirect activities are not bound by these limits. This allows super PACs, specifically, to raise and spend unlimited funds communicating with the public to elect Candidate X or to vote against Candidate Y. As long as there is no coordination between the super PAC and the campaign, which is extremely hard to prove, these groups can spend as much as they want supporting or opposing any candidate for any federal office.

DARK MONEY

Funds from anonymous donors that go unreported effectively hide large donations from wealthy individuals who would rather not complicate their personal and professional lives with their political contributions. This is a key reason why big money goes to tax-exempt nonprofits and super PACs to spend money independent of candidates—it provides donors public cover.

Dark money flows through 501(c)(3)s that operate as religious, scientific, or educational groups but are limited to voter registration. 501(c)(4) organizations can engage in uncoordinated politics, as long as it is not their primary purpose, as can 501(c)(5) labor organizations and 501(c)(6) business organizations. Again, there are no limits to donations or spending, and it is dark because the donors do not get outed by FEC reporting.

CONSULTANT STORY

The two most visible impacts from independent groups are their ability to raise money and their spending on communications. The most conspicuous recent example was the super PAC Right to Rise, which allowed Jeb Bush to raise and spend more than $100 million on his campaign. When Bush announced his candidacy in June 2015, leadership of the super PAC passed over to Mike Murphy, his consultant, and then the two couldn't formally coordinate. But everyone in politics knew that Murphy was fully informed of what Bush might want, so this independence was strictly on paper.

The amount of money raised was staggering, and in most elections would have scared off opponents, but few shied away from the fight. The super PAC spent a lot of money on advertising, Murphy's specialty. Many of the ads took on Bush's in-state rival, Marco Rubio, making the path to the nomination easier for Donald Trump. What all of the spending didn't do was help Jeb Bush, who never seemed to find his footing and was savaged for "low energy" by Trump in debates for his laid-back demeanor. Bush and his super PAC tried to run a traditional campaign with a closely affiliated super PAC—and lost.

Despite the high-profile loss, independent groups have proliferated and, according to Dr. Alan Rosenblatt, much of the "buzz" in a race is generated outside the campaign. Rosenblatt estimates that about 4 percent of digital content is created by the campaign about the campaign, while the remainder is created by outside groups, unaffiliated surrogates, and partisan media. The bottom line is this: Independent groups have a lot more influence now than ever because the money flows with less friction there and they can be more aggressive. Campaigns are operating with less because the rules of direct donations are more stringent.

CAREERS

With the growth of PACs, specifically super PACs, the number of jobs available outside the parties and campaigns has grown exponentially. As I alluded to earlier, it has also fed an expanding consultant class because PACs, parties, and campaigns all write cashable checks. What this means for aspiring politicos is that you need not work for the parties and campaigns directly to make an impact on an election cycle. In some cases, unless you have a strong preference for red, blue, or a particular person, the better move is to join a PAC that supports a wide range of candidates who support a cause. Most of my students are mission driven, not candidate obsessed. For them, a job with a PAC offers an opportunity to meet like-minded people and work on issues, not just races.

As with campaigns, there are quite a few options in terms of jobs. Some well-funded PACs will send field staff to competitive races to encourage local voters to support their candidates. PACs generally run lean, so you can move up in the ranks relatively quickly, particularly if you stay with the PAC after a cycle, when job movement is expected.

Moreover, you can gain experience in working with and, at some PACs, managing vendors and consultants, which is great training if you would like to run campaigns as either a campaign manager or a general consultant.

Jobs at PACs are advertised widely on the websites I've included in this book. Beyond those, the key is to network. The best way to get an entry-level job at a PAC is to go to one of its events and get to know those who already work there. During the cycle, there is a constant need for talent, and if you are willing to do grunt work early, it pays off relatively quickly. Take it from experience: Smart people with great résumés are easy to find; finding people who are willing to work hard is much more difficult. Finally, before you approach a PAC for a job, make sure you have done your homework on the mission of the PAC as well as who it supported last cycle. If you miss doing either one of these, you may end up either working with a group that doesn't fit you or be asked to work on behalf of a candidate you don't support.

THE FUTURE

What's next for independent groups in the United States? More than likely, we will continue to see the number of PACs and super PACs group grow, and it is not unreasonable to believe the money will follow there as well. That's basic politics under our current rules. As these groups mature and integrate all of the tools of modern political campaigns, we will begin to see them grow as gatekeepers to candidacies. In some respects, that has already happened among a select subset of independent groups like the United States Chamber of Commerce. Get the endorsement from them and in Republican circles it's like you've been branded with a big red approved stamp. And as independent groups become more professionalized, they will have more influence.

Beyond that, one can envision blowback on unlimited spending. It might not be today or tomorrow, but once in a generation some enterprising member of Congress or presidential candidate attempts to bend the money tree, and super PACs might just end up on the wrong side of that debate. Any limits to super PAC's raising or spending money would stunt their growth, and political money would need to find another home. As long as money and speech are viewed within the same context, a conservative Supreme Court will uphold it, so the tug of war against unlimited money in politics will go another round, and what super PACs do currently may end up under a different name. The history of money in politics is that it always finds a way.

Successful campaigns will find ways to better predict the behavior of and manage the income from independent groups. Again, what we will do versus what they will do is too simplistic in modern political campaigns. As groups mature, they will be able to work down the ballot, which means that state legislative campaigns as well as local elections will become more complex. Taking into account what groups might play in your race will become an increasingly standard way of planning and executing political campaigns. The more independent groups add professionalism, technology, and speed to the mix, the more dangerous they could become to a campaign. In future campaigns, it will no longer be okay to ignore them. The days of two-dimensional campaign chess are over.

What the most successful independent groups will do is double down on their focus on membership, creating stronger bonds with individual voters, who they will be able to activate during campaigns to support candidates. While the tools are there today, few organizations do a great job of managing what they know about their membership, which is viewed as a lower-level function than fund-raising or lobbying. As the tools become commoditized, we will see better representation by individual groups, and this will make politics more personal for their members.

ASSIGNMENT

Choose an open race for county commission in your area and focus on which groups will be active in the campaign in the primary and the general election. Focus on professions and industries that are key to the local economy as well as other independent, more issue-focused groups. What issues might bring them out to work for or against your candidate? Which groups are essential to lock down for your campaign and, conversely, to keep away from your primary opponent? Are the groups that will be active on your behalf better funded than those that will run against you? Which groups might decide to pass on the primary but engage in the general election? Who are the leaders of these groups and what kinds of relationships could you leverage to get in their ears?

Once you have the list, plot them out on a scale from least likely to most likely to participate in the election on the x-axis and whether or not they will support you on the y-axis. Groups closer to the top right of the grid are the best independent groups to approach for support, while those in the bottom left quadrant are to be ignored. Once you have plotted the groups that will support you, try to guess what they are most likely to contribute to your campaign in terms of money, services, and field staff. This will influence how you will spend your own money, because if you feel confident in that group and that they will do the right things to support you, then you will need to spend less in those areas. If you don't trust them to *really* help your campaign, then it doesn't matter what they will do and you can ignore them as well.

SOURCES AND FURTHER READING

Bai, Matt. "How Much Has Citizens United Changed the Political Game?" *New York Times*, July 17, 2012. https://www.nytimes.com/2012/07/22/magazine/how-much-has-citizens-united-changed-the-political-game.html.

Center for Responsive Politics. "2020 Election to Cost $14 Billion, Blowing Away Spending Records. October 28, 2020.

———. "Foreign-Connected PACs." Retrieved April 19, 2020, from https://www.opensecrets.org/political-action-committees-pacs/foreign-connected-pacs.

———. "Outside Spending." Retrieved April 19, 2020, from https://www.opensecrets.org/outsidespending/fes_summ.php.

———. "PAC Dollars to Incumbents, Challengers, and Open Seat Candidates." Retrieved April 19, 2020, from https://www.opensecrets.org/overview/pac2cands.php?cycle=2018.

———. "Super PACs." Retrieved February 12, 2021, from https://www.opensecrets.org/political-action-committees-pacs/super-pacs/2020

Dalgo, Emily, and Ashley Balcerzak. "Seven Years Later: Blurred Boundaries, More Money." Center for Responsive Politics, January 19, 2017. https://www.opensecrets.org/news/2017/01/citizens-united-7-years-later/.

Duffin, Erin. "Total Number of Political Action Committees (PAC) in United States from 1990 to 2015. Statista, March 17, 2020. https://www.statista.com/statistics/198132/total-number-of-us-political-action-committees-since-1990/.

Evers-Hillstrom, Karl. "Outside Spending Reaches Record $2 Billion as super PACs Hammer Trump." Center for Responsive Politics. October 19, 2020. https://www.opensecrets.org/news/2020/10/super-pacs-hammer-trump/

Federal Election Commission. "Political Action Committees (PACs)." Retrieved April 19, 2020, from https://www.fec.gov/press/resources-journalists/political-action-committees-pacs/.

———. "Statista analysis of Political Action Committees—Number by Committee Type via FEC Press Release." Retrieved April 2020 from http://www2.census.gov/library/publications/2011/compendia/statab/131ed/tables/12s0422.xls.

Garecht, Joe. "How to Write a Fundraising Plan for Your Political Campaign." Local Victory, February 8, 2016. https://www.localvictory.com/fundraising/political-fundraising-plan.

Internal Revenue Service. "Restriction of Political Campaign Intervention by Section 501(c)(3) Tax-Exempt Organizations." Retrieved April 19, 2020, from https://www.irs.gov/charities-non-profits/charitable-organizations/the-restriction-of-political-campaign-intervention-by-section-501c3-tax-exempt-organizations.

MacColl, Spencer. "Citizens United Decision Profoundly Affects Political Landscape." Center for Responsive Politics, May 5, 2011. https://www.opensecrets.org/news/2011/05/citizens-united-decision-profoundly-affects-political-landscape/.

Microsoft. "Public Policy Engagement." Retrieved April 18, 2020, from https://www.microsoft.com/en-us/corporate-responsibility/public-policy-engagement.

Pruitt, Sarah. "The Founding Fathers Feared Political Factions Would Tear the Nation Apart." History, last updated March 7, 2019. https://www.history.com/news/founding-fathers-political-parties-opinion.

Rosenblatt, Alan. Interview with the author. May 8, 2020.

Statista. "Number of Political Action Committees by Committee Type." 2015. http://www.statista.com/statistics/198140/number-of-us-political-action-committees-by-committee-type/.

Vandewalker, Ian. "Since Citizens United, a Decade of Super PACs." Brennan Center for Justice, January 14, 2020. https://www.brennancenter.org/our-work/analysis-opinion/citizens-united-decade-super-pacs

Zieger, Robert H. *The CIO 1935–1955*. Chapel Hill, NC: University of North Carolina Press, 1997.

FIVE

Vulnerability and Opposition Research

"I do full-research books on people running for office. I'm going to look at everything. I'm not going to go digging into trash cans. I'm not going to follow you around like a detective. But anything that's public record, online, anything that I can order, I will do. I'm not going to follow you around and see if you are screwing another woman. That's what a private detective does. That's not what I do. I put together research reports, so you have a good, solid, understanding of who the person is."

—Erik Milman, Democratic opposition researcher

As Erik Milman describes above, modern vulnerability and opposition research is not the stuff of campaign legend, where staffers break the law to get the goods on a candidate. As you will see in this chapter, it is a much more professional, technologically advanced, and speedy enterprise than hiring an undercover operative to track someone in the hopes of finding the one thing that will kill a campaign. In reality, there are few campaigns that turn on one bit of information, and the best information is almost always readily available in public documents. Let's begin with a discussion of the relative power of negative information, as it is what is most likely to derail your campaign as well as your opponent's.

NEGATIVE INFORMATION

Most candidates are relentlessly positive people. They have to be because of the constant challenges and rejection they get from the general public as well as a justifiably skeptical media. They want to talk about what they want to do, or at the very least why they're so great and therefore worthy of election to public office. But positive information often comes across as unsurprising, because *of course* candidates believe in what they're selling, and they tend to aggrandize their background and experience. Politics is part salesmanship, so voters take the positive within that context.

Positive information is often too general to matter much in the heat of a campaign. Most of the time, things candidates say are easily dismissible, like that they are great parents or are successful, which simply confirms what we expect to hear. If positive information is too detailed, voters tend to look at it with an eye to determine what is fake: *You're such a great parent that your kid has never gotten a B? No way! You are the most sought-after accountant in Virginia. Oh, c'mon!* This is why positive information tends to be general—if you get too specific, you invite negativity.

This is why negative information can be powerful and why campaigns need to go find it on opponents as well as their own candidate. It's more engaging, interesting, and powerful than positive information. This chapter will cover vulnerability and opposition research as well as how it is practiced in the modern era. The first thing to understand is that no one oppo nugget sinks a campaign by itself; it needs to have context.

According to Jeff Berkowitz of Delve, one of the best firms in the business on the Republican side, this kind of research is about finding information about "the things we say, the stories people tell, and the trail we leave behind." But more importantly, it's about turning research into action through storytelling. As you'll see in the discussion in chapter 7 on focus groups and polling, this is the way I tend to look at it as well. Remember, most voters do not think about politics all the time. Consistent narratives are crucial to helping voters understand why negative information should be considered as they make their decision among candidates.

Disparate moments of a candidate's life may be interesting by themselves, but they become more powerful when they either create or double down on a narrative. The reason news of a 1976 drunk driving charge, dropped on George W. Bush late in the 2000 campaign by Al Gore's press secretary, Chris Lahane, was so powerful was that it reinforced the preexisting narrative that Bush wasn't serious and had a drinking problem when he was younger. The idea that he had withheld this from voters became a big issue late in the cycle and, according to some analyses, cost Bush a clean victory on Election Day; instead he had to wait until the Supreme Court awarded the victory in its 5–4 decision in *Bush v. Gore*.

THE TOUGHEST QUESTION

I've asked this question of candidates, and it has never shown up on a poll (at least not directly): *What do we need to know about you that they will use against you?* Candidates never want to give you the goods on them, as they know their right to privacy ends when a campaign begins. But we all have things in our past that we would rather not see on a website, in print, or on video. Yes, there's a photo of me on my twenty-first birthday that I hoped would never surface, but it did. Friends of mine had copies made and placed them all over my parents' home on New Year's Eve in the most epic gag of all time. Was it criminal? No. Was it embarrassing? Of course! But it was all in good fun because I wasn't running for office.

No one wants to face up to their childhood, young adulthood, or even adult lapses or personal issues. This is why my clients have always lied to me when I've asked the question. This is why you need to hire a professional to make sure you find what is findable before the opposition does. When you know what might turn up in a negative story or ad, it helps the team plan for responses to limit the damage. If it is truly something that needs to be addressed, it is good practice to release it yourself to better frame what happened; otherwise you're leaving your opponent to do that for you, and it absolutely will not be kind.

As an aside, this is the one class in my course that truly freaks out my students—once they understand how vulnerable they are, they are much more likely to be circumspect about their political futures. My students, and most people who grew up Millennial or Gen Z, do not understand why this would be a problem for them. In most cases, everyone they grew up with had a phone with a camera and all kinds of crazy was captured, including things they might regret. The theory goes like this: *Sure, I have done stupid things, but so has my opponent. Why would this matter at all?*

The problem is that you have no idea how the information will be combined with other available data to paint a picture that skews who you really are, which, presumably, is someone we would all be proud to represent us. One bad decision or bad day *usually* does not kill a campaign. But if you do not get ahead of it as early as possible, you can end up on the wrong side of it, and for most campaigns there is no way to recover. Without an information advantage, answering the toughest questions about your candidate and your opponents, the story of the campaign can get lost very quickly.

OPPONENT FRAMING

So much of winning in politics depends on which ground the debate is engaged. Framing the debate over what is important in an election—which issues, candidate characteristics, and proposed solutions—is essential to winning. Framing your opponent is just as important as framing the issues and solutions debated. Some candidates want to shy away from negative campaigning, and there is some intrinsic appeal to this, but it is unrealistic given the nature of the modern political campaign.

In most cases, as we learned in chapter 1, voters are less tied to political parties and specific issues than they are to the people holding them. Therefore, making sure that your candidate's narrative is as positive as possible and your opponent is not given a free pass is just as important as framing the debate more broadly. Remember, many of the same people who voted for Jimmy Carter in 1976 voted for Ronald Reagan, who defeated him in a landslide, in 1980.

In the heat of a campaign, journalists and the opposition are doing their very best to answer the question of what will be used against your candidate or an opponent so it's best to drop it before they do. In some cases, you can drop opposition research early enough, through quiet channels, and encourage an opponent not to run against you, which happens all the time. If the opponent is not cowed by the research, then it's truly off to the races and you're well advised to leak it to the media before they can reframe it for voters.

One of the under-the-radar reasons why Barack Obama won reelection against Mitt Romney is that the president's reelection team turned Romney's business success on its head, showing how his firm had laid off workers to achieve profitability for his clients. That story was sent to the press and they ran with it. The story about his putting his dog on the roof of his car was an oppo hit. A secret tape of Romney telling a fund-raiser audience that 47 percent of the nation wouldn't vote for him because they got free stuff from the government was leaked to the magazine *Mother Jones*. Romney was framed by the Obama campaign as someone who was insensitive and selfish, caring only for himself. It worked because Romney had changed parties and was personally awkward and stiff, reinforcing the existing frame.

RESEARCH STRATEGY

So how do we begin? Like with polling, we start with a set of core questions. I'll simplify them into two: Who are the candidates in this race? What kinds of documentable activities have they engaged in, and can we get them? Most voters have no idea who candidates are, especially if they have never run before but also when they are incumbents. Never overestimate how much politics lives in busy people's minds, especially in down ballot races where voters *might* remember the people's names on the ballot, let alone what they know about the candidates. What you are creating here are impressions of people, positive and negative, based on information and the feelings you might be able to create.

There is a big difference between knowing something and being able to document it. For years, Senator Amy Klobuchar of Minnesota was widely known as someone who treated her staff poorly. This was not a problem for her in statewide races, but it landed, early, in the 2020 presidential race. A widely read story was dropped that documented, in graphic detail, just how Klobuchar handled stress and how she took it out on her staff kneecapped her campaign and she never broke into the top tier. She was not able to deny what she had done because the opposition research was solid. The campaign sought to reframe it as her being tough, but that was not successful.

Beyond staffer stories, there are a lot of public records available if your team is committed to finding them. If someone has been in the public eye for a while, there are media interview quotes, social media posts, photos, and videos. If they've previously served on a commission in or legislature, there may be interesting "hero" votes, where they voted alone or with a very small group against a popular measure or for an unpopular one. Beyond that, there is sponsored legislation to mine, and known associates who might include donors with complicated histories and interesting stories to tell. Beyond these there is the personal: financial records, criminal records, lawsuits, and businesses. Families, friends, and other known associates might be investigated, uncovering caches of data to be analyzed and contextualized.

All of this adds up to a research plan. First, construct a wish list of documents you would love to have to support that what you are finding may be true. Today, the low-hanging fruit is not found in a dumpster but is generally found online, as much of our recordkeeping has moved online and is searchable. But everything will not be available there, and time and money are limited, so you will need to prioritize which supporting evidence is worth searching for offline. Remember, how this information is collected is just as important as whether it exists at all, so going over the line to land a document is never worth it. Violating the law for oppo is a poor decision, and most campaigns will and should fire you for even attempting to do that, even on their behalf.

DESKTOP RESEARCH

Since the dark art of opposition research is always evolving, let's look at some of the favorite sources pros use online. The following is a nonexhaustive list of websites where you can learn *a lot* about both your candidate and your opponent. Each offers something a bit different, and I'll put them into context below as well as some tips on how to leverage the most out of them. I am half-joking when I say these are dark arts, of course, as these are public datasets. What your candidate told his third-grade girlfriend about her ex is likely unavailable here—unless it was posted on Twitter, and why in the world would a third grader have a Twitter account in the first place?

- Advanced Google Search (https://www.google.com/advanced_search): Do not waste too much time with the dot-com and instead invest some time in the free advanced search from Google. Not only can you search for names of candidates, you can search for them within a context, within a specific time period, and on specific websites. Boolean searches can mandate or exclude certain words or phrases to keep search results uncluttered, particularly if you have a common name like "Michael Cohen."

- People Finder (https://www.intelius.com): Running against an unknown is very challenging, so the first question that needs to be answered is: Who are we dealing with here? People Finder, now owned by Intelius, provides anonymous searches of public records that can uncover a person's full name, phone number, addresses, age, date of birth, aliases, work experience, and college attendance. For a small fee, you can do quick searches of social networks and e-mail address, marriage and divorce records, criminal records, liens and bankruptcies, and court lawsuits and judgments. What's even more important than the data you can get here is where it might lead offline, where some of the best stuff about people can be tracked down.
- WhoIs.net (https://www.whois.net): Beyond checking to see if your preferred domain name is available, this is an underrated political resource, which can show not only what individual or entity owns a domain name but where it was registered. In some cases, it offers you a way to purchase the domain name you want rather than a clunkier .net or .us alternative. Sometimes, this site can reveal who the opponent's consultants are and helps you size up the race, and occasionally, when the oppo gods shine upon you, the domain is registered outside of the district, which opens up all kinds of questions about candidate residency, inappropriate use of corporate funds, or carpetbagging.
- Internet Archive/The Wayback Machine (http://web.archive.org): What did a website look like last year, last cycle, or even ten years ago? This is a useful website if you think a candidate has changed positions on issues or to expose embarrassing campaign oversights such as Photoshopping Getty Images in as supporters or—and this has happened—swapping out an aggrieved ex-spouse for a current, younger one. Overall, this gives you a good sense of how your opponent sells him- or herself, which provides insight into how to run your race.
- Federal Election Commission (https://www.fec.gov): For federal candidates, the unassailable source of campaign finance information is the official FEC website. This is the best way to see who is open to donating to your opponents and what kinds of work they do. Even better, it is great to see where they are spending their money, which helps to give you a clearer picture of their strategy. The biggest problem with the site is time is that reporting is quar-

terly, so this isn't the stuff of rapid response, but it can help uncover things that opponents would rather not publicize.

- Center for Responsive Politics (https://www.opensecrets.org): The CRP's website is an aggregator of money in politics from the FEC, so it does not include any nonfederal candidates. While the data is from the FEC, what the site adds is analysis and grouping of contributions in terms of industries, geography, demographics, and PAC support. CRP also does a pretty solid job of analyzing expenditures. All of this gives you a quick overview of the financial operations of the campaign, while the FEC website is better if you are searching for something specific, like a contributor, organization, or vendor.
- National Institute on Money in Politics (https://www.followthemoney.org): This site does the difficult work of aggregating statewide and state legislature elections. The data isn't as rich as what you will find on the federal level, but it can show you the top donors as well as broad sectors from where that cash was donated. For some candidates, it offers up associated filers, which could include a campaign committee, independent expenditure campaigns, and self-funding.
- LexisNexis (https://www.lexisnexis.com): If your candidate or opponent is a public figure, chances are that they have been in the news or have been quoted by a reporter for a story. LexisNexis is *not* cheap, but most firms have subscriptions to get the good stuff, which adds scope to the legal issues you can search, as well as a full search of available media and paid web content that might include your candidate or opponent. For low-dollar campaigns, most college students have some access to the platform, so it is always worth a search here.
- Legistorm (https://www.legistorm.com): The Political Research section of this site is expensive but extremely interesting. It includes staff salaries, which could open the door to knowing whether, for example, a member of Congress pays staff equal pay for equal work; searchable personal financial disclosures, which can give a view of their personal wealth; private travel, which can show who is giving an opponent special favors; and foreign gifts, which can help a campaign understand whether an opponent is getting freebies from foreign governments. This site also tracks town halls and public events so you can get a sense of who the opponent believes is important.
- Social media platform searches: By design, most social media platforms allow users to search for other people. This is great for a variety of reasons and also helps campaigns get a sense of their own candidates' public and private lives, as well as those of their opponents. The default setting to most social media is public, which means that at some level we are all searchable. One of my favorite

sites is Politiwoops (https://www.politwoops.com), originally published by the now-defunct Sunlight Foundation but now updated regularly by ProPublica, which tracks tweets that politicians all over the world think better of and delete.

- Specialized sites: There are dozens of other websites that track everything that has a public component to it. You can check to see how an organization used federal funds (https://www.usaspending.gov), whether a company or organization has had Occupational Safety and Health Administration issues (https://www.osha.gov/pls/imis/establishment.html), or how solid are the charities a candidate or opponent gave to or worked for (https://www.charitynavigator.org). If it involves a public transaction, chances are you will be able to find someone with that information.
- Special mention: Larry Zilliox's list of Research Starting Points (http://researchops.com/Links.html) is somewhat outdated (there are several broken links) but helpful in giving underfunded campaigns additional ideas of where to begin their investigation.

One important note: no matter what you find, the very best information is documented by someone outside the campaign. This allows voters to double-check credibility and encourages them to make their own decisions. Again, negative information is far more powerful than positive information because it engages the mind—we expect politicians to tell us how great they are, but if we are told something negative, it makes us wonder if it is true. A subset of voters will take the next step and check the documentation, so if it is true, the message has a better chance of influencing votes.

Still, while third-party testimony can be powerful, the voice that can absolutely kill a campaign is the candidate's own. These are the nuggets you live for in vetting and opposition research, and they are not always available online.

While it is tempting to believe in the veracity of claims you find on the internet, make sure you have multiple sources, if not the definitive source. Anything you learn from third-party websites needs to be verified with official documents or with interviews so that you do not unwittingly set up your candidate for a boomerang effect because the claim was incorrect. The only thing worse than the candidate's voice is oppo that is verifiably false. This goes for offline research as well.

FIELD RESEARCH

Not all that Twitters is research gold. In some cases, a lead will not be enough or the original documents will not be accessible online, so the campaign will have to decide whether or not it is worth sending someone to go and get them. It is one thing to believe something is true, to get an online lead, and quite another thing to actually be able to get verifiable information. While you might have learned part of the story online or through another person's recollection, where it leads may be decidedly offline, to a place far away from your campaign and among people you do not know.

Taking this kind of research on the road is not dumpster diving, but it generally involves visiting a government office and asking for a document that might not be able to leave the building unless you photocopy it or request it from the clerk. "You need to understand the public agency that you are submitting the request to and kill them with kindness," says Erik Milman. These conversations are a little closer to the line, but pros tell me that there is no reason to cross it because there is no law that requires someone to say, "This is for opposition research purposes."

Documents are accessible by any citizen, and all you need to do is fill out the right forms. If someone asks the uncomfortable question of why you want to see them, you can simply say that you are doing research, which is objectively true. You are under no obligation to say that it is for a political campaign. You have just as much right to see those documents as any other citizen. If they're public, you should be able to get them. The best way to construct a story on this information is, as veteran opposition researcher Alan Huffman says, to act like an elite reporter, get multiple data points, record interviews, and provide context: "We operate on two basic premises: Only documented facts truly matter, and everyone knows something we don't know."

The future of field research is remote. Jeff Berkowitz, CEO of Delve, says that over the past three or four years his firm has been able to build the capacity and relationships to get about "95 percent of what they would normally want to collect in a field program" via e-mail, phone, mail, and fax. This "virtual field research program" was built as a response to clients' not wanting to "put a researcher on a plane, even in normal times, to go and pick up records." While this approach takes more time and there are usually mailing costs, campaigns are willing to deal with both because the cost savings is so substantial. "In our experience, campaigns are more willing to put up with the additional time rather than put in the additional money," says Berkowitz.

ORGANIZATION AND ANALYSIS

While the collection of candidate research has modernized with the ability to do relatively simple internet searches, the art of analyzing that data remains. First, make sure whatever system you use limits access to those who are doing the investigating, preferably a small group plus the campaign manager and the candidate. If you go beyond these people, it is likely that the research will show up somewhere at a time not of your choosing.

Next, ensure the information is well organized. Come up with a system of tagging files so that your team can easily search them. What you find early in your research may become more interesting weeks, if not months, later, so retrieval is important to allow the campaign to react with speed. Finally, make sure that there is a link or background on where the information was found. This will help not only with documenting that it is from a source outside the campaign but will help you return to it should there be more to find.

Despite the advances in technology, many consultants continue to deliver the traditional book on a candidate, quite literally a printed or electronic document detailing all of the findings. This will pull together the strongest potential threats (if it is a vulnerability study) or opportunities (if it is opposition research) and include all of the supporting records and content. It will prioritize the strongest information available, including an analysis of why it is important and how it fits into the campaign themes. As the best in this field will tell you, this is where consultants make their money.

DEPLOYMENT

Research used to be a siloed activity where the team produced a book that would then sit on a shelf until the communications team needed content for a mailing or another set of advertisements. Today's vetting and opposition researchers are integrated into the communications teams, so they not only have a seat at the table but are able to advocate for the best approaches in real time so that it is in the daily drumbeat of narrative building. Earned and paid media teams now have live ammunition to deploy rather than rusty research gathering dust on a shelf.

Before this kind of research sees the light of day, it is assessed to determine where it fits within an assessment of strengths, weaknesses, opportunities, and threats, or SWOT analysis. Vetting research lives in the internal section of the grid, in strengths and weaknesses, which helps to define how to message, build coalitions, gain endorsements, and respond to any incoming attacks. Opposition research is the realm of opportunities and threats, external forces that might impact the campaign. Honest, documented, and pressure-tested vetting and opposition research opens up the playing field so the campaign knows when to attack, how to defend, and what is worth avoiding.

As we will discuss in chapter 7 on focus groups and polling, the raw data is reconfigured into overall narratives and specific messages to be tested with targeted voters. The results of this testing provide playbook of options for the campaign as well as evidence that they might work on different platforms under predictable conditions. As modern campaigns have learned, voters with the same don't necessarily react the same way to the same messages, so it's important to be able to handicap what will work with whom and when.

Beyond individual voters, winning over coalitions and endorsements is an important outcome of vetting and opposition research. Quiet, behind-the-scenes pitches are often where this work is done, and the vetting and oppo books are a part of them. Getting groups and high-profile endorsers to leverage their names on your candidate's behalf is enhanced by the knowledge that they will not have to disavow your candidate and can better understand why the opponent is the wrong choice for them.

The most visible use of vetting and opposition research is in media and rapid response, both of which are crucial to delivering and staying on message. Radio, television, and mail remain the best way to reach the widest audiences during campaigns, and selectively deploying opposition research is both cost-defensible and compelling. However, traditional broadcast media often takes too long to produce, so modern political media—text, social, search, and quick-turn video—has become the best venue for fighting back against attacks because of its ability to reach the most engaged voters quickly.

LIMITS

Sometimes you just miss. In 2016, the Ted Cruz campaign felt it had to pull an ad called "Conservatives Anonymous," which dinged Senator Marco Rubio of Florida for claiming to be a Tea Party hero, only to "cut a deal on amnesty." Another advised, "Maybe you should vote for more than just a pretty face next time." The person who the second ad was referring to was Amy Lindsay, who turned out to be an actress in softcore pornography films, not exactly someone Ted Cruz, campaigning as a traditional conservative, would have preferred to appear in his ad during the GOP primary for President of the United States. The campaign pulled the ad, but unfortunately, it had already run, so the damage was done. Campaign research teams, even ones at the presidential level, cannot vet every single actor in an ad, donor, or volunteer.

It's even worse at lower levels, where the planning for this type of research is more limited. This is how Virginia governor Ralph Northam was able to escape scrutiny of a 1984 medical school photo in which he was wearing either blackface or a Ku Klux Klan robe, neither of which Northam was able to (or willing to) confirm or deny. The photo was easily found in the yearbook, if you were looking for it. The problem was that Northam's opponent, a former RNC national party chair Ed Gillespie, didn't give his team enough time or money to do the kind of digging that would allow them to find it. According to Will Caskey, a Democratic opposition researcher, it would take more than the standard five weeks and roughly $10,000 to $12,000 to go to the level necessary to find that photo.

The information found through vetting and opposition research has its limits as well. While we'd all like to believe that the truth will move voters, modern campaigns now operate in a broader political environment that is far more skeptical of *any* information, even from traditionally trusted sources like broadcast and print mainstream media. Imagine what President Richard Nixon would have done with Woodward and Bernstein—"FAKE NEWS!" Monica Lewinsky's blue dress might have ended up as a mini-conspiracy—Who planted Bill Clinton's DNA? The bottom line is that while negative information can be powerful, only the best data will really move people, and it has limits.

The most striking modern example is the 2016 release of Donald Trump's *Access Hollywood* tape, in which he brazenly describes how he manipulated and harassed women because he was a celebrity. The release of the tape was well-timed for maximum impact in October. Under the unwritten rules of oppo, this was a coup of a drop. But what it did not account for was that views on Trump were already baked in, as voters knew their candidate for years as someone who "might just do that" and so the information was discounted. It did not shock their candidate view and did not separate him from Hillary Clinton, who had given her husband a pass on his own dalliances. Moreover, partisan media rallied to Trump's defense, and he was able to survive the damage and win the presidency.

The timing of the Access Hollywood tape release highlights the basic issue of how important getting the word out on opposition research is and the timing of its release. Well-funded or well-connected campaigns can buy or create an audience for it, but timing is just as important as the potential voter interest for the content. Will anyone care if a candidate for state representative cheated on their taxes? Maybe, if it is the only thing we know about the candidate and if the details are salacious enough to break through their literal and figurative reality TV screens. This is why the story of Aaron Schock broke through: It was a reality TV episode come to life. It was also dropped at just the right time, when he was at his apex and reporters were looking for something to bring balance to their coverage.

On the Democrat side, 2018 congressional freshman class president Katie Hill found herself exposed—literally and politically—when someone leaked compromising photos of her smoking marijuana, revealing a Nazi-era iron cross, and brushing her staffer's hair while naked. Texts were also leaked showing an embarrassing "throuple" relationship among Hill, her husband, and the staffer. Hill and her husband posted photos of themselves on wife sharing websites in 2016. It was a mess of an oppo dump and led to Hill's resignation as well as Republicans picking up the seat in a special election in May 2020. An audience for this did not need to be purchased, as nothing sells like a novel sex scandal with proof. Strangely, it landed in the *Daily Mail*, published out of London, but the story was written by reporters based in the United States. Opposition research knows no national boundaries. As one might imagine, it quickly found itself top news worldwide.

Finally, it is important to note that while the Schock and Hill scandals were obvious, not everything you, the team, or the candidate finds appalling will be to voters, which is why it should be pretested in focus groups or in polling. Once your team has decided that these are the best hits, road-testing the messages and countermeasures with real voters is an essential gut check. Again, the best tests are ones that take place within the timeframe where it will be released, but before that, you can make sure you are on the right track by gaining feedback before launching into messaging that might just boomerang.

CONSULTANT STORY

Let's loop back in with Erik Milman before we cover careers in and the future of opposition research, because he truly has an epic story to tell. Even better, it's about a candidate few followed, which lands an important point: Opposition research is sometimes more powerful in campaigns where the media spotlight is shined on them infrequently, because whatever gets covered has a greater impact. While I'm sure other states have great campaign stories, this one is about a Florida man named Howard Warshauer, who was a county commissioner running for mayor of West Palm Beach in 1999.

Milman was representing the Florida Police Benevolent Association at the time. Strangely, Washauer hated cops. There was no obvious reason for the enmity, but he voted against every police contract, and his public comments were kind of out there. "The guy hated police officers. In the meetings he would just grill them. There were some weird things he used to say. Things like, we've got to close down the police department if we're in a recession. We can't afford them. Okay, this guy is nuts. Why does this guy hate cops so much?" he remembers thinking.

Of course, there was a reason, but it took some digging. It turned out that he was a former New York City public school teacher. After he retired, he went to Florida, sold jewelry, and lived on a houseboat. Washauer had applied to become a stockbroker, but he "didn't fit the profile." It turns out, decades earlier, while he was a public school teacher, he had been a stockbroker in New York City. Milman says, "Howard and his partner were cheating little old ladies out of their savings. So, we found he had been arrested."

Milman sent a retired police detective to New York to get more information and found that the arrest was sealed. But they found out from the Securities and Exchange Commission that Washauer was barred for life from being a stockbroker because of stock fraud, so he couldn't reapply to become one. Milman found a *New York Times* article on it. Then Milman got someone to go out and find the microfiche to get the old complaint from twenty-five years before and it showed how he sent his partner to jail. "It was all right there," Milman says.

The reason Washauer didn't go to jail was because "he made a deal. We got the SEC files and they were running Ponzi schemes. And to top it all off, they formed a corporation in Florida, and they were running it in New York and Florida. We knew if we went public with it, Howard would say that it was the police lying to them."

Milman and the team found a reporter who was writing about the race and fed it to him. The result: Washauer finished third, missing the runoff between two candidates by less than seven hundred votes. In a close race, opposition research, expertly deployed, can make a big difference. All the information Erik was able to track down would have been inconceivable from a technical standpoint years ago, and it would never have been put together with the speed necessary to make a difference in the primary.

CAREERS

Vetting and opposition research often is handled at the political party so that the campaigns can spend their money and effort elsewhere. For campaigns without large bank accounts, this is extremely helpful, especially when the opponent is an incumbent and there is already a book on that person. But it even happens at the highest levels for campaigns with historic fund-raising, like the Trump reelection campaign, and this is an opening for young people looking to start their careers in research.

As reported in early March 2019 by *Axios*, the Republican National Committee was "taking the lead" in opposition research, funding a network of trackers in all of the early states. The goal was to film all of the leading Democratic candidates, trying to catch their mistakes at events in small towns or rural areas, which would be missed by national news media. In most cases, trackers are people who are either in college or just out of college, can travel at a moment's notice, and are willing to get paid relatively poorly so they can work on a campaign. Many of them move up during the cycle into other roles.

Outside groups play a significant role in disseminating opposition research as well. In 2012, American Bridge 21st Century, funded in part by Democratic donor George Soros, was able to take down Todd Akin, a Republican running for US Senate in Missouri, after tracking and packaging a gaffe where the candidate used the phrase "legitimate rape." Of course, no rape is legitimate, and although Akin later tried to explain he meant "forcible," the damage was done, it went national, and Akin lost the election.

After Mitt Romney lost election, his former campaign manager Matt Rhodes joined with two RNC officials to start America Rising, which would become the semi-off-the-books Republican rival to the semi-off-the-books Democrat group American Bridge. With some leftover funding from the Romney campaign, they were able to raise even more to hire researchers and trackers. In 2016, America Rising produced anti–Hillary Clinton materials, while American Bridge defended her. Both groups, and those like them, provide opportunities to break into the world of this type of research.

Many well-funded campaigns, however, hire outside firms to do the difficult work of vetting and opposition research, and that work pays fairly well. The kinds of skills needed include an extreme attention to detail and an ability to thread it altogether. The very best in this space have an intuitive sense for what is important and how it can bolster a candidate narrative.

The best advice to build a career in this kind of research is to take it slow and learn. As Berkowitz puts it, "I think there's a tendency for young people now to think it looks really easy. You click these things and, poof, you can do it. I think the people that are going to have longevity are the people who appreciate learning the craft and take the time to identify smart people. The reason I am where I am is because early in my career, I got to sit at the feet of people like Barbara Comstock and Tim Griffin, who revolutionized research for that era."

You can get experience in research at the local level, too. As Milman remembers, "I first got involved in research around 1995, 1996. A friend of mine was running for the state senate in Florida. He was running against a multimillionaire trial lawyer. He had asked me to look into his opponent to see if he missed any votes on the state ethics commission and things like that, and I really enjoyed it. Back then nothing was online, so I went to the state office where the guy served, and I enjoyed pulling the records to see what he did." Today, an opposition researcher could get that information at http: //ethics.state.fl.us. Milman concludes, "I think the way you break into this field is you definitely need to get involved with campaigns. Then when you move on to the research side you have an idea of how everything fits together."

Professionals in this space tend to do a lot more than candidate work. Companies like Delve, for example, help corporate clients with crisis communications as well as when competitors attack them. As there are millions, and in some cases billions, of dollars at stake, even large contracts for deep research are cost-benefit bargains. There is a good mix of one-person shops and small, medium, and large firms in the space, and, as one might imagine, the larger firms are more competitive for the larger corporate contracts. Still, in politics, relationships matter most, so it is not unheard-of that a former party staffer or retired candidate-turned–government relations professional has preferred vendors, even if they are small.

THE FUTURE

The future of vetting and opposition research has already arrived. As you can see, there is a great deal of information readily available on all of us, and, as we will see in chapter 7 on focus groups and polling, there is a wealth of information already aggregated on individual voters, including voting histories, modeled preferences, and some financial information. The data portfolio on all of us is very deep, which gives vetting and opposition researchers additional threads to pursue that were unimaginable even five years ago. While Cambridge Analytica imploded, the methods did not all of a sudden go forgotten. Beyond the available data is the social, contextual information that can be immediately accessed simply because we are all somehow connected online. While a particular individual might have a private account, *someone* is connected to that person, and all of us have either made mistakes or earned enemies.

Even the way this information is shared with campaigns is evolving. Berkowitz sees an evolving future where the venerable book is just one deliverable in a secure online portal where the campaign can access all the underlying data so it can be pulled when it's needed. "The more you track these things along the way, the more you can focus on analyzing what it means to the political context," he says. In addition, services like Quorum and GovPredict now have vote histories on incumbents going back a few years, making them more valuable to researchers. Connecting these platforms with original consultant research makes for a powerful suite of resources for modern political campaigns.

Still, as technology has improved and the speed at which information is available has increased, professionalism and the quality of the analysis have declined overall. Pros know what lines they should not cross, and inexperienced consultants using the latest tools may make poor choices, leading to either losing decisions or throwing good money after bad. The barriers to entry have lowered but the premium is now on the professionalism and analytic quality of the research.

Extending this future is the ease with which unsavory political operatives might hack an opponent's background or data. While this might seem unlikely, WikiLeaks remains operational, and every e-mail sent, every smartphone photo shared, notes on private platforms like Evernote, purchases on websites, and browsing activity all leave data trails. There is no guarantee that these online portals or services are safe from competing campaigns. Again, campaign plans get leaked and so does opposition research.

No electronic service is 100 percent secure, and if you do not think that your information will get out somehow, you are mistaken. It might not come from a stand-up firm like Delve or others, but an individual or rogue hacker could have just enough know-how and interest to find the one thing the campaign missed. There is no escape from this future. The best you can do is to be honest about the dumb things your candidates have done and prepare for the eventualities that they will not be kept secret.

How this information is further tailored to smaller groups of voters, even individuals, is the next wave of the use of opposition research. At this point, this kind of information is a blunt instrument and needs to serve an old-school broadcasting model where everyone gets the same message. But the more we know about voters, the more we will be able to target opposition research to move them. While focus groups and polling will always be helpful, improved data will allow campaigns to put more of the opposition research playbook to use, knowing that it is relevant to the voters getting this information.

ASSIGNMENT

Your best friend has asked you to be his campaign manager for state assembly. He won't have a lot of money to pay you or an opposition research firm, so it is up to you to dig dirt on him that is documented and widely available. It is, of course, the very worst thing a best friend can ask a friend to do. You already know a lot about him that you cannot say and could not be verified, anyway.

Setting a limit of one weekend, and setting aside any travel for this, please conduct your search using available websites in this chapter as well as your own social connections to him or her. Put together a book containing any of the following: personal, business, financial, political, and anything else you can find on social media connecting him to someone or something damaging. Then draft a short narrative of how you might attack your best friend if you were an opponent. Fill out a SWOT analysis grid of at least three strengths, weaknesses, opportunities, and threats.

Finally, sit down, just the two of you, and lay out what you found, why it could make your friend vulnerable to attack, and the various lines you think may end up being most damaging. Context matters in these conversations, but stay on target and take it from the perspective of a voter, someone who knows very little about your best friend. This is the moment where the serious candidates will understand what they're up against and where those who are less so will reveal themselves as great friends but terrible candidates.

SOURCES AND FURTHER READING

Access Hollywood. "Access Hollywood Archival Footage Reveals Vulgar Trump Comments from 2005." October 7, 2016. https://www.youtube.com/watch?v=NcZcTnykYbw Footage available on YouTube at https://www.youtube.com/watch?v=NcZcTnykYbw.

Allen, Mike. "Rove Suspected Gore Aide of DUI Leak." *Politico*, March 4, 2010. https://www.politico.com/story/2010/03/rove-suspected-gore-aide-of-dui-leak-033946.

Axelrod, David. "What is Opposition Research?" MasterClass. 2019. https://www.masterclass.com/articles/what-is-opposition-research-understanding-the-tactics-used-by-political-campaigns-to-conduct-and-use-opposition-research#how-is-opposition-research-used-by-campaigns.

Berkowitz, Jeff. Interview with the author. May 6, 2020.

Boswell, Josh, Martin Gould, and Jennifer Van Laar. "Shocking Photos of Congresswoman Katie Hill Are Revealed Showing off Nazi-Era Tattoo While Smoking a Bong, Kissing Her Female Staffer, and Posing Nude on Wife Sharing Sites." *Daily Mail*, October 24, 2019. https://www.dailymail.co.uk/news/article-7609835/Katie-Hill-seen-showing-Nazi-era-tattoo-smoking-BONG-NAKED.html.

Caskey, Will. "Why Didn't Ralph Northam's Yearbook Photo Surface Earlier?" *Campaigns and Elections*, February 4, 2019. https://www.campaignsandelections.com/campaign-insider/why-didn-t-ralph-northam-s-yearbook-photo-surface-earlier.

Corn, David. "SECRET VIDEO: Romney Tells Millionaire Donors What He REALLY Thinks of Obama Voters." *Mother Jones*, September 17, 2012. https://www.motherjones.com/politics/2012/09/secret-video-romney-private-fundraiser/.

Cruz, Ted. "Conservatives Anonymous." Campaign advertisement from the 2016 presidential primary campaign. Retrieved from https://www.washingtonpost.com/video/politics/ted-cruz-conservatives-anonymous--campaign-2016/2016/02/11/e3124d52-d107-11e5-90d3-34c2c42653ac_video.html.

Economist. "Digging Dirt, Digitally." July 12, 2014. https://www.economist.com/node/21606854.

Flegenheimer, Matt, and Sydney Ember. "How Amy Klobuchar Treats Her Staff." *New York Times*, February 22, 2019. https://www.nytimes.com/2019/02/22/us/politics/amy-klobuchar-staff.html.

Huffman, Alan, and Michael Rejebian. *We're with Nobody: Two Insiders Reveal the Dark Side of American Politics.* HarperCollins: New York, 2012.

Krieger, Hilary. "An Introduction to the Dark Arts of Opposition Research." FiveThirtyEight, October 31, 2017. https://fivethirtyeight.com/features/an-introduction-to-the-dark-arts-of-opposition-research/.

Milman, Erik. Interview with the author. April 29, 2020.

Moore, Lori. "Rep. Todd Akin: The Statement and the Reaction." *New York Times*, August 20, 2012. https://www.nytimes.com/2012/08/21/us/politics/rep-todd-akin-legitimate-rape-statement-and-reaction.html.

Moyer, Justin W. "Cruz Kills Campaign Ad Featuring Former Softcore Porn Star." *Washington Post*, February 12, 2016. https://www.washingtonpost.com/news/morning-mix/wp/2016/02/12/cruz-kills-campaign-ad-featuring-former-softcore-porn-star/.

Our Campaigns. "West Palm Beach Mayor—Primary." Retrieved May 20, 2020, from https://www.ourcampaigns.com/RaceDetail.html?RaceID=247008.

Rucker, Philip. "Mitt Romney's Dog-on-the-Car-Roof Story Still Proves to Be His Critics' Best Friend." *Washington Post*, March 14, 2012. https://

www.washingtonpost.com/politics/mitt-romneys-dog-on-the-car-roof-story-still-proves-to-be-his-critics-best-friend/2012/03/14/gIQAp2LxCS_story.html.

Treene, Alayna. "Inside the Trump Campaign's Plan of Attack." *Axios*, March 27, 2019. https://www.axios.com/inside-the-trump-campaigns-plan-of-attack-03364e8d-99ea-418b-b6e7-510c117dc0bf.html.

Westen, Drew. *The Political Brain*. New York: Public Affairs, 2008.

Zilliox, Larry. *The Opposition Research Handbook: A Guide to Political Investigations, Fourth Edition*. Investigative Research Specialists, LLC. 2012.

SIX

Data and Analytics

"Think of data and models in terms of not having a model. The purpose of a model is to be more efficient and make better decisions than you otherwise would be able to make. We need to think in terms of probabilities and efficiencies, instead of absolutes."
— Matt Knee, Director of Analytics at Republican firm WPA Intelligence

While political fund-raising has increased exponentially, we do not live in an age of unlimited campaign dollars, especially at the state and local levels. To maximize the campaign's potential, the lifeblood of modern political campaigns is data. Modern data, modeling, and analytics provide insight into who voters are so campaigns can meet them where they are: at home, online, and politically. These tools can save someone from running a race that cannot be won. In tight races, it can be the difference between winning and losing. For all campaigns, it provides avenues to contact voters most likely to support the candidate, which issues may be important to them, and which media they consume.

THE VOTER FILE

Political data begins with the voter file, a list of names that can also include addresses, party affiliation, and voting histories within a specific geographic area. The file can be as broad as a national database or as narrow as a town or municipality. In practice, its most basic use is to understand the universe of potential voters and put together a targeting strategy for identifying a majority to support a candidate. Advanced campaigns will combine the data with other political, commercial, and other information they collect to model voter interest and refine outreach.

As we learned in chapter 1, there is no national system of voting, so there is no single voter file. There are many. States compile Election Day reports from counties across the country, and it's not easy to cobble together a usable list for a campaign. Nationally, there are about 190 million voter records in the United States, and there is no common format or set of data points. In its raw form, the data contains errors and incomplete information. A name might be misspelled, a street address might not be current, or the voter may have died after the last election, making that person unavailable for the next one. Moreover, there may not be a live telephone number or a current e-mail address included.

A well-organized or well-funded campaign will have field staff or hire consultants to identify voters to check the voter file, fill in gaps, and discern who is for and against each candidate and who says they are undecided. It's a lot of work, but it pays off to refine who should or should not be on the target list. The better the list, the fewer dollars wasted on contacting or advertising to voters who will never vote for the candidate. Also, some voters change their minds during the campaign, sometimes from one candidate to another but usually from undecided or soft support to a candidate.

In addition to IDing voters, firms like Aristotle, L2, and i360 can provide a wealth of additional information, connecting a raw or refined set of data with additional political and consumer databases. These firms first filter what the campaign has through basic checks against the national change of address database and deceased voter lists. Then they match the voters to sources that can provide historical turnout and donor information, organization membership, and buying patterns. Some firms can match voters to social media accounts. There are literally hundreds of data points on all of us.

The next step, which is expensive but worth it if the campaign can raise the money, is to hire a firm that can add behavioral and opinion data for predictive modeling. This amplifies the data you have to infer anything from the strength of their party identification to issue interest and preference to media preferences to religious service participation. Note that while statistical modeling is scientific, it is not perfect, and what the models predict will shift during the campaign as the field team gains more information about voters. The key is to ensure a feedback loop back to the team constructing and analyzing the voter data so that the analytics are closer to reality.

In sum, political data is used to target voters and save resources. The data from official sources can be messy, but campaigns can either clean it up themselves, by having staff make calls or visit homes, or hire consultants or a firm to do it for them, by filtering the available information and combining it with other databases. Predictive modeling can help campaigns answer additional questions like which issues matter and which media voters prefer.

IDENTIFYING WINNABLE VOTERS

Voter file data reveal that we live in neighborhoods that have become more politically homogeneous over time. As we have become a more politically polarized nation, Democrats and Republicans have self-sorted into separate areas. Gerrymandering has made these patterns even more stark; many districts are reliably more conservative or liberal than they would have been if they had been constructed more on geography than on political strategy. Any effective targeting of voters will take into account where people live, not just who we appear to be, so field teams can spend their time and campaigns can spend their outreach dollars in areas that could have the most impact.

An initial approach to identifying potential voters is to categorize them into three groups: opponents, supporters, and undecideds. Begin with the voter file to see who has voted consistently in primaries for one party or another and map them based on where they live. For those who switch primary voting or skip primaries altogether, put them in the undecided bloc. This is the first pass of identifying who to spend time on during the campaign. You want to activate your base of supporters, ignore groups of opponents, and spend time understanding what issues drive the undecideds, who are typically not tied to one party or another.

It used to be the practice that supporters would not get voter contact outreach, but this has changed in the modern era. The theory was that these people would vote for your candidate regardless of what you did, so time or money spent activating them was wasted. The dominant theory today by practitioners is to maximize the potential vote total out of this group because persuasion is so difficult. In other words, ignore the opposition, as all you can do is activate them to the polls. Instead, focus on the small group of true undecideds and those either leaning toward or fully supporting your candidate who are most likely to vote.

Ignoring the opposition, check to see who has voted in the past several elections and how often. Voters with long participation histories are much more likely to cast ballots in the next election. The voter file will usually show how eligible voters have voted in the past four elections, and the commercial databases show even more. Whether it is the last four elections or the last ten, choose the races that look most like your campaign. In other words, if your candidate is running in a presidential election year, the previous elections that are most like yours will be quadrennials, not off-year elections. In Virginia, for example, state legislative races are run the year after a presidential, so looking at even-numbered contests for perspective is generally a waste of time.

Some states provide information on how people voted, in-person or by absentee ballots. This data is key to understanding how the campaign will approach voter contact as it defines whether a strong get-out-the-vote operation is meaningful and how much time should be spent in registering voters to vote by mail. It directs your field operations toward definable goals and helps bank votes before Election Day.

Next, cast aside registered voters who haven't voted by absentee or shown up on Election Days like your race, as it's not least cost-effective to focus on them. Trying to get someone to vote who is committed to avoiding elections is not worth your time or donor money. Target voters who are most likely to vote, who have perfect voting histories, and who are most likely to choose your candidate. Then move on to those with good voting histories say, 60–80 percent of the time. After that, move on to undecideds who have perfect voting histories and then those who vote at a high rate as well. These are your targets to ID.

From there, have your team call or visit each of these voters in the neighborhoods that make the most sense based on your preliminary mapping. You might find that the information you get from IDing voters does not match your initial expectations based on voter histories, but that's okay. This is why you ID or hire a team to do it for you. In addition to party affiliation, asked in terms of, "In general, do you vote Republican or Democrat?" (randomize the party order), find out what issues are important to them and gauge which messages appear to be most effective. Refine your expectations and targeting accordingly, and make sure this data is added to whatever you have from other sources to amplify the voter file with your field research.

CALCULATING VOTE TOTALS

To begin coming up with a plan for voter outreach, you need to know how many votes it will take to win. This is not as simple as halving the pool of registered voters and adding one vote to your side. It is a behavior-driven approach that begins with voter registration but involves patterns of votes cast. You also need the total number of ballots cast in the previous elections that look like your campaign's, as well as the number Republican and Democratic votes cast. Finally, you want to make sure you look up ballot at campaigns that headline a ticket to determine if voters chose one from the top but skipped the seat your candidate is running for.

As an example, let's say that a state house district has 100 registered voters. In the last race that makes sense to compare with yours, the Republican won 35 votes and the Democrat won 30, for a total of 65 votes cast in the race. That election also featured a governor at the top of the ticket. The Republican won 45 and the Democrat won 44, for a total of 89 votes cast.

Total registration: 100 voters
Total ballots cast: 89
Republican votes cast: 45

Democrat votes cast: 44

So while there was an 89 percent turnout for the governor's race, only 65 percent of registered voters cast a ballot for state house. Those who didn't may not have had enough information to make a choice or may simply not have liked either candidate—we don't know the answer, and it doesn't matter for our purposes here. What does matter is that there is an undervote, a difference between the top of the ticket and the state house campaign. These are votes left on the table and the easiest to reach.

If you ran the Republican in that race, the previous candidate for state house left 10 votes on the table, which would have led to a bigger victory. It's even worse for the Democrat, who could have won the election in a landslide by picking up the 14 undervotes. If you're advising a candidate, this race is winnable by either the Democrat or Republican without changing the composition of the electorate.

Let's look at another example. Say the state house district has the same number of registered voters and ballots cast, but the previous race was won by the Democrat. The Democrat got 45 votes and the Republican got 20, a wipeout. The governor's race also flipped and the Democrat won 50 and the Republican won 39, another landslide. The undercounted votes would not have mattered, as the Republican would have still lost by six votes.

What happened? There are several options. The Republican candidates could have been lackluster while the Democrats were outstanding in the previous race. Alternatively, something could have been going on underneath the surface in terms of demographics and political affiliation; one or both may have shifted. Something changed, because the total number of registrants and ballots cast did not; that the composition of the electorate changed, not its size.

Another way to close the gap would be to grow the participation rate. In our example, that would mean getting closer to 100 voters from 89. Let's say every voter cast a ballot for state house. To estimate the expected number of votes, you take the number of nonvoters (11) and divide it by the percentage of the vote. In the first example, the Republican would have earned 53 percent of the vote for the state house election— 5.06 more votes, rounded down to 5 because we can't count parts of a vote. That alone was the margin of victory. This is why GOTV efforts are so important—they help close the historical gaps in undervotes and nonparticipation.

MODELING VOTE TOTALS

At the federal level, most campaigns are running predictive models to estimate the impact of closing the gaps in undervotes and nonparticipation within the context of partisanship, issue preferences, and a host of other salient questions on the minds of voters. Firms offer a variety of models, with some off-the-shelf based on previous races and others tailored to a specific campaign, which are custom made and more expensive. All of these models are based on voter probability scores from enhanced voter file data and questions asked, usually on live or short interactive voice response (IVR) surveys, which are covered in greater detail in chapter 7.

Turnout models are constructed to paint a picture of what the composition of the electorate will be on Election Day. In most cases, firms will offer a range of models, from low turnout to high, and some will focus on turnout for a specific candidate rather than the overall electorate. Ballot models assign probabilities from 0 to 1, with 0 being that the voter will definitely vote for the opposing candidate and 1 meaning the voter will definitely vote for your candidate. Media consumption models show campaigns where they should put their money to reach the voters they need to win.

More interesting are models that help campaigns understand where voters are and where they might go after additional information is given. Consideration models involve predicting who will be open to a candidate based on a set of biographical and issues, while persuasion models attempt to show who might be swayed away from supporting another candidate, which is more expensive to accomplish. Issue models focus on current laws, policies, or proposals under consideration and their relative impacts on potential support for a candidate.

Beyond modeling vote totals for the campaign strategically, the output of modeling is a tangible list of voters who have been scored, along with all of their relevant contact information, so campaigns can prioritize outreach and direct communications budgets accordingly. Once again, this all goes back to a usable voter file. As we will see in the earned, paid, and social media chapters, knowing who to target and where makes the best use of these modern platforms.

CONSULTANT STORY

The value of wide access to voter and consumer data runs counter to what political scientists say is important in a political campaign. As Matt Knee put it to me in our interview, "Academics who criticize modeling will say, look at all of this consumer data that's not really that relevant. Yeah, we know. The vast majority are things that make sense, like partisanship and demographics and past election results, donation histories, and how the economy is doing in that area."

But the important thing to remember—and this is what separates the academics from the practitioners—is that data, modeling, and analytics can be helpful in close races or ones that tip on a specific issue: "We have a lot of data that are often not relevant until an issue comes up that is suddenly incredibly relevant. Most of the time it doesn't matter if somebody likes camping. However, if you are on a local race where there is some issue about campgrounds, then, yeah, good to have!"

More broadly, after the Romney loss, Knee remembers that there was a lot of experimentation around data and modeling: "Okay, we have someone's likelihood to turn out to vote. Well, where do we get our best ROI? And the answer is a bell curve centered around somewhere between 30 percent and 40 percent likely to vote. But we had to go and find that out, and that's what our target universes were going to look like, what a swing universe looks like. We had spreadsheets with numbers. Now we had to figure out, what are all the things we can do with this?"

All of the work Knee and others on both sides of the partisan divide are trying to answer revolves around these questions. We have a lot more data now than we had before, and better analytical tools. Right now, access to these tools is expensive and the expertise is in its infancy. The data is there but the professionalism and speed of delivery are catching up to what most campaigns, beyond federal and statewide races, will need.

CAREERS

The field of political data, modeling, and analytics has exploded in the past ten years. Viewed previously as an adjunct to field operations or polling, it now has its own seat at the campaign table. For political science majors who like math, this is a unique opportunity to apply *Moneyball* tactics to campaigns. If you are someone who likes politics but are more introverted and thoughtful and have a talent for finding patterns in data, then this is a great way to contribute.

You can break into this field by working on a campaign or with a political party or firm that specializes in data, modeling, and analytics. Direct campaign experience will show you how political data, modeling, and analytics are used, but will likely limit the amount you can learn. You get exactly one chance, which does not allow for a margin of error. Remember, if you are responsible for the data, you're likely working with a voter file that has all of the inefficiencies and errors described in this chapter. At best, your team includes a consultant or vendor from whom you can learn a thing or two, but they get to do all of the interesting things and you are the client.

Working for a political party or firm that specializes in data, modeling, and analytics gives you the opportunity to learn, fail, and improve in relative anonymity. You'll also get the benefit of working with a team of professionals who have training materials and systems in place, which is like getting a master's degree on the job. Finally, you'll get various opportunities at all levels of campaigning that you can then bring with you to a larger race as a data director if you want to work on a campaign directly.

THE FUTURE

Data, modeling, and analytics will become more pervasive in campaigns as the cost of data hosting, collection, and analysis drops and the speed at which usable political lists can be deployed increases. The professionalism of the industry has increased to the point where standards are becoming commonplace. The difference among campaigns, parties, and firms is going to be in their ability to deploy solutions that help target voters and maximize campaign budgets.

I'm bullish on the future of political data. It is more likely than not that getting a better voter file will become easier over time and that the money will be made in how parties and firms extend it to include more comprehensive nonpolitical information that will give campaigns more insight into voter interests and preferences. Some of this has already happened, but it's costly. My guess is that those costs will come down as it will become easier to construct and maintain deep databases of voters.

One area that needs improvement is data on adults who are voting for the first time. Some may land in the voter file during an election season as they register, but by definition historical information on them is weak. New approaches need to be taken to improve information on first-time voters, including specific identification programs and better utilization of nonpolitical databases to provide insight into the interests and leanings of young voters.

Moreover, by some estimates one-quarter of eligible voters are not registered and cannot vote in elections. Connecting the available data in specific geographic areas and constructing registration programs can grow the available votes, even areas perceived as noncompetitive, to give candidates a fighting chance. Remember, registered voters do not always reflect the larger population of the general public politically and demographically.

Basic voter models are also becoming increasingly commoditized. Whereas five years ago ballot and consideration models were relatively new, now they are standard, utilizing some of the same math. The most interesting work being done in political modeling focuses on specific geographic areas or is able to identify swing voters outside the traditional data points of partisanship and voting behavior. Those who can uncover insights in seemingly solid districts will win the next wave of upsets.

The keys to victory may go through the specific analytics, customized for each race. It still amazes me that my former boss's thirty-year-old insight about "soccer moms" remains an analytic descriptor that candidates still reach for in today's elections. The next wave of definable, repeatable analytics will be modeled from data that is just being combined for the first time. Again, those who are able to win close elections and pull upsets will define the future language of campaigns in terms of analytics on voter groups we didn't target because we couldn't see them.

ASSIGNMENT

Contact your Secretary of State or Department of Elections office and find out how to get the statewide voter file. For example, the Virginia Department of Elections offers a "Client Services" page (https://www.elections.virginia.gov/candidatepac-info/client-services/) that offers "Data available for sale." While it does not list pricing, it gives a contact name, email address, and telephone number to purchase a dataset. Once you get the data, browse through it in your neighborhood and try to spot inaccuracies for people you know and then spend an hour calling through a few dozen in your area to see if the information is still accurate. Now you'll have a sense of how much it might take to make sure official data becomes usable data for voter outreach and mobilization.

SOURCES AND ADDITIONAL READING

Desilver, Drew. "Q&A: The Growing Use of 'Voter Files' in Studying the U.S. Electorate." Pew Research Center, February 15, 2018. https://www.pewresearch.org/fact-tank/2018/02/15/voter-files-study-qa/.

Green, Joshua. "The Science behind Those Obama Campaign E-Mails." *Bloomberg*, November 29, 2012. http://www.bloomberg.com/bw/articles/2012-11-29/the-science-behind-those-obama-campaign-e-mails.

Knee, Matt. Interview with the author. May 18, 2020.

Issenberg, Sasha. "How President Obama's Campaign Used Big Data to Rally Individual Voters." *MIT Technology Review*, December 19, 2012. http://www.technologyreview.com/featuredstory/509026/how-obamas-team-used-big-data-to-rally-voters/.

———. "How Ted Cruz Engineered His Iowa Triumph." *Bloomberg*, February 2, 2016. https://www.bloomberg.com/news/articles/2016-02-02/how-ted-cruz-engineered-his-iowa-triumph.

———. *The Victory Lab*. New York: Random House, 2012.

O'Connor, Patrick, and Dante Chinni. "Election 2014: Results Show Limits of Big Data." *Wall Street Journal*, November 9, 2014. http://www.wsj.com/articles/election-2014-results-show-limits-of-big-data-1415585721.

Quinn, Sean. "A Word on Voter Files." FiveThirtyEight, June 21, 2008. https://fivethirtyeight.com/features/word-on-voter-files/.

Porter, Dan. Interview with the author. May 22, 2020.

Shaw, Catherine. *The Campaign Manager*. New York: Routledge, 2018.

SEVEN

Focus Groups and Polling

"In terms of technology, the most dramatic change has been getting computerized, moving online for interviewing, mixed-mode. The rapidity [with which] you can turn around the data, the modeling, the statistical analysis, all of that has increased."

—Celinda Lake, Democratic pollster

After the vulnerability and opposition research books are delivered to the campaign, the next big question to answer is: What will voters find interesting? Sometimes it's obvious—a nasty affair, clear evidence of cheating on taxes or breaking the law, or some obvious corruption. All of these are fair play and will likely get a second look from voters. But what will actually move voters away from a candidate is a subject best left up to the voters themselves. To learn what is not only interesting but compelling, you need to conduct research with voters using focus groups and/or polling.

In addition, well-funded campaigns do quite a bit of work testing campaign themes, slogans, messages, attacks, and responses. The goal here is to minimize the risk of alienating voters and maximize the potential of turning out supportive voters. Specifically, this leverages the best content options the team can agree upon prior to its initial release, when strategic decisions need to be made. This is not to test one ad over another. That's too tactical for this purpose at the early stage, although top campaigns will do this as well.

There is an important distinction between focus groups and polling: The former is qualitative and the latter is quantitative. Both are important. Focus groups provide information from open-ended questions, which allows voters to tell you what they think without much direction. In a sense, the output of focus groups are stories that can give direction. Polls, however, direct respondents to specific answers that roll up nicely into percentages, which are quantitative. Let's take an in-depth look at both options in terms of how they are used by candidates and their teams, how they are constructed and fielded, and what the latest techniques offer for modern political campaigns.

FOCUS GROUPS

Focus groups are structured meetings led by a professional researcher who moderates, either in person or online, discussions with voters about various aspects of candidate backgrounds and messaging. Their history dates back to the late 1930s as academics began to question the results from traditional interviews, which were conducted with prewritten scripts and closed-ended questions. The intent of this approach was to get a set of standardized perceptions that could be projected to broader populations, which it did.

The concern was that respondents were being directed too much, and if they were given a different way of providing feedback, their answers would be not only closer to each person's individual truth but more expansive and relevant to the questions being asked. Since people are social and many decisions are made collectively, putting a group of people together and having them interact around subjects, not closed-ended questions, opens up ways to test more real-world experiences.

The development of focus groups as we know them today would take the better part of the next two decades. One of the first known uses outside an academic setting was by Paul Lazarsfeld, who was hired to conduct focus groups of World War II propaganda messages. But it was the market research industry that quickly saw the utility of this methodology to get feedback from potential customers, which was less expensive than doing individual interviews. They began to use focus groups to gain insight into designing consumer products as well as packaging and advertising. It was much more compelling to show a set of options to a group than to describe them to one individual in an interview script.

Focus groups were rediscovered much later by political campaigns and came of age in the 1980s. Ronald Reagan, known as the Great Communicator, had help from focus groups. Reportedly, his team spent more than $1 million per year on research, which included focus groups, while the incumbent he defeated, Jimmy Carter, spend only one-quarter of that amount. Reagan pollster Richard Wirthlin tested his client's words and phrases for persuasive impact, using focus groups to better tap into people's values and emotions than polling could do with a script and limited response options.

Four years later, former vice president Walter Mondale deftly used focus groups to fight off a challenge by Senator Gary Hart. Mondale pollster Peter Hart (no relation to Senator Hart, though that would've made for a better story) found that the polling wasn't giving the team an understanding of how to beat the upstart challenger, so they commissioned a set of focus groups. They learned that Hart was seen as young and dynamic, which presented problems for the older Mondale.

However, when asked who they would want to answer a call at the White House at 3:00 a.m., focus group participants went to Mondale, which became the focus of the strategy in beating Hart. This strategy would be used by Hillary Clinton against Barack Obama by my former boss Mark Penn, albeit with a less positive outcome.

The goal of focus groups is to best understand how participants react in real time and how they react to each other. What spontaneous reactions move a room? Which kinds of voters are moved? How do they talk about the information they are getting, in their own words? The best way to use focus groups is to give guidance as to how to further explore voter opinions and an inkling into how to construct polling questions, not to make decisions on these alone.

Components

According to Richard A. Krueger and Mary Anne Casey, who wrote the best book on the subject, there are five main characteristics of focus groups. First, a focus group should be a small group of people—they suggest five to ten—so that the group is large enough to get a diversity of opinions but small enough so that side conversations don't break out in the middle of a session. In most cases, political groups will be more in the range of eight at the low end and twelve at the upper end. In my experience, this keeps the side conversations to a minimum and gives more input into decision-making.

Second, focus group participants should have something in common in terms of their demographics, political leanings, or some other quality that the campaign has identified as important. This builds trust within the group and focuses the analysis on that distinguishing characteristic. Particularly on sensitive topics or with candidates who are viewed as arousing strong opinions on either side, it is important for these sessions to be relatively safe places where participants can be honest in a group setting, or you'll get garbage data.

Third, as discussed above, focus groups provide qualitative data through open-ended questions. The goal is to solicit natural as opposed to prescriptive feedback, which is what polls will do later. With the rise of big data and analytics, qualitative research has often gotten a bad rap. There is a place for it in a campaign, an exploratory and humanistic approach that puts voters at the center and allows them to guide us. In fact, it's one of the few places in a campaign plan where we do more listening than testing or communicating. It's vital.

Fourth, while they seem like natural discussions in practice, focus groups are very structured, moving from the general to the specific and guided by the moderator. Think of focus groups as less like polls and more like meetings with a relatively strict agenda. They need to cover certain topics and get perspectives, and then a moderator is assigned the task at the end to roll up the notes into a report so decisions can be made.

Finally, focus groups are organized to understand specific topics. In politics, this is most often discussions about candidates and messaging. Voters will tell you what they think about both if you ask the right questions and give them enough time, within reason, to respond. The topics can include everything from the candidate's background and experience to specific proposals and messages to help explain them. Rough cuts of ads can also be offered, but if they're in print, make sure to get them back at the end of the session so they don't show up in the media.

Sometimes you'll simply get a weird group that, while they bring up interesting ideas, has preferences that are just a bit off. This is because focus groups are held with a relatively small number of people sharing the same demographics or behaviors, and you cannot project how the larger population will react. At times you'll get groupthink, which is to say that one dominant person will influence others in the room in a way that they would not in real life. Still, testing vetting and opposition research and targeted messages within a small group lowers the chances that the least effective stuff will find its way out into the public domain.

Organization

Putting together focus groups is relatively straightforward. Most major cities have a choice of facilities, and your general consultant and research teams will know them well. The very best ones ensure that whoever shows up in the focus groups has not done one in about six months, so that you're not getting "professionals" who really don't care about your questions or the topic but are just looking to get paid that evening. The facility is usually in charge of recruiting voters to be in the focus group, and I've seen facilities do that themselves or from lists the campaign provides, which is the better choice because it ensures that they are selected at random and fit the targets more closely and ensures, at a greater level of confidence, that the people you put in the room will not be ringers from an opposing campaign or members of the media. Generally, food and beverages are offered to the voters before the sessions, at an additional cost to the campaign.

In-person focus groups take place in a meeting room where the moderator and voters meet and has an adjacent room where the campaign team can view the proceedings. Virtually all modern focus groups audio- and videotape the sessions, with most providing a way to download the files as soon as they are completed. At the front end of my career, nights were longer as we had to wait for the facility to make copies of the sessions for the client as well as the team analyzing the sessions. Now it's super quick.

In addition, most facilities now provide a paid option to stream the focus groups to teams that might not be able to make it to the sessions. This is extremely helpful when the candidate or top staff cannot make it to the facility but have a bubble of time to watch it. It's generally pretty expensive, so skip the additional cost if you can. Sessions usually go about two hours, and two sessions are held each evening because if you do more than four hours of focus groups, your brain starts to go to mush and there is only so much junk food you can eat behind the glass.

I suggest taking a break about halfway through each session to see if the campaign team has any feedback or wants the moderator to pursue a line of questioning that is not on the list of topics to cover. It's also helpful to give the voters in the room time to take a break and spend some time talking with each other.

Moderator's Guide

It's important to understand that a focus group is not a survey. Researchers are not giving voters a set of questions to answer, tallying up the results, and giving them to the campaign team. Instead, the goal is to first create a sense of openness and respect so individuals can freely speak their minds. The moderator is there to guide the discussion, not direct it. Questions asked of voters are open-ended, so they can, in their own words, react to the question as well as to their fellow voters. Follow-up questions are encouraged to ensure that reticent voters in the group speak up as well. Great moderators know not only how to get voters to talk but how to keep the conversation moving and not allow one person to dominate the session.

The other thing to remember is that what the campaign will want to ask is often too much to cover in a two-hour session. Break the sessions into blocs of time where the moderator will take the first ten minutes to go over ground rules and introductions, then move to an easy question such as the political environment or the state of the economy to get the group moving, before feedback on specific points from vetting and opposition research, messaging, and content options. In addition to the opening and easy question, I'll usually cover two main topics, take a break, and then show content after the break to reengage participants' focus.

While focus groups are not surveys, it is okay to ask at the end of a bloc for a show of hands on roundup questions such as candidate and message preferences. This is helpful to wrap up blocs before moving on, and it gives those behind the glass some context for what they just saw. It is also helpful in writing the report, which the campaign should expect to be delivered within a few days after the sessions.

The report should follow the moderator's guide in form, with an executive summary at the front that brings together the common themes learned in the sessions. The report can also include a transcript, which is an additional charge to the campaign, for those who like to read all the details. Generally, the video of the session is just as good, if not better, because you get facial expressions, tone, and interactions among the voters that a stale transcript won't provide.

POLLING

This is why polling is so compelling: It is the only tried and tested way of understanding what large groups of voters think, how they react to campaign messages, and who they might support. Modern surveys are conducted with hundreds, sometimes thousands, of voters by telephone or internet and are projectable to wider populations such as registered or likely voters. Polling is used not only to check vetting and opposition research findings but to evaluate the political environment, the state of the race, messaging, and the impact of messages on potential turnout and intent to vote for a candidate.

Polls are subject to various levels of sampling error, which involves how the voters are chosen for the survey and is reported as the margin of error. In addition, polls can go haywire for a variety of other reasons, such as bias in the wording of the questions, the order of the questions, and the day of the week and time the poll is conducted, as well as more subtle biases such as social desirability, meaning voters give a response they think interviewers want to hear rather than their own opinions. Moreover, some survey firms are known for survey results that are generally more favorable to one party or another.

Data Collection

Polls can be assisted by interviewers or self-directed by the respondent. Assisted means that someone reads the questions and records the answers, assisting voters in taking down their data. This tends to be the most effective way to get surveys completed because people respond to people. It is much easier to dismiss an invitation to do a survey by text, e-mail, or interactive voice response because you do not have to reject another human being outright by saying, "No thanks; I'll pass." Generally, the less assisted the interview, the cheaper it is for the campaign.

In addition, where polls are conducted matters quite a bit, as does the time and the day of the week. Nationwide polls are conducted over a two-to-three-day period to ensure representation of the population and to capture any changes that might happen due to unforeseen events that could influence the results. Researchers and their clients can get this data by day, just in case something intervenes, and can choose to add a day onto the back of the study if it has had a significant influence.

To that end, small batches of voter phone numbers or email addresses are released over time to vary the day of the week and time of day, ensuring everyone chosen to participate has a chance to do the survey. If the survey is conducted online, the questionnaire is pretested and then you're good to go, but if it is done by live interviewing, some time is necessary to train the team doing the survey to know the content and how it should flow, as well as how to probe if respondents do not want to answer certain questions.

Most campaigns hire pollsters who then hire a separate field shop that actually programs and serves up the polls to voters. It is a fair question to ask the pollster who they use and why, as well as what quality controls they take to collect data. Overall hiring and training methods show a level of professionalism that is important in terms of how much weight you put into the data you get at the end. If a pollster will not name or is purposefully opaque about who their partners are, pass.

Another thing to check is where they get their sample, because this, too, could be subcontracted out further. While most will go with a recognized data vendor, if the field shop does their own sampling, ask them to give you an overview of how they approach it. What you are looking for is whether they use the voter file, which is the best way, or if they are relying on your team to supply the universe of voters from which to take a sample, which can work as well if you have it. More often than not, a good field shop has a strong relationship with their sample vendors and are willing to share this information.

Construction

Polling begins with a population, the group of people you want to interview. This can be registered or likely voters or some demographic or geographic subgroup. For the early benchmark poll, I'd suggest registered voters. From there, the polling firm and their field shop will select a sample from that population, ideally giving every registered or likely voter the same chance to be chosen for the interview. This is called random selection, and it provides the poll an important check on potential error.

The commonly reported margin of error reflects the size of the sample vs. the population. For example, a sample of one thousand voters among a very large population will result in a margin of error of +/-3.1 percent, which is the lowest standard for a national poll that the media will report. For statewide polls, you can go smaller, eight hundred interviews, and be safe at under +/-3.5 percent margin of error.

There is another line that is reported, and it's such a standard that it's usually in the methods section of the report and generally ignored by the media. This is the level of confidence. It is almost always 95 percent, meaning if the poll was done one hundred times under these conditions with the same sample size, the results would fall within the margin of error ninety-five times out of one hundred. For medical studies, the confidence level is 99 percent but for politics we don't need that and it would be cost prohibitive.

Cost drivers for polls are how difficult it is to qualify the sample to be in the survey, the number of questions, and the number of completed interviews. Generally, in-person polls are more expensive than mobile phone surveys, more than landlines, more than mail, and more than internet. Moreover, if a survey needs to be delivered overnight, that kind of speed comes at a premium cost.

Questionnaire

Standard benchmark polls follow similar outlines of questions, beginning with a greeting then checking to see if the voter meets the criteria for participation. From there, questions go from general to specific, usually starting with the political environment and testing the ability to identify candidates in the race. From there, an initial preference will be taken, called the ballot test. Then messages and content options can be tested. After each set, the ballot test gets rerun to see if there was any movement. Finally, at the end, a set of demographics will be asked, going from basic to sensitive, and then the voter is thanked for participating.

- *Greeting.* Opening a survey with a short welcome and expectations of the poll, as well as an accurate estimate of how much time to complete it is both essential and respectful of the voter who is going to take it. To ensure that the time estimate is fair, ask to take the survey before it is fielded to test the flow as well as time. Have at least two members of the campaign team check it before it goes live.
- *Screening.* Screening questions ensure that the right people are taking the poll. You do not want someone who no longer lives in the campaign location doing the survey, a member of the other campaign's team, or a journalist taking it. You also want to ensure the right distribution of key targeted demographics, so asking a few questions up front can go a long way. If you ask them late, you will have to throw out data or weight it more aggressively to fit the voter population.
- *Political environment.* The general question of whether the voter thinks things are going in the right direction or are on the wrong track is a well-researched question and sets up any political poll very well. Ask this nationally, statewide, and in the district where the candidate is running, as voters often have very different opinions at each level.

- *Candidate identification.* Who the voters recognize is the benchmark for having more detailed conversations with them. Generally, first-time candidates have low name identification, which is something their communications campaign will build over time. Learning where this is at the start versus the incumbent and other competitors shapes how aggressively the team spends its budget initially to get into the conversation on who might earn voter support.
- *Ballot test.* After asking voters who they know, you can ask who they might support. This can be put before the candidate identification question as a generic ballot test where voters are asked whether they would support one party's candidate or another for a given race. If asked after the candidate identification, the names are specified as well as their party, if appropriate and/or if the team determines it wants to lean into the label. The question can also be offered in terms of who a voter thinks will win the race. This is sometimes even more interesting because in situations where there is a polarizing candidate, it allows the respondent to give an honest answer that might indirectly be reflective of their own preference. This strategy is used in situations testing risky or socially unacceptable behavior such as smoking or recreational drug use and sometimes provides a better estimate than asking the questions of a person directly.
- *Message test.* This is where the candidate and opponent research and message options are put before voters to see what they find most believable, whether or not they agree with it, and, more importantly, whether or not it moves their support. More often than not, voters will not be honest with themselves or a survey, whether it's being offered by phone or electronically, because they are not aware of what moves them. They know what they think is believable but not necessarily what might change their minds, because the content is being viewed in isolation and it is not presented the way it would be during the campaign in paid and earned media. Moreover, the sequencing of the messages will not be randomized, as they should be in a survey, so that no one message biases the next. Remember, voters see hundreds of ads each day and political campaigns will be among them.
- *Ballot retest.* Because of the issues noted above, the ballot question needs to be repeated after each message test. This will allow voters to simply retake the survey question about who they support rather than estimate how much of an impact it will have on them.
- *Demographics.* With modern polling, much of this information can be lifted from the voter file and attached to the survey data. However, there are several data points—including age, gender, geographic location, and household income—that should be double-checked at the end of the survey to ensure that they are correct.

There are other demographics that may be missing in the data set but crucial to the campaign, including religious service attendance, number of children, employment status, and split ticket voting history.

- *Thank-you.* Finally, you want to offer the voter a short thank-you for participating in the study and reiterate that what was said is confidential and will not be released to the public. This is an important bond with voters, protecting them for being honest on the survey. If the survey is done online, give a link to the campaign. Regardless of mode, do *not* ask for a donation at the end.

Mixed Mode

While it is cleaner to do surveys by phone or internet, modern campaigns are increasingly using mixed mode, which means using a variety of techniques to survey voters. This allows research teams to hit their contracted number of completed interviews and, in most cases, lower costs. Some populations, such as older voters, are better reached by landlines than by text. The reverse is also true. Moreover, busy people do not have time to take a survey in the moment during the day and might prefer to take it on their own time at night or over the weekend. Self-administered internet surveys are the solution there. The important point is to be open to a certain amount of flexibility.

The downside of mixed mode is that it can take more time during the fielding period as well as on the back end to integrate the various methods into one data set for analysis. In a time crunch, this is a significant drawback. Considering the time pressure campaigns are under, it might not be a possibility as the campaign rolls toward Election Day. However, during the planning stages of the campaign, in that window where the research and messaging are being tested for the first time, a mixed-mode survey is the right way to make sure you get input from all subgroups in a population without having to make significant adjustments with weighting the data after the field period is completed.

MODERN TECHNIQUES

The latest advances in focus groups and polling have involved moving them online. Utilizing the new technology is a work in progress, as the new tools have been available for less than ten years and there is wide variation in how they are used. Basically, online focus groups allow researchers to conduct these sessions without the need to round up the team or the voters as everyone participates individually. Internet polls have been available for longer than online focus groups, but the latest advance has been in using text messaging to recruit voters to take them.

Online Focus Groups

The use of online focus groups has become more of an option, particularly with COVID-19 during the 2020 election campaign. Generally, you are able to interview more people online than in person, which eliminates some of the problems with in-person focus groups that are limited to eight to twelve people per session. Online focus groups can run into the dozens. With larger numbers of participants, it is easier to have confidence in the results, but the methodology flips some of the assumptions of qualitative research on their head, so you have to be careful in interpreting what is reported.

One of the big reasons why qualitative research works is that it allows voters to be themselves and answer questions within a group setting. In-person moderation provides the opportunity to view nonverbal cues and react to them in real time, spend time clarifying and following up on questions asked, and modify the script should interesting issues arise within a group. In an online setting, many of these are either impossible or far more difficult to implement. Still, the ability to get more data at a lower price makes this an interesting and at times compelling option.

Up front, the campaign has a choice to make for online focus groups: synchronous or asynchronous. Synchronous online groups are completed in real time, conducted by video chat. Asynchronous groups take place over a few days and are more akin to doing a long qualitative session, but with a recorded interviewer. In most cases, a campaign will opt for synchronous groups, as there's usually not enough time to dedicate to this phase of a research plan, let alone multiple days. Also, make sure you have a moderator who has conducted more than a few online focus groups, as they are very different than in-person groups.

If the campaign plan allows for more time, asynchronous online focus groups provide time for moderators to probe, allowing individuals participating on their own not to feel the social pressure and that they can therefore answer questions about sensitive subjects like their opinions of a polarizing candidate or give more honest assessments of opposition research. Basically, the voters have more time to think, so the quality of the insight you can glean from these groups is greater. Moreover, the questions can be modified along the way, as asynchronous sessions are not handled in a group setting at all.

Text to Survey

As we discussed above, the biggest problem today in polling is falling response rates. As we all have mobile phones and are most likely to respond to texts, researchers are trying to improve contact rates by starting where the voter's eyes are, which is on their smartphones. Text-to-survey allows for fast feedback and forces your questions to be short and to the point, so they're not great for highly complex message testing.

A survey can be completed either in the text or SMS window by a link provided to voters to take it in their browser. My suggestion is to use these surveys for short questions, as some SMS services cannot handle texts with more than 160 characters, and that they be questions that are not hard to think through, like candidate awareness and support, as well as getting demographic information and checking e-mail addresses.

The text window is best for completion rates, as you already have them there and people have become suspicious of opening links due to privacy and hacking concerns, both of which are valid. Still, most of the major survey platforms offer the ability to conduct surveys by text and they mitigate these concerns by utilizing their opt-in panels, who have agreed to get these kinds of invitations and links.

Most importantly, the survey needs to be very short, a max of five questions, based on my experience. More than that and you get a lot of drop-offs. Federal Communications Commission regulations have made it illegal for companies to send text messages without express consent from the voter—an opt-in. This means if you text instead of call people for a survey you are breaking the law. In some states, like California, and overseas, like in the European Union, the rules are even more stringent, so make sure to check with the vendor before choosing this as an option.

Still, your mileage may vary. Gallup ran a test of response rates from text-to-web surveys and found they were three times lower than what they got by phone. Gallup also found that text message surveys did not improve the composition of the samples in terms of gender, race, and income level, but they did find that respondents were slightly younger and more highly educated. Take note that this is from Gallup, whose brand is much stronger by phone than by text. If someone calls you from the Gallup Poll, you are much more likely to answer than if someone sends a text claiming to be from Gallup. The personal element is important there. However, taking the Gallup results into account, it is clear that text-to-survey helps in getting younger voters to participate, which is the single toughest group to reach right now.

Both of these techniques have a long way to go before we understand how much they can add, as well as how they operate in a changing regulatory environment. Still, under the right circumstances, they can be viewed as forward-thinking supplementary options for campaigns that have healthy research budgets and more time before launch.

PRECISION AND NONRESPONSE BIAS

Low response rates have led to a great deal of angst among pollsters and voters who see inconsistencies among the results. Response rates are down across the board, even among government surveys. A study completed by two researchers at Mathematica Policy Research for the US Department of Health and Human Services found rates that on national surveys for the Centers for Disease Control, the Bureau of Labor Statistics, and several others found response rates all down significantly from 1995 to 2015. In my discussions with field shops on nongovernment surveys, like the ones we do for political clients, response rates are far worse.

No longer are surveys bound to the telephone or probability sampling, where every respondent has the same chance of being selected for the poll. Today's surveys are more likely to be multimodal, which means that some people will be contacted on a landline, others on a mobile line, and others by text or e-mail. This presents a lot of data quality issues that are beyond the scope of this book, but it does complicate the math behind the margin of error, even if it is not reported.

Firms are attempting to grapple with these issues by rethinking who is sampled. In an e-mail conversation I had with Patrick Ruffini of Echelon Insights, he told me his team is moving toward estimating the likely electorate, not registered or likely voters. This shifts the onus from the data file to modeling what is likely to happen on Election Day, including both likely voters and "the right share" of unlikely voters at any one time. This is an interesting move, because polls missed some of Trump's support in 2016 because many voters deemed unlikely to cast ballots actually did. Ruffini and his team at Echelon Insights did rather well, providing a path for how we might do future polling. Their final Verified Voter Omnibus poll released on October 29, 2020 predicted Biden would get 50 percent of ballots cast, and he got 51 percent. Echelon predicted that Trump would get 44 percent and he got 47 percent. Both results were well within the margins of error and almost nailed the spread between the two candidates.

When I first began my career in polling in the late 1990s, mobile phones were expensive and the service was cost-prohibitive for many. Mobile phones were limited in what they could do, and each text sent cost the user money. If you went above a certain number of texts, the hit could be enormous. Call screening and blocking was available, but in limited form as well. You might recognize the number, but in most cases you would pick it up because early mobiles did not show names. This limited technology allowed calls from survey research firms to go through relatively unimpeded, and our contact and completion rates were much higher than they are now.

TOOLS

Despite the relative dark age of survey completion rates, we are living in the middle of a golden age of polling technology experimentation. When

I started in the business twenty-five years ago, there were three accepted methodologies. Most expensive was in-person surveys, where interviews would be conducted face-to-face. This was followed by telephone polls on landlines, assisted by computers, which was a leap forward because you could move quickly through data entry and gather large amounts of data in a relatively short period of time. Finally, there was mail, which was cheap but slow, and the response rates were relatively low compared with the other two options. All three are active today, but less so for mail because internet is cheaper and faster.

Generally, people are more likely to do something if there is another person attached to it. However, for some surveys, it is better to have people take the surveys themselves without human intervention because social influence is removed. An example of that is the "shy Trump voter" effect, where some voters were embarrassed to admit to another person that they intended to vote for Trump but were more likely to write it down on their own. In today's polling environment, sometimes the methods are mixed, leading to this effect sometimes being a factor and other times not, depending on the campaign.

Beyond this overview, let's dig into your options a bit deeper. They basically break down to delivery systems: a telephone or an internet-assisted mobile device. What we'll find is that the closer you get to human interaction, the more expensive the option becomes. Still, there are additional positives and negatives with each, and they're briefly summarized below.

Telephone-Based Options

- Telephone polls conducted with landlines have become a nonstarter for political clients because you cannot get coverage of most young voters. Since 2004, the percent of US households with landline phones has dropped by more than half, from 93 percent to 42 percent. The holdouts tend to be older, so it no longer makes sense to do a survey on landlines alone. Still, people who own landlines are easier to contact, so that helps to keep the pricing of surveys relatively low.
- Mobile telephone polls have become a bigger part of the mix because of the trends listed above. However, it is far more expensive to call mobile numbers than landlines, so when you get sticker shock on a polling budget, this is the most likely reason why. However, if the results do not have a significant percentage of completes polled this way, you can fairly question its accuracy. Political shops will try to sell their clients on a 50/50 split between landlines and mobiles, if not more skewed toward mobiles. It's the right call but it's also not budget friendly. This is where campaigns make trade-offs between what they'd like to have and what they can afford.

- Interactive voice response has become a low-cost alternative to interviewer-led landline or mobile polls. Respondents get a phone call and take the survey by using the keypad on their phones. As anyone who has been through an extensive customer service nightmare knows, this limits how many questions can be reasonably asked. Still, if the questions are short and few, this is a relatively good option and removes interviewer and social influence bias.

Internet-Assisted Options

Surveys can now be offered via e-mail and text as well as on websites and social media. While I was there, Gallup looked down upon internet surveys because of concerns about representing the population fairly. But with the growth of the internet from computers to mobile devices, those concerns have abated, and sampling techniques have improved. The dive in telephone survey completion rates significantly increased costs because it took much more time to reach the desired number of voters for a survey and have them complete it. This made it cost-prohibitive for clients so research firms needed to adjust their methods.

The shift from landline telephones to smartphones has been a game changer for polling, mainly because it opened up other ways to contact potential survey respondents. While the percent of US households with landline phones has dropped by more than half since 2004, as mentioned above, those that only have cell phones has risen elevenfold, from 5 percent to 55 percent. Virtually all Americans—96 percent according to the Pew Research Center—own a mobile phone, and more than 80 percent now use a smartphone, meaning they can take a self-directed survey on the device. In response, surveys have gotten shorter, generally, from when I started in the industry in the late 1990s, because our always-on lifestyles no longer permit us the luxury of time. Internet-assisted options give us the opportunity to take surveys on our time, not the interviewer's.

- Internet polls have become a more accepted option over the past twenty years because the cost is so low compared with telephone, no matter the mix between landline and mobile. In some cases, it can be more than five times cheaper to go with an internet poll because once it is programmed, the surveys are self-administered, without other people involved in the process. Internet surveys are generally quicker to complete, and there are no interviewer transcription errors because the respondent enters the data. Respondents can mess up an answer on their own, of course, but if they do that's on them, not the pollster's team. Well-designed internet polls are hardware agnostic and work well across platforms and browsers. The one caution I'd make at this time is that social media polls do not offer researchers the ability to define a sample, so you end up with data that cannot represent wide groups of voters.

- As we are all hyperattached to our mobile phones and smartphones, SMS or text polls have become the latest wave of technological innovation. Like IVR, they're cheaper than regular polls, and can be even cheaper than internet polls. The text is sent to invite someone to participate in a short internet poll, and we have seen higher response rates than just e-mailing the survey link, as texts are more immediate. Another option for short polls is that they can be completed in a series of texts and responses. Due to the intrusiveness of this version, I would say the poll needs to be three to five questions, max, but several other researchers I've spoken with have found good results with longer surveys. The problem is that you cannot test audio or video content, only text, so it is somewhat limiting to testing messaging. Still, you can easily use it for IDing voters and getting their awareness of and preferences on candidates.

- What has virtually disappeared is the mail invitation to do a survey, unless, of course, it is the US Census. But I keep mail polls in here because this has become another way to prod people to complete an internet survey. Currently the only times I consistently see mail invitations to do surveys are either by political parties who are really trying to fund-raise instead (a bait-and-switch practice called frugging), or the US Census, which is a legitimate government function specified the US Constitution, in which you, or someone on your behalf, likely participated in 2020. Even there, most of the invitations provide a link and a code so it can be completed online. In the past ten years I haven't seen a political poll conducted by mail in the United States.

CAREERS

As we have seen in previous chapters, the best way to break into a specific part of the business, like being the researcher in charge of focus groups and polling, is to get on-the-ground practical training on a campaign. If you want to be a strategist, which is what most modern pollsters sell themselves as, you need to have a deep understanding of how the polling connects to other parts of the campaign and what it says the team should do next. Without it, a pollster is relegated to saying, "Here's what voters think" and letting the rest of the team figure out what to do.

The elite pollsters get paid not only for the data they bring but the insights they glean from and add to the data from focus groups and polling. This is the point of view of both Tony Fabrizio, a Trump pollster and one of my mentors, and Celinda Lake, a leading Democratic pollster and someone I crossed paths with when I directed the political management master's program at George Washington University. I interviewed both for this book, and they were expansive in how important working on local campaigns was to their development.

Fabrizio's first campaign was a local town supervisor race where he served as the youth coordinator; he was in the local Young Republicans chapter at the time. He says that he was "working on a congressional campaign and I was asked to be, basically, the field director and it was the first time I met my mentor, Arthur Finkelstein."

Young and brash, as opposed to seasoned and brash, as he is now, Fabrizio asked Finkelstein directly, "What do we need a pollster for?" Finkelstein, to his credit, laughed off the question and responded with a question of his own: "Do you even know what a pollster does?"

Fabrizio responded simply, "Yeah, public opinion. Kind of like that Gallup guy."

It was then that Finkelstein began to teach him the ins and outs of name identification, message testing, and the more interesting nuances of polling and focus groups. A couple of campaigns later, Fabrizio was working for Finkelstein as a pollster and a general consultant, and another legendary career was launched.

Lake echoed some of Fabrizio's political upbringing. She was involved in the College Young Republicans, working on the Massachusetts for Nixon effort in 1972 and on Gerald Ford's campaign for president as well. During her junior year abroad, she came across scholars involved with some of the original seminal voting research featured in *The American Voter*, originally published in 1960. She fell in love with it and returned to the University of Michigan, where she immersed herself in the field while maintaining her extracurricular activity on campaigns. She kept taking leaves of absence to go work on them while working toward her degree.

"Get some training in sampling and question wording because you will be a better pollster for it," Lake says. "And get some campaign experience. I think it's really helpful to combine those two pieces. But I would just say, in general, follow your heart."

Of course, I'm biased here, but careers in voter research are extremely interesting as well as portable to noncampaign arenas such as government, nonprofits, academia, and business. Familiarity with the techniques and tools can go a long way, and starting in politics opens up opportunities in the other fields. Most noncampaign organizations understand how much speed plays a role in winning elections, and that ability to turn around projects quickly is an advantage over those who haven't had to work under that kind of pressure. In addition to speed, the level of understanding of modern techniques and professionalism is very high because there is so much riding on the data.

That said, working for a political shop in voter research can be grueling. There can be full days and weeks where you're going without breaks because of the rigors of the election calendar and demanding candidates. Still, you can learn a lot in a short period of time and gain exposure to extraordinarily interesting ways of approaching focus groups and polling and get enough chances to make mistakes and learn from them within the span of one election cycle. I usually counsel my students and those I've mentored along the way that, no matter what, you should commit to the cycle, because the type of focus groups and polling varies as you get closer to Election Day. If you drop out early, you're not only hurting your team but limiting your own learning.

In the long term, careers in voter research tail off in off-year elections, and some firms are not forward-thinking enough to take advantage of their extremely valuable offerings to folks outside the business of elections. A great firm understands that it needs nonpolitical clients, even if they are public-facing ones like public affairs firms, interest groups, and trade associations. This is where you want to work, because not only will you have a job in the off year but you will learn additional skills and have exposure to clients who have different needs and expectations.

As we saw in chapter 6, the opportunities outside of politics are substantial, and you may find that one cycle is just enough to realize that you either do not love elections as you might have once thought or would like to have a life as well. Professional affiliations like the American Association of Public Opinion Researchers (AAPOR), tools, and techniques translate to the private sector. Most of the time, careers live in the insights groups of large organizations, but there are also firms that focus on market and marketing research for nonpolitical clients. You might think that your political affiliation might put you at a disadvantage, but in most cases employers and clients who hire you outside of politics care about what you know, not the political affiliation of your former clients.

THE FUTURE

Focus groups and polling will remain important components of strategic campaign planning. There is no substitute for asking voters what they think about the political environment and what they think of each candidate and their messages. While there are other metrics people use to evaluate how a campaign is performing, voter support remains the core of what a campaign is attempting to accomplish. Every time you read that focus groups and polling are dead (again) dismiss it. There are always going to be predictions that will go wrong, but the alternative is just to ignore the voters, which is antithetical to why people run for office in the first place.

Instead, what I see is professionalism of the industry increasing all of the questions surrounding the different methodologies, I can consolidation around processes that work and keep costs down. Pollster will get better at using phone and internet together, and better understand how to balance the results from both to achieve something close to a mirror of reality at a particular point in time. With better voter data, pollsters will be able to improve sampling, which should lower the number of incorrect predictions we see on Election Day. Importantly, this will lower the worry pollsters have that somehow the voters who take our polls are different in some way than those who do not.

The technologies will change as well. Over time, opt-in panels will grow, which will lead to greater representation in sampling. With upcoming regulations to texting, we will move to an opt-in world where certain populations will be less reachable because they choose to be left alone. Survey firms will need to become more creative in how they build their panels, how they incentivize them, and how they cycle through people so they do not get burned out on doing surveys for firms like mine.

The upcoming leap forward in the speed of internet connectivity with 5G as well as faster home internet speeds will offer the ability to serve up more complex messaging and reliable ways to test video, which right now is lagging. Improved web connections will also help with drop-offs within surveys, making it easier and cheaper to complete survey quotas. This will improve access to Generation Z. more of half of whom are already eligible to vote and will become more political active as a group as more of them reach voting age.

Anecdotally, participation in online focus groups and completion rates for surveys is up significantly during the COVID-19 pandemic. Locked up at home, people are simply more available and have more time to spend. AAPOR's Listserv is replete with stories about voters and consumers being much easier to contact. One example showed landline response rates up 10 percent, while cell phone surveys were up marginally in Washington State for the Behavioral Risk Factor Surveillance System (BRFFS) survey, the largest health survey in the world. A survey field vendor I have worked with for many years said that their response rates are up across the board, particularly on political campaign studies.

What I'm seeing in my research and hearing from others is that people are craving more connection, and this is another way to participate politically, since they cannot do it in person. This is happening across the research world in campaign, government, and commercial research. My guess is the bump will last as long as the virus dominates our lives. I am hopeful, however, that some voters who reengage will find the experience as valuable as we do and continue to participate.

ASSIGNMENT

net browser, go to Real Clear Politics (http://
:s.com), and find the section where the presidential
addition to seeing what the trends are, look at the ten
d the organizations that sponsored them. See if there
are any patterns then go deeper and look at their methodologies. What
do you see? Are there any differences in whether they were conducted by
phone, and if so, what was the split between landline and mobiles? For
internet surveys, how were they conducted? What do you think influences their results?

Then go to FiveThirtyEight and look at the pollster ratings (https://
projects.fivethirtyeight.com/pollster-ratings/). Start with the Read More
section (https://fivethirtyeight.com/features/the-state-of-the-polls-2019/),
where Nate Silver runs through the state of the polls as of 2019 and get
his take on how the industry performed. Then head back to the previous
page and look through the rankings, sorting by "538 Grade." Which firms
are rated best by the site and why? Which polls that are in the Real Clear
Politics tracking are the most biased one way or the other? Do they cover
a wide range of bias, or are we seeing a slanted view on that site?

SOURCES AND ADDITIONAL READING

Campbell, Angus, Philip E. Converse, Warren E. Miller, and Donald E. Stokes. *The
American Voter*. New York: Wiley, 1960.
Collabito. "Advantages and Disadvantages of Online Focus Groups." Accessed on
February 16, 2021. https://www.collabito.com/advantages-and-disadvantages-of-fo-
cus-groups/
Czajka, John L., and Amy Beyler. *Background Paper: Declining Response Rates in Federal
Surveys: Trends and Implications*. Mathematica Policy Research for the U.S. Depart-
ment of Health & Human Services, June 15, 2016. https://aspe.hhs.gov/system/files/
pdf/255531/Decliningresponserates.pdf.
Dillman, Don A., Jolene D. Smyth, and Leah Melani Christian. *Internet, Phone, Mail,
and Mixed-Mode Surveys: The Tailored Design Method*, Fourth Edition. New York:
Wiley, 2014.
Echelon Insights. "October Verified Voter Omnibus—Election Update." Released Oc-
tober 29, 2020. https://echeloninsights.com/in-the-news/october-omnibus-election-
2020/.
Fabrizio, Tony. Interview with the author by phone. May 4, 2020.
Featherstone, Liza. "How the Powerful Learned to Launder Their Reputations Using
Focus Groups." *Baffler*, February 13, 2018. https://thebaffler.com/latest/listening-
con-featherstone.
Kish, Leslie. *Survey Sampling*. New York: Wiley, 1995.
Krueger, Richard A., and Mary Anne Casey. *Focus Groups*, Fourth Edition. Los An-
geles: Sage, 2008.
Lake, Celinda. Interview with the author via Zoom. May 2, 2020.
Marlar, Jenny. "Using Text Messaging to Reach Survey Respondents." Gallup, No-
vember 1, 2017. https://news.gallup.com/opinion/methodology/221159/using-text-
messaging-reach-survey-respondents.aspx.

Pew Research Center. "Mobile Fact Sheet." Retrieved April 24, 2020, from https://www.pewresearch.org/internet/fact-sheet/mobile/.

Ruffini, Patrick. Interview with the author. May 22, 2020.

Salant, Priscilla, and Don A. Dillman. *How to Conduct Your Own Survey*. New York: Wiley, 1994.

Silver, Nate. "The State of the Polls, 2019." FiveThirtyEight, November 5, 2019. https://fivethirtyeight.com/features/the-state-of-the-polls-2019/.

Stambaugh, Alex. "Getting the Most Out of Focus Groups." *Campaigns and Elections*, March 25, 2012. https://www.campaignsandelections.com/campaign-insider/getting-the-most-out-of-focus-groups.

Statista. "Landline Phones Are a Dying Breed." May 17, 2019. https://www.statista.com/chart/2072/landline-phones-in-the-united-states/.

———. "Smartphone User Penetration as a Share of Population in the United States from 2018 to 2024." Retrieved April 24, 2020, from https://www.statista.com/statistics/201184/percentage-of-mobile-phone-users-who-use-a-smartphone-in-the-us/.

EIGHT

Earned Media

"The interest in politics has intensified over the past five years but it goes back even to President Obama. The big change I've noticed in cable TV is you used to have two segments an hour on politics and now some networks do sixty minutes an hour."
– Alex Finland, nonpartisan cable television booker and media trainer

Americans are more interested than ever in politics. A Fox News poll published in April 2019 showed that more than three-quarters of voters were already interested in the upcoming election the following year. What was particularly striking was that 57 percent of voters who had supported Hillary Clinton and 57 percent of those who supported Donald Trump in 2016 were *extremely* interested in the 2020 election. Generally, you see that kind of intensity a few weeks before Election Day, not one year and seven months ahead of it.

What is the best way to reach these high-interest voters? The most powerful and impactful media is free yet earned. Earned media is unpaid coverage by the news media through any distribution channel: online, on television, on the radio, or in print. Coverage from the news media about the campaign, candidate interviews, and mentions by high-profile influencers is valuable not just because it doesn't hit the campaign budget *directly*, but also because those who consume this content are more likely to believe it, value it, and make decisions on who to support because of it.

Modern political campaigns have gone a step further with this, extending to social networks. This personalizes the content because it automatically comes from someone you are connected with, if not trust. A survey conducted by Nielsen found that 92 percent of respondents in fifty-six countries say they trust earned media via recommendations from someone they know far and above any kind of paid advertising. This is a higher bar than some random website or post; it is something from someone you know. News can be dismissed as inaccurate or even fake, but it is much harder to do that when you know the person who shared it with you.

Types of earned media are endless but fall into certain categories, including endorsements, which can appear in the planning stages of the campaign but may not materialize until later, on someone else's time-table. A lot goes into other events like rallies, town halls, and smaller gatherings, but whether or not those are covered or shared—and what parts of them are covered or shared—is up to others. The news can drive additional earned media if the candidate has something interesting to say or offer as a solution. Finally, an opponent may say something that requires a reply or opposition research may drop, which requires a rapid response, and while all of this media is earned, it is also uncontrollable.

While earned media is free in its delivery, it is not random, and it is not free in its preparation. Modern campaigns create moments they know will be covered by the news media, like big policy speeches and rallies. These events cost campaigns time and money because paid staffers write the speeches and advance teams, also on the payrolls, need to plan the public events. One does not just show up and hope everything goes well. Moreover, the creation of sharable content is a very expensive activity. On well-funded campaigns content is tested with smaller groups to see which versions produce an action, such as a donation or a share with a personal network. This content may be seeded to supporters for free, but creating, testing, and promoting it has real costs to a campaign.

The hardest part of earned media is how little control you have over it once it goes live. You have no idea who will pick up the event you're planning or how viral the content you post will go. It takes time. This is the earned aspect of this. If it's great, then you'll have a shot at getting your message out to the people you hope will get it. But you have no control over who receives these messages, under what circumstances they are received, or the slant of how they are shared. News media may view the speech as uninteresting and ignore it or inaccurate and challenge it. If it is done poorly, the shared content may become something different than it was originally intended. Even worse, it could become a complete joke, hurting the campaign.

TOOLS

The toolbox of earned media is endless, but here are some examples of how a campaign can grab media attention without paying for it. In all cases, there are traditional norms and modern ways of earning media coverage, most of which are now blending together. We'll start with the earned media opportunities that are most controllable by the campaign, and create the least risk, and then move to those that are more challenging to pull off well, which create greater risks.

Announcement

For most campaigns, the only earned media they can count on will be the formal speech announcing the candidate is running for office. The speech itself must be carefully written not just for the audience but for the media who will cover it. Straightforward answers to why the candidate is running and what the policy priorities are will help lay out a story that can be told by someone covering it. If the announcement is going to be before an audience of supporters, there is advance work required to ensure that enough people show up to make a good impression and that the staging and audio are professional. Moreover, specific invites should be made to the local press.

Announcements have shifted to hybrid in-person and online events, with some choosing to announce online and having a live event to celebrate afterward. This gives the candidate a two-bump shot at getting earned media and it focuses on separate audiences. The first drives news since it is actually new. The second demonstrates how a campaign can organize and pull off a complex event. The live event, of course, can be recorded, streamed, and shared afterward in total or in key moments for building voter support and fund-raising.

Events

The lifeblood of earned media is events. Giving a speech to a local VFW on veteran's issues, meeting with voters at the county fair, having coffee at supporters' homes, or meeting with local business leaders are all examples of ready-made candidate events for earned media. Expect private events with donors to become public, so be mindful of Mitt Romney's 47 percent mistake and don't say anything behind closed doors that the campaign would not want to see on the front page of the local paper or tweeted out by a respected community activist.

Like announcements, live events can be streamed, recorded, and shared online. There is nothing like the candidate being out and meeting voters, listening to their concerns, and directly asking for their support. All of this is repackageable content that can be used in a variety of ways. Again, while the campaign is out in the field, expect opposing campaigns to find a way in and stream or record whatever is said so it can be used against the candidate.

News Coverage

Earning media coverage is highly dependent upon what is going on in the community. During the 2020 campaign season, the only thing on voters' minds as they went through the COVID-19 pandemic was when and how we were going to be able to resume our lives. A candidate trying to get news coverage on any other issue would not find a willing audience of media gatekeepers, who also wanted to know what the candidates would do about COVID-19. The best strategy in any situation is to match up what is in the news instead of trying to drive it in a completely different direction.

Successful news coverage is powerful because it is in a setting where one expects to be challenged. Within the current media environment, however, news coverage of the candidate will be skewed for and against, so what modern campaigns do is share clips from friendly outlets. Being aware of not only the national but local news sources' biases and leanings, including those of the journalists themselves, will help position the candidate's expectations of how much positive media they can earn. Remember, voters consume news on their time and then share it. The news cycle is eternal.

Press Conferences

When a timely event happens, calling a press conference where the candidate makes an opening statement and then takes questions is another strategy to gain earned media. The reason for a press conference can vary, but in most cases, it will be to announce a new member of the team or a significant policy rollout, or to respond to an attack by an opponent. Opening up the candidate to questions from the media is a significant risk, as what might be asked cannot possibly be controlled. Be ready for anything off-topic.

As President Trump saw during COVID-19, it is impossible to control a news conference, and a hostile relationship with the press is not good for the candidate. Bits and pieces of news conferences find their way into the social media and news coverage streams and take on lives of their own. Do not expect the best candidate moments to find second lives outside of the press conference. Most press conferences are high risk and low reward because of the modern dynamics of campaigning, where very few people will watch the whole thing.

Endorsements

High-profile endorsements are a surefire way to gain earned media. Endorsements from people who are not well-known are not. This might seem straightforward, but in down ballot races most people do not know the local leadership that a campaign is soliciting support from, so they are easily ignored. A former president giving an endorsement is news. The local fire chief is a great asset to an existing event but will not get earned media on its own unless the chief is a local hero. If there is a group of local leaders endorsing a candidate, one endorsement event is more likely to get the campaign earned media coverage because the story is the combined weight of the group.

With modern e-mail, SMS, and social platforms, endorsements can have productive second lives. Based on voter research, the team should be able to find out which endorsers are most likely to move or strengthen support for the candidate. These endorsers can then be deputized to fill up specific voter inboxes, smartphones, and social media feeds with friendly faces who will help the candidate.

Candidate Interviews

The sit-down interview for either an endorsement or a news feature is a staple of traditional campaigns. The candidate preps for this like it was a debate, knowing all of the issues as well as understanding the reporter leanings and interests. As with any news coverage, the prep for who is interviewing the candidate is just as important as the candidate's understanding of what might be important or for a "gotcha" question like: How much did the county spend on mowing services last year? Everything is fair game because it is not the campaign's ink, mic, or platform.

The nightmare scenario is former Alaska governor Sarah Palin, whose great announcement speech raised voter expectations of who she might be as John McCain's running mate. Her sit-down interview with CBS's Katie Couric was a disaster. In her book *Going Rogue*, Palin claims that Nicole Wallace talked her into doing the interview, while Palin would have preferred to do interviews with Fox News or the *Wall Street Journal*. Wallace disputes this, of course, but the basic error here is that Palin was unprepared for what Couric might throw her way because the venue was out of her comfort zone. It got replayed everywhere and was the beginning of the end for the campaign. One study showed Palin cost McCain 2 million votes.

Web Properties and Organic Search

The "media you own" also serves to earn additional voter interest. Static websites and dynamic content such as blogs are important tools not just for introducing the candidate, conveying messages, and asking for donations but also to build up credibility within search networks like Google so that voters can find the candidate organically. In the final days of an election, the most common search queries are who is running for this office and the names of the candidates. Constructing a web presence that directs searches to the candidate's website helps answer these questions. Remember, most voters do not think about politics until they have to.

Search engine optimization (SEO) is a strategy to create links back to the website so that it will get a high ranking on sites like Google. In addition to mentioning the name of the candidate on each page and having a clean, rational organization to the site, links that exist offsite that point back to the main website help to improve the ranking. Therefore, the best URL for the website is the candidate's full name and dot-com. If that URL is unavailable and the team cannot buy it, add the office to the name. Former Senate majority leader Mitch McConnell's website is team-mitch.com, which is not ideal. His 2020 opponent, Amy McGrath, has AmyMcGrath.com, which is. During that election, the first several pages of results in a search for "Mitch McConnell for Senate" were ads from WinRed, ActBlue, and McGrath. McConnell's website came up fifth, after his Wikipedia page. There is no good reason for this other than a failure of SEO. Switching out the names, McGrath's campaign got four out of the top five search results: ActBlue's ad, the website, and her YouTube and Facebook pages.

CONSULTANT STORY

Despite all of your best intentions to earn media, maximizing the amazing reach of modern political vetting and opposition research campaign tools, it all falls apart if your candidate isn't being straight with you. As outlined in chapter 4, the most important question you need to ask of your candidate is, *"What do we need to know about you that they will use against you?"* As one might imagine, this is the one question candidates don't want to answer, but you have to ask. The reason you ask it is not only might it show up in a negative ad, it's more likely to show up in media. If your candidate doesn't tell you the whole truth, what happens next is well earned.

A friend of mine from college, who I won't name here, reached out to me a few cycles ago to ask if I'd be interested in doing the polling for an upstart Chamber of Commerce kind of candidate against Ted Yoho, who represented the Third Congressional District in Florida. As an independent pollster, campaigns were tough to come by so this is the kind of gig you get when you don't spend your entire life pitching candidates. That was my life at one time, so I said yes.

While we weren't close in college, my friend and I were very familiar with each other in campus politics at the University of Florida, which became a proving ground for several pols over the years at the local, state, and national levels. It was more real than any of us had anticipated, and at times, the two of us were on opposite sides. But it was always respectful. That he came to me about this campaign was kind of neat—a full-circle moment where two kids were about to become pros.

The problem was this, and we didn't know it at the time: Our candidate was a vampire.

After my friend and I made our business pact, I was introduced to the client. We exchanged short versions of our life stories, as one does in these kinds of meetings. *Oh, you've known your friend for how many years? Hey, here's my dad, who's advising me on the campaign. We have a baby on the way!* After the get-to-know-you part, it was down to business: Who really was this guy?

So I asked the question. His answer? "Well, if you must know, I'm a little nerdy. I play video games." Even at the time, that really didn't raise any red flags for me. In college, my roommate and I once had a tough semester because we were consumed with playing the OG version of RBI Baseball on a Nintendo system connected to my tube TV. Exasperated after some bad grades, my roommate, who continues to be one of my favorite people to this day, put it outside our room and mock melted down with, "I just can't do this anymore! It's ruining my life!" I told that story and the candidate laughed. No big deal, we're cool. Our guy is a computer game nerd. Whatever.

So we did the benchmark poll without asking the question, "If you knew Candidate X (we named him in the poll) dressed up as a live action role player (LARPer, I learned, belatedly) and there were these photos of him dressed up as an undead zombie, vampire, and a truly disturbing other thing I never got clarity on from anyone, would you still be open to voting for him?"

Our candidate was running for the first time so he may not have thought LARPing was potentially damaging or, worse, thought it could be a problem but didn't tell us about it or show us any of the pictures. So we did a poll without that information and our candidate did poorly but there was a narrow path to victory. He said, "Let's do this," and we said, "We're in with you."

Then one fine morning a conservative website posted the photos, ID-ing our guy as the vampire. I called my friend from college and asked, casually, "Hey, did you read the thing this morning?"

"What thing?"

"Uh, the thing on RedState.com."

"Oh, let me punch that up." Pause. Grunting. Expletives exchanged. "Is that him?"

"Uh, yeah, it's him. Now what?"

The answer to that question ended up not being what I had hoped for our candidate. I argued that he should drop out as LARPing isn't exactly the activity you'd want a squeaky-clean mainstream Republican trying to knock off an ultraconservative to be doing. My friend talked with the candidate, who didn't see the problem, so the campaign continued, albeit without any additional polling. We had no data on the impact of this earned media but, again, if you know the answer, why ask the question? So we didn't.

Confident in the knowledge that, although the candidate wasn't there yet, the campaign was over, I moved on to my corporate clients. It's amazing how comforting helping to sell more burgers and T-shirts for a national brand is when your last candidate was spooky as hell.

A few weeks later I got another call from my friend with a question that you should never, ever, answer honestly: "Am I genius or am I an idiot?" The correct answer is, *Well, this is a very bad idea for our candidate* and, *Hey, why is he still in the race?*

This is why this story is in this particular chapter: Satirist Stephen Colbert, who was hosting *The Colbert Report* on Comedy Central at the time, wanted to interview our vampire. Really. A sit-down. With our guy. The segment was innocuously called "Get to Know a Candidate," which was an absolute lie. The real title should've been "Watch Me Make Fun of a Candidate and Attempt to Ruin His Life."

My mind raced and I laughed audibly as I described what the show really was about and how it would go. My friend instead believed that going on the show could reboot the campaign and give our guy an opportunity to show who he was (e.g., not a vampire) and laugh at himself on the show. It would be humanizing—a great contrast to the incumbent, who was kind of a jerk.

"Okay," I countered, "What if it all went badly? Our guy isn't really funny, and Colbert is. They get to cut the tape so even if our guy lands a good one, it won't make the show."

"Oh, Mike, you're worrying too much. We'll coach him. He'll be great."

"Oh, so this is going to happen, isn't it?"

Yes. Yes, it did. Our guy lost by a ridiculous number of votes in the primary, but the worst thing about it is this: If you Google "Jake Rush," his creepy photos show up and the interview with Colbert remains the top-ranked search item, years later. There's nothing good there about him. His public life was ruined and any chance of running again when Ted Yoho decided to retire was squandered.

Jake now goes by Jacob on LinkedIn, which is terribly sad. He's a good man and would have made a good congressman. Remember, I know how a name can get ruined, particularly when it's not your fault. The other Michael Cohen went to jail and my @michaelcohen Twitter account gets annihilated every so often. But Jacob could have still been Jake today if had we talked him out of it. That's the power of earned media gone bad. With apologies to P. T. Barnum, all publicity (and earned media) is not good.

CAREERS

One of the most consistently lucrative jobs in modern political campaigns is in earned media. While making great paid advertising is valuable, earned media is cheaper and more powerful, resulting in high value for clients. Even better, the jobs are plentiful for those who would like to transition to the private sector, where you can be paid even more by corporations with larger budgets than political campaigns. Corporate social responsibility campaigns are essential components of a healthy public-facing organization, so if you are good at this when money is tight and time is even tighter, imagine what you could do with a big budget and plenty of time to plan.

If you would like to stay in politics, opportunities are everywhere, from campaigns to parties, PACs, public interest groups, and consulting firms. Creating something out of nothing is a very, very difficult thing to do, and everyone remotely engaged in politics recognizes this and is willing to pay for it. Starting on a campaign is a great way to get sea legs before you jump into the larger ocean of possibilities.

You can take a number of paths to break into earned political media, but beginning on a campaign will let you make mistakes out of the national spotlight. I can't relay all of the interviews I've had with consultants about an awful first event they ran or how unprepared their first candidates were for a press conference or an announcement that had such a low attendance it became the news itself. No one wants to talk about that on the record. What they will say, myself included, is that it is great training for recognizing what is really news and the value of preparation.

Consultants and media bookers suggest that before you try to earn media, consume it. Track which journalists cover public figures, which ones do well in their presence, and what the interviewers' interests are. Keep a spreadsheet of who's who in the local market and then pitch them individually. National reporters are easier, as they all have easily accessible reputations, but local media sources vary quite a bit. Building relationships with media bookers, being fast when they say yes, and understanding who is doing the interview helps everyone. Take it from someone who tried to save a vampire from Stephen Colbert.

THE FUTURE

With the breakdown of trust in advertising and news coverage, the challenge to earn media attention is likely to grow even more over the next few years. This will require a lot more planning, research, creativity, and luck to break through the complex haze of media we all consume. When I was growing up, we had two televisions, a few radios, and printed content where we consumed our media. Today, we literally carry the world's media in our pockets, and audiences have become so splintered now that most families do not watch the same television shows, listen to the same music, consume the same content, or participate on the same social media platforms. Breaking through all of this, reaching the people you need to reach in order to win, is incredibly difficult in today's environment.

This is why earned media pros have the edge. They can create something from nothing with little control over the outcome. In the corporate environment, events that build buzz are termed public relations functions. In campaigns, this doesn't translate perfectly, as everything candidates do has a public posture. What does translate is the creativity and professionalism necessary to navigate the media environment to move people. Future technology will allow campaigns to better track the ROI on earned media outside of news monitoring services and counting the sharing of hashtags. What won't change is the speed at which events are needed to come together and the uncontrollable tempo of how the public finds and reacts to it.

ASSIGNMENT

Let's play earned media matchmaker: Choose a federal candidate from the past five years and come up with a local and national media list. Choose five news- or opinion-centric outlets and target specific people for a sit-down interview. Find out all you can about the organization, match what your candidate believes to what the media outlet usually covers. Then, read all you can about how specific journalists or opinion writers cover candidates like yours. From there, choose one that you must have and one that you'd like to have. Write a one-page pitch to the campaign for the interview.

SOURCES AND ADDITIONAL READING

Blanton, Dana. "Fox News Poll: Interest in 2020 Already at Election Day Levels." Fox News, April 18, 2019. https://www.foxnews.com/politics/fox-news-poll-interest-in-2020-already-at-election-day-levels.

Bump, Philip. "Sarah Palin Cost John McCain 2 Million Votes in 2008, According to Study." *Washington Post*, January 19, 2016. https://www.washingtonpost.com/news/the-fix/wp/2016/01/19/sarah-palin-cost-john-mccain-2-million-votes-in-2008/.

Confessore, Nicholas, and Karen Yourish. "$2 Billion Worth of Free Media for Donald Trump." *New York Times*, March 15, 2016. https://www.nytimes.com/2016/03/16/upshot/measuring-donald-trumps-mammoth-advantage-in-free-media.html.

Couric, Katie. "CBS Exclusive: Gov. Sarah Palin." CBS Evening News, October 31, 2008. https://www.youtube.com/watch?v=-ZVh_u5RyiU.

Iyengar, Shanto. "How Television News Affects Voters: From Setting Agendas to Defining Standards." *Notre Dame Journal of Ethics & Public Policy* 6, no. 1 (1992). https://scholarship.law.nd.edu/cgi/viewcontent.cgi?article=1468&context=ndjlepp.

Palin, Sarah. *Going Rogue.* New York: HarperCollins. 2009.

Nielsen. "Consumer Trust Online, Social, and Mobile Advertising Grows." April 11, 2012. https://www.nielsen.com/us/en/insights/article/2012/consumer-trust-in-online-social-and-mobile-advertising-grows/.

Tyndall, Andrew. "Why Donald Trump Is King of All Earned Media." *Hollywood Reporter*, March 16, 2016. http://www.hollywoodreporter.com/news/why-donald-trump-is-king-876134.

NINE

Paid Media

"If you let an attack go, and not answer it. It's sort of a subliminal thing. The voter will just start to accept that it must be true because I'm not hearing a counterargument.

"To me, bells and whistles don't make an ad more convincing. If anything, you want it to be as authentic as possible. You want it to look not highly produced. You want it to look well-made, but I don't need special effects, things disappearing or magically appearing, or three-dimensional graphics traveling down a road. I don't think that works because it looks too technical and it looks too unbelievable."
— Mark Putnam, Democratic political advertising consultant

For most of my students, this is the section of the course where everyone looks up from their computers, puts down their smartphones, and pays attention. The development of political campaigns in the United States can be traced to the evolution of media options and the technology to produce, place, and track their effects. Media is so important in a campaign that it often becomes the story itself; to paraphrase Marshall McLuhan, the paid media becomes the message. The amount spent on paid advertising by super PACs supporting Jeb Bush before Iowa and New Hampshire in 2016 was the story, not necessarily what was in the ads.

Campaigns, with good reason, closely follow each other's moves in terms of the strength of ad buys (how much money is spent) in addition to the content. The messages a campaign can best control are delivered through paid media, but this is a deeply crowded marketplace and spend is a reflection of the broader political environment because it affects access to money to pay for ads. For example, political advertisers spent $5.25 billion during the midterm cycle in 2018, which was 17 percent more than they spent in 2016. As a result of the discontent with the governing party, Democrats outspent Republicans 53 percent to 46 percent, flipping margin in 2010, when party control was inverted. By mid-

May 2020, political spending was predicted to run ahead of 2016 and 2018 by $1 billion, and that was during a pandemic when most ad spending was sharply down.

DEFINITION

Paid political media is anything the campaign buys that conveys support for a candidate or their message. It could be as traditional as a yard sign or as modern as a paid social media post, anything that drives interest or behavior in the campaign or a candidate first into this category of activity. As outlined in previous chapters, campaigns are not the only ones who buy political media, so this definition includes any group, PAC, super PAC, or individual who is purchasing advertising to influence an election. Beyond the scope of this book, but also fair to say, is that paid political media also includes ads that seek to move public policy, a growing beyond-the-election-cycle service campaigners now provide.

Televised political advertising grew out of documentaries about campaigns. Cameras followed the candidate, collecting B-roll video while they met with voters or gave speeches. The content would later be spliced together with a script and then the ad would be manually spliced, mailed, and then aired. But the soul of the industry was telling a story about a candidate that made you feel like you had been in their presence and got a sense of the person along the way. We've come a long way from that, and various techniques have moved the candidate off-screen, particularly when the message is negative, but that's where it began.

HEARTS AND MINDS

The very best political advertising targets affect first, an emotional reaction, which acts both as a screen for messaging and a way to bond with the voter. This is a voter's availability to be reached. Next comes cognition, which is the brain's way of sorting out the information in a message and drives decision making. This is the reason to vote. Paid media must do both to be effective and to break through the overcrowded advertising landscape, especially close to an election. What I've found over the years is that most paid media do a solid job at rationally conveying who the candidate is and what they want to do, but only the most creative and empathetic pros find a way to draw an emotional response first.

There is no clean formula for this but there are ways to test paid media before it is finalized. No good campaign will go up with messages and ads that were not tested with focus groups and polling. Again, these are not cure-alls and mistakes can be made, but in most cases, you can tell whether there is a strong response to a paid media option or if it's *just okay*. The great AT&T ad maxim works here: If the options the campaign is considering elicit *somewhat* positive responses but not *extremely* positive ones, send the creative team back to the drawing board to find better options to consider.

The way to test affect in a focus group is to ask for what kind of emotional response the ad triggered in them. Most voters will dutifully give an answer, but only the best paid media options will draw out impassioned responses. Generally, the words themselves can be ignored, but the team should pay attention to the nonverbal response. Did voters seem truly shocked, excited, or engaged, or were they just answering the question posed to them? This takes a moderator who can also probe for the why here—you need to understand what prodded that response, what words or phrases or visuals mattered most? Then you can test the cognitive response with more straightforward questions about which parts of the message made the most sense to voters and why.

It is more challenging to test content with polling, as we are either testing messaging in an artificial situation such as reading it on a screen or hearing it from an interviewer. Optimally, the paid media options should be presented to voters the way they would interact with them, so the best mode is an internet survey. There, you can show any kind of ad as well as test audio messages. Still, with no moderators to probe or affect to decipher, we are relying on asking the right questions and hoping that voters will be fully honest with us, and we know from years of study that we are unable to get their emotional responses on self-administered surveys precisely.

One way to approach it is to show the messages in a group of others that are either from another campaign (so you can compare) or from media that you are considering. At the very least the campaign will be able to make a decision among several messages. Still, if one does not pop out from the group then it is fair to say it is not going to when there is a budget attached to it, either.

CALL TO ACTION

All paid media should offer the voter something to do beyond listening to, reading, or watching a campaign message. Any media that does not do this results in donations wasted. Depending on the strategy, voters should be directed to a website, a telephone number, or some way to either donate to the campaign or invest in it. That said, what the call to action (CTA) should say can be situational, and voter subgroups will react differently to some appeals than to others.

Online media will offer options to A/B test, which allows you to split a buy between two designs, sending half the voters to one page on a website and the other half to another, both of which can be tracked to see what was more effective. Modern e-mail outreach platforms also have this available as well as statistics on what links were clicked so you can know quickly whether one kind of appeal is working over another.

Beyond online media, mailers can replicate this, too, with small-batch printing of the same ad with two different CTAs. Broadcast CTAs are more difficult to track, requiring the cooperation of the stations you're buying. Offline media such as yard signs can be varied, but you can't A/B test at the same house. At best, you might be able to get two different ones on a block, and by then you've already spent too much money.

POSITIVE VERSUS NEGATIVE POLITICAL ADVERTISING

Positive advertising depicting candidates has been a staple of campaigns for decades. Positive ads increase knowledge about candidates, their positive traits, and the policies they support, and encourage voters to participate in the campaign. As a bonus, voters say they like positive ads, even if the academic research is all over the place on their effects. One study published in 2016 found that running "positive ads can increase a candidate's margin of victory," but this was done within an academic fantasy of a campaign where both candidates stay positive and out-advertise their opponent. A fact of campaign life is that in the heat of a race, it is difficult to avoid negative ads and usually unwise to go 100 percent positive.

A hot debate in academic circles continues to be whether candidate or interest group advertising is more effective if it is negative. Having studied this for both my master's thesis and my dissertation in the 1990s, I'm struck by how stale the arguments continue to be after working in and around politics for the past twenty years. Conventional wisdom has moved from *it doesn't work* to *it works* to *it may or may not have unintended effects on the political system.* A meta-analytic "reassessment" found that the research shows that negative ads don't work, "even though they are more memorable and stimulate knowledge about the campaign," and that it found no "reliable evidence that negative campaigning depresses voter turnout, though it does slightly lower feelings about political efficacy, trust in government, and possibly overall public mood."

The professionals know whether or not an ad works is related to the content, campaign, sponsor, and the timing. Most campaigns begin with a round of positive biography-driven advertisements aimed at boosting name recognition and positive sentiment toward the candidate. As the campaign progresses, they will begin to deploy negative ads; "contrast messaging" is the current professional term. Then, at the end, they will close with a positive get-out-the-vote message or drop the nastiest opposition research they have. The reason this is backloaded is that some attacks boomerang back on the sponsor, so the timing is a damage mitigation move.

The mix of positive and negative advertising is now all over the place due to the fact that independent groups, in some races, take up the majority of the spend. The way the industry appears to be going, the outside groups hit opponents with negative ads while the candidate's campaign attempts to put out mostly positive ads. Again, this changes from race to race, but the basic idea is to protect the candidate's image and give the campaign wiggle room to disavow ads they don't like or cannot like in public. That said, the academic research conflicts as to whether negative ads from a candidate or a group are more powerful. One study found that PACs are less effective in producing higher voter shares and influencing voter turnout. Still, it found myriad intervening factors. The bottom line is this: negative advertising is a fact of campaign life.

Overall, the important internal figure for campaigns is share of voice. While the message itself is important, so is how much of it finds its way to targeted voters. While ad placement technology has been refined over the past few years to include nontraditional platforms like over-the-top television and social media, where the technology is going in political advertising is toward tracking not only your team's spend but the opponent's, so that changes can be made. With better information, campaigns can find ways to tweak their spend along the way rather than just react to ads as soon as possible. The overall weight of your message versus the opposition's will become the crucial metric as this information becomes more widely available.

As campaign advertising moved online and into social media feeds, it became difficult to figure out who was sponsoring which ad. Leaving aside the heated debate over how much it mattered, it is clear that foreign actors sought to influence the 2016 presidential election and that this had a self-regulatory effect on the platforms in the aftermath. Facebook continues to allow political advertising, but with restrictions on tools for targeting voters. On the other side, Twitter has banned them. Most platforms in 2020 banned political ads fairly universally, even extending to my Congress in Your Pocket apps, which are not published on behalf of a campaign. Still, paid teams were very effective at posting sharable content that had some of the effect without as much control of paid ads. An example of this is the "Reply Guys," which included my former student Tyler Giles, who worked on behalf of the Ed Markey for Senate primary campaign and found viral ways to grab attention that could not be bought with advertising this cycle.

CONSULTANT STORY

In my extended interview with Democratic consultant Mark Putnam, he talked at length about how making ads for campaigns has shifted during his career. On his way up, he used to watch MTV, which at the time showed almost exclusively music videos. They were creative, visually, so he used to watch them with the sound off to get a sense of the techniques used and what audiences might expect to see in one of his political ads. Some of them also told short stories, which was a skill that translated to political advertising as well.

As for what's next, Putnam doesn't think we know yet what the next big thing in political ads will be. "It's so hard to predict the future, because who would have guessed ten years ago that long-form video on the internet would be such a thing. The conventional wisdom in the early 2000s was that something online had to be short, fifteen seconds because of everyone's short attention span. Who could predict that you could do two-minute, three-minute, five-minute ads? But if the content is good enough, people will watch it," he says. We seem to be going back to the future here. "It is part of the evolution back to documentary storytelling," he concludes.

In the kind of high-concept, high-production advertising like he produces, Putnam has not seen the hypertargeting of online ads that was predicted. "A campaign would have to make twenty ads to talk to all of these small groups of people, and you can target them very efficiently. That hasn't come to pass to the degree people thought it would. We're not making Senate ads for senior citizens that they only see on Facebook. I haven't seen that be successful," Putnam says.

"But an ad that you're going to run pre-roll on a program on Hulu or it's going on television that has to rise to a higher level of production. That costs money. A campaign doesn't have unlimited funds to make ads," he explains. Putnam thinks the kind of content you can make for social media, like filming a candidate on the way to an event, is very low cost and fits the platforms well. From my vantage point this kind of content, while not traditional advertising, will become a greater share of what campaigns will pay to produce. It comes off as more authentic, and that's where the eyeballs are.

CAREERS

Jobs in paid media are plentiful, and it is a great career path to running campaigns. As the keepers of the message and the largest chunk of the budget, the person in charge of the paid media is the most important person on the campaign aside from the candidate. A successfully packaged candidate and message is for all to see, so if a campaign wins, credit instantly goes to the media team after (and sometimes before) the candidate. It is a high-risk, high-reward, high-profile career.

The very best paid media professionals are storytellers by nature. They understand that every ad needs to have a hook to draw in the voter, a story, and an ending. What the best consultants tell me is that advertising is so ubiquitous now that the bar for getting attention to a campaign ad rests on its ability to be creative while remaining authentic. With all of the visual and auditory tools available on our mobile devices, we have become desensitized to glitzy appeals jammed with tricks. Great stories and ads don't need them.

There are various paths to a career in paid political media, but they generally run through consulting firms. Small campaigns do not have the money for advertising beyond mail or digital, so doing higher-level paid media is not something you can learn on a county commission race. The political parties are another way in, but they just hire consultants, so it is best to start there. Most firms will want some fluency with production technology, but what they really want to know is this: Can you tell a compelling story with creativity and edge?

Republican consultant Sue Zoldak says that in her business, campaign experience is overrated and talent is underrated: "I think people who are better had naturally a gut instinct all along. I'd rather have a twenty-one-year-old who has that gut instinct than a sixty-one-year-old who has no gut instinct but has a lot of experience. To me it's about that feeling. Are they able to understand what a good piece of creative is versus a bad piece of creative? If someone is able to do that, I don't really care about what their experience is. Some people can do that right out of the box."

While talent is important, even Zoldak began her career as an intern working for one of the best ad makers in campaigns, an innovator named Ben Goddard, whose "Harry and Louise" ads depicted a married couple sitting at a kitchen table working through the Clinton healthcare reform proposals in 1993 and 1994. It was the first instance of political campaign-style ads run during a public policy debate, and the ads are widely credited with derailing the effort. What Zoldak and I recognized, a few years apart, was that public affairs organizations were going to adopt these media habits because the campaign was so successful.

The Goddard Claussen firm spent only $14 million, but the impact was much larger as the paid media was picked up by news outlets, becoming an earned media event. Today, public affairs media is a multi-billion-dollar political industry. As my now-dusty dissertation argued, there's nothing in politics like adopting something new like this that works. As for Zoldak's career, Goddard nurtured her gut instincts and she now owns her own agency.

Putnam had a similar path. At the front end of his career, he was able to land an informational interview with Geraldine Ferraro, the first woman on a national ticket. It turns out, he had a good friend in the same college dorm who was Ferraro's daughter. Putnam asked Ferraro, "Should I work on a campaign? Should I go work on the Hill? Should I go work for a regular ad agency?" And she said, "No, you should go work for a political media firm."

Then Ferraro proceeded to give him a list of people to contact, which Putnam did. One of them was legendary media consultant Bob Squier, who hired him for his first campaign as an intern, and his career began there. Putnam saw some opposition research on an opponent and thought it might make a great ad. Squier agreed and asked Putnam to write it. He did, and it was cited in postelection analysis pieces as one of the reasons why the candidate won.

But it begins with a passion for politics. "This is a crazy business to be in. I feel like I'm doing something meaningful," Putnam says. He has found that there are people who come from the campaign management or earned media side to ad making, figuring it is the lucrative area to be in a campaign, but find it to be more complicated. "It requires such an overwhelming focus on it to teach yourself the tools, to develop the political, strategic side of your judgment as well as the creative side of it. There aren't enough people, frankly, in this business that come in understanding creative. They haven't studied how to make advertising, how to make film. You have to have a willingness to really learn the craft, if you want to be successful, and make a good ad. And then you do have to spend time on a campaign." Putnam never did that, but he wishes he did at the beginning of his career because it helps you understand campaigns as they are, on the ground, and helps to build your political network of consultants and campaign managers.

THE FUTURE

The growth in paid media for political campaigns is online. By now, most firms can place ads for a campaign, and the best ones do an excellent job of leveraging data and modeled audiences to maximize budgets. But there is always going to be a market for great storytellers, and that is what we are not seeing online so far. In the pursuit of CTAs, campaigns have not yet figured out great ways to tell stories that are emotionally engaging as well as persuasive. Sadly, most campaigns now believe the best way to reach voters is to prime their base with tried-and-true messages. The future of paid media belongs to those who can move voters we do not already have.

For consultants, the biggest challenge to the future of paid political ads is the restrictions of internet and social platforms. The aftermath of the 2016 presidential election moved the most-visited platforms to reconsider their rules on political ads, landing on more restrictive policies. Some have banned political ads altogether, while others have removed the ability to target lookalike audiences, which allows campaigns to upload a list and reach people like them. While these are works in progress, it is notable that the largest, Facebook, has resisted much of this pressure.

Still, the backlash is coming, and what might result from the changes is that it will cost more money to reach voters when the platforms remove some of the technology used to target, reserving it for businesses and apolitical nonprofits. Is this fair? Probably not, and there will be litigation, to be sure. In the meantime, it will simply be more expensive and will favor campaigns with the largest paid media budgets.

What won't change is the need for speed. Attention spans have shrunk, particularly online, so it will be important for campaigns to be quick in grabbing attention so they can emotionally connect and convey a message. Campaigns will need to be even more nimble in having all kinds of content prepared and ready to launch, given the shrinking nature of the news cycles that is now minutes, not hours. A team that can move on a dime will be important to not only producing and placing the content but making sure that it is being tested along the way. The future is going to be very busy for media teams.

For voters trying to make sense of the ads they see or hear, it is a more complex picture. Two factors are at play: Trust in the media has declined and the number of local media outlets covering local races has plummeted. Fewer journalists are writing about political ads' consistency, so holding ad makers to their claims made has become increasingly dicey. As Putnam put it in our interview, ad watches were "a way of bringing professionalism and accountability to political advertising for many, many, years, but the death of newspapers has actually led to a decline in accountability and a lot more dishonesty in political ads over the last few cycles."

ASSIGNMENT

What was the best political ad you've ever seen, and why did it work for you as a voter? Break down the storytelling, where it was released, and if it earned news media attention. What lessons did you learn from it that you could bring to another campaign? Now compare that ad to a similar one run by an opponent in the race on the same characteristics. Why did it not do as well; what was missing? Were there differences in production technique that mattered, or was it just that one candidate was better than another? Look at the two of them critically and compare your notes with news coverage of the race. Were these ads impactful? Why?

SOURCES AND ADDITIONAL READING

Advertising Analytics and Cross Screen Media. "2020 Political Spending Projections." *Politico*, May 15, 2020. https://www.politico.com/f/?id=00000172-150d-d57a-ad7b-5f2fd9520000.

Birnbaum, Jeffrey H. "Returning to the Genre He Started." *Washington Post*, November 29, 2004. https://www.washingtonpost.com/wp-dyn/articles/A18417-2004Nov28.html.

Cohen, Michael. *Directly Negative: Effects of Political Advertising on Party-Based Expectancies on Candidate Evaluations*. Master's thesis. University of Florida, 1993.

Cohen, Michael. *The 1993–1994 Health Care Reform Campaign: The Influence of Political Advertising and News Media Coverage on Public Opinion*. PhD dissertation. University of Florida, 1996. https://ia801705.us.archive.org/2/items/19931994healthca00cohe/19931994healthca00cohe.pdf.

Fineman, Howard. "My Former Newspaper Is Struggling—and Is More Important Than Ever." *Washington Post*, May 5, 2020. https://www.washingtonpost.com/opinions/2020/05/05/my-former-newspaper-is-struggling-is-more-important-than-ever/.

Goddard Claussen Public Affairs. "Harry and Louise" commercials. Last updated July 31, 2011. https://www.youtube.com/playlist?list=PL9D25B09ECD13EBFF.

Jamieson, Kathleen Hall. *Dirty Politics: Deception, Distraction, and Democracy*. New York: Oxford, 1992.

Kaid, Lynda Lee, and Anne Johnston. "Negative versus Positive Television Advertising in Presidential Campaigns, 1960–1988." *Journal of Communication* 41, no. 3 (1991). https://onlinelibrary.wiley.com/doi/abs/10.1111/j.1460-2466.1991.tb02323.x.

Lau, Richard, Lee Sigelman, and Ivy Rovner. "The Effects of Negative Political Campaigns: A Meta-Analytic Reassessment." *Journal of Politics* 69, no. 4 (2007): 1176–209. https://www.researchgate.net/publication/227686152_The_Effects_of_Negative_Political_Campaigns_A_Meta-Analytic_Reassessment.

Lynch, Jason. "Advertisers Spent $5.25 Billion on the Midterm Election, 17% More than in 2016." *Adweek*, November 16, 2018. https://www.adweek.com/tv-video/advertisers-spent-5-25-billion-on-the-midterm-election-17-more-than-in-2016/.

Malloy, Liam C., and Shanna Pearson-Merkowitz. "Going Positive: The Effects of Negative and Positive Advertising on Candidate Success and Voter Turnout." *Research & Politics*, February 1, 2016. https://doi.org/10.1177/2053168015625078.

McLuhan, Marshall. *Understanding Media: The Extensions of Man*. New York: McGraw-Hill, 1964.

Montellaro, Zach. "Political Ads Expected to Explode, Even as Economy Tanks." *Politico Pro*, May 15, 2020. https://subscriber.politicopro.com/article/2020/05/15/political-ad-spending-increases-as-economy-tanks-259653.

Putnam, Mark. Interview with the author. May 4, 2020.

Wang, Yanween, Michael Lewis, and David A. Schweidel. "A Border Strategy Analysis of Ad Source and Message Tone in Senatorial Campaigns." *Marketing Science*, May 9, 2018. https://pubsonline.informs.org/journal/doi/abs/10.1287/mksc.2017.1079.

Zoldak, Sue. "In Memory of Ben Goddard." LinkedIn, June 16, 2018. https://www.linkedin.com/pulse/memory-ben-goddard-sue-zoldak/.

———. Interview with the author. May 7, 2020.

TEN

Social Media

"I think the winners of the campaign technology arms race are the things that make reaching voters faster and easier. They're going to prize things that are cheap, free, and fast. Things like Twitter, Facebook ads to help raise money and get some message testing."
— Patrick Ruffini, Republican digital strategist

The internet can be a weird place, but we've unintentionally yet collectively decided it'll be where we live a great deal of our lives. It's also an important venue for the modern political campaign and a blend of earned media, where a post can spontaneously find a wide audience, and paid media, where you can promote specific posts in the hopes of driving activity such as signing up for e-mail from campaigns, offering to donate time or money, or other kinds of campaign behavior.

Social media has come to dominate our shortening attention spans, moving us from attempting to avoid broadcast commercials with channel switching or fast-forwarding to skimming our feeds for content from our family, friends, colleagues, and brands we follow. Embedded in all of these feeds is advertising, of course, and in many cases, candidates we follow.

As most readers know, the platforms vary widely. While Facebook has the most users, other platforms, like Instagram and TikTok, skew much younger. The content you'll find on social media is so diverse that it's on the verge of becoming too generic a term to hold together music, photos, video, and the written word as one *thing*. The business models are so different and what you can do on these platforms varies so widely that your levels of integration and activity don't port. We can heart a song on Spotify or a post on Instagram, but they mean qualitatively different things. We can react to a post on Facebook with several choices, which influences the algorithm of what we see next in an effort to maximize the time we spend there. Social media is not designed for you to stop by, look around, and leave. Its main goal is to keep you there, and it's quite good at it.

Political content is now part of this stream of social media in a core way. While platforms moved in 2019 to restrict the tools political ad makers have, no one can stop your adorably crazy uncle from sharing a Moscow-designed Trump or Pelosi meme or your kids from sharing brief TikTok videos that are even funnier after they explain them to you. (Okay, that's just me.) While advertising on social media has become more complicated, unpaid posts that can earn your attention are even more important.

DEFINITION

Without getting too technical or earning a Captain Obvious Halloween costume, social media is an electronic platform where self-organized groups of people share content. The platforms have different rules on accounts ranging from closed personal accounts, where you must ask to follow a user, to open personal accounts, where you do not need permission to follow the user's content. For the purposes of campaigns, most platforms have some version of a company or organization account where you may post as a group on behalf of a candidate. While most social media accounts are run by staff or consultants, the candidates may choose to keep their personal accounts open to interact with users directly.

This is an important choice to make, and it impacts how social media platform users react to posts. One of the top reasons why @realDonaldTrump was a leading account on Twitter is because it was actually used by its namesake. In general, the more authentic an account is, the greater the follower opportunity, and engagement with the account is much higher. Trump understood this for years, often writing tweets himself or dictating them to staff for *light* editing. What we saw on @realDonaldTrump was the real Donald Trump. It's also the reason why the account was ultimately banned by Twitter after the January 6, 2021 insurrection. Twitter understood that the posts inciting and supporting the rioters were coming from him, so they needed to act.

Despite the ban, other elected officials and candidates have taken the lead from Trump on Twitter, with more personal engagement there, if not on other social media platforms. Still, the vast majority of candidates do not post their own content, leaving that to staff, which is why followers are less engaged. If you have an opportunity to reply to an elected official, that is a draw on social media. Replying to their staff is less so. In the early years, candidates and members hid behind their staff, so you had to guess what was authentic and what was prepackaged. Usually now, content shared by the officials directly includes their initials at the end, and on other platforms the expectation is that it is staff and not the candidate. For example, who believes that Donald Trump or Nancy Pelosi post videos to YouTube? But everyone can tweet, which is why initials at the end are best practice—except if you are Trump, of course.

All social media activity should be intentional and in service of voter contact or fund-raising goals. Alan Rosenblatt notes that "there is a difference between knowing how to use social media and using it strategically." Just posting *more* on social media is not going to help the campaign. What is posted, on which platforms, and when are the keys to using social media effectively.

TOOLS

Optimally, campaigns should own the same username on every social platform so a voter following your candidate on one can find the candidate on any other. In practice, this is rare among established officeholders but has become increasingly common among first-time candidates. As discussed earlier, the best SEO for a website is simply the person's name, which has the virtue of being portable should the candidate move on to run for a different office. Even if the campaign chooses to go a different way, the candidate should find a way to lock down their name so they don't end up getting spoofed by an opponent or one of their supporters.

The social links will be different, however, but should be consistent. The candidate's name on its own is the best way to go, too, but going with @LastnameForPosition throughout the social media ecosystem works well, too. Note that elected officials have gone to separating their official and campaign accounts, so @NancyPelosi and @SpeakerPelosi are used for different purposes.

With that branding preamble, let's look at the social media platforms (as of spring 2020) that would qualify as must-participate, which are optional platforms, and which ones you could avoid.

The Major Platforms

You can buy advertising on each one of these, and we will cover them in detail in the following sections, focusing on what each one is in brief and what it offers a campaign.

- *Twitter.* This platform has the advantage of immediacy. Twitter has tried to curate its user timelines with algorithms set to push "top tweets," but most users hop on Twitter to see what is going on right now. When a candidate or campaign tweets, it is an official statement that goes directly to followers and haters alike, as well as to the news media covering the race. When it started, tweets were limited to text and 140 characters. Now they can go up to 280 characters and include links, video, and up to four photos. Brevity is key and snark is rewarded. With President Trump and most major national, state, and local leaders active on the platform, Twitter has become a highly political space, if not the most political one online. Campaign tweets often become the subject of earned media, showing up in news stories in traditional formats like television, radio, and print. These blasts of content find their way off-platform easily and can go viral on their own without the campaign's prodding. After the 2016 election, Twitter was the first to outright ban political advertising. Their definition appears to be airtight: No ads for candidates, political parties, elected or appointed government officials, elections, referenda, ballot measures, legislation, regulation, directive, or judicial outcomes are allowed at all. PACs, super PACs, and 501(c)(4)s are explicitly banned. The only exceptions appear to be for news publishers referring to political content, but even that is likely to be reviewed with strict scrutiny, as one could imagine Russian TV trying to place an ad under these guidelines. Still, for our purposes, campaigns are going to have to engage on Twitter through posting on the platform.

- *Instagram.* This is the most visual platform available and increasingly the social media of choice among Millennials and Generation Z. The timeline is curated, so what is happening *right now* is not necessarily at the very top of the feed, but Instagram does an outstanding job of pushing photos and short-form videos up to a few minutes. Captions are less important but provide context. Keep them short to maximize impact on the short attention span.
- *Facebook.* The dominant social media platform is a catchall for all online content. Again, the platform controls what voters will see and when, so whatever is posted on Facebook should complement what is being posted on other platforms. As we'll learn later, the best reason to be on Facebook is its 1.69 billion users worldwide and 221.6 million in the United States. If you want to reach a voter, chances are they are here at some point during the month. Facebook owns Instagram, so their policies on ads are the same. Overall, they've taken a largely hands-off approach to political ads, allowing campaigns to continue to pay for posts on both platforms. Their rules reflect those generally accepted on television and radio and in print. They include "paid for by" labels on political and issue ads, and they are offering an archive for all political ads that is searchable by the public. Custom audiences on Facebook allow political campaigns to upload their own enhanced voter file lists to create a specific audience they want to reach. All the hard work of the data and analytics teams pay off here. Look-alike audiences is another tool Facebook has, but it takes the campaign's list one step further.

Using a proprietary algorithm, Facebook takes the campaign's list and creates its own based on information the advertiser cannot see and expands the pool of users the post can reach. Finally, ads can be placed directly with basic demographics such as age, education, zip code, income, and relationship status. Personal interests of users are also in the mix as well as stated political leanings. Advertisers need to reveal their identity and location, and, in my experience, this can be a very stringent process so give your team enough time to get through it. At the end of 2020 it was not clear that Facebook had settled on political campaign advertising going forward and it is likely that some of their best tools may remain restricted for such use.

- *YouTube.* This is where all long-form video lives and where few people subscribe or browse. Voters are generally clued in to campaign ads and videos from somewhere else, but they need one home and it is YouTube. Once there, voters may leave comments on campaign videos, so make sure that a staffer is watching out for trolls or choose to turn off the ability to leave comments as a safe option. Voters who land there may dig a little deeper and see other videos, so have a consistent, branded, approach. Google owns YouTube, and they have taken the stance that their policies on political ads are the same as "selling office furniture." They do not offer "granular microtargeting of election ads," limiting potential audience targeting to the basics: age, gender, and postal code level location. In short, they offer up the basic Facebook suite without the ability to upload your own list or create look-alike audiences.

Secondary Platforms

- *Medium.* If your campaign is pushing out policy substance, this is a great place for it to land and be discovered by others who like to read and take their content seriously. Medium is Twitter founder Jack Dorsey's apology platform, where the written word is paramount and quippy is devalued for thoughtfulness. Several members of Congress have Medium pages, but most do not post there often. This is an excellent place to leverage a candidate who wants voters to understand why they support a policy. While Medium launched with advertising, it shuttered the practice in early 2017, laying off one-third of its team and moving to a subscription model. Founder Ev Williams, who was one of the cofounders of Twitter, said in an interview with *Digiday*, "It's clear that the broken system is ad-driven media on the internet." Political advertising was not cited as a rationale for the move, but Medium is now limited to a channel for political earned media.

- *TikTok*. The hottest new social media platform is also the least political—for now. This is where Generation Z goes to take a break, catch up with what's going on, and share the latest jokes, memes, and hot takes. Vine famous has now become TikTok famous. The videos go up to about a minute and loop like Vine did, but these are much more engaging. The downside is that the company is Chinese owned, which created a host of privacy concerns. In response, the Trump administration temporarily banned TikTok before bringing it back through a long review process, ultimately leaving it to the Biden administration to decide what to do next. Of course, this makes the app even more attractive to those you might want to reach. Sensitive to perceived influence, the Chinese-owned platform wants nothing to do with political advertising, banning it in fall 2019. Any ads that support or oppose political candidates, current leaders, political parties or groups, issues, and advocacy are not allowed there because "the app's light-hearted and irreverent feeling" does not match up with politics. Like Medium, TikTok is now an earned media platform.
- *Snapchat*. Not long ago, this was the platform that caused parents the most worry and was viewed as too seedy to use for campaigning. No more. The app that broke the barrier to disappearing communication remains a force among Generation Z, who do not want to have their online lives live forever. One of the best uses of the platform is location stickers, which can be used to help capture a snap at a campaign event. Snapchat has gone the Facebook route with a public library of political and advocacy ads and "paid for by" tags. It "encourage[s] political advertisers to be positive" but "don't categorically ban 'attack' ads." The exception? "Political ads must not include attacks relating to a candidate's personal life," according to their guidelines. Like TikTok, dropping personal oppo on an opponent just seems weird for the platform, anyway. Avoid it, even on unpaid campaign posts. It's just not the place for it.

Avoidable Platforms

None of the following are great fits for elections and they are even worse for a campaign budget. No information on advertising on these platforms is given below as pro-to-pro encouragement for your campaign to avoid spending donor money there.

- *LinkedIn*. Don't mix business and politics is an axiom of both. While that is true most of the time—don't post negative ads here—you might use the platform to write about how your candidate will engage the business community or post about business-friendly proposals. Still, be very careful and remember that the campaign is opening itself to quick scorn. Moreover, as engagement on the platform is generally low and is confined to brands and job seekers, posts are least likely to go viral here.

- *Flikr*. Instagram basically killed Flickr, which campaigns used to use for showing off candidate and event photos. Skip it.
- *Tumblr*. A microblogging site that amounts to a short-form Medium post. Campaigns can integrate Tumblr into their websites, but generally, few people will visit a website to read a campaign blog unless it is really compelling. In most cases, they'll skip reading the posts and find your content on other platforms.
- *Pinterest*. A campaign having an official Pinterest is a bit odd. While there are 88 million monthly active users on the platform and it is now the third largest social network in the United States, this goes back to a core question of why. If your candidate is trying to reach a predominantly female audience, that would be one reason. But the platform is organized by what users find elsewhere on the internet and "pin" to a board. The most popular items pinned are home design and clothing, as well as food and recipes. There was some coverage of groups and candidates using Pinterest for political visuals, but they're probably best shared elsewhere as this is one of the least political social media platforms.
- *Reddit*. This is a nerdy and risky play, but Reddit is a platform where discussion is king and comment section is on full throttle. Barack Obama once took questions on the platform and it was, in his words, "NOT BAD!" (https://www.reddit.com/r/IAmA/ comments/z1c9z/i_am_barack_obama_president_of_the_ united_states/). Most campaigns, however, can easily avoid it because most voters are simply not on it and those who are may not be the people your candidate is targeting.

CONSULTANT STORY

When you signed up to take my course or buy this book, many of you did that half-double take: Is he *that* Michael Cohen? Most of you figured out right away that the other guy couldn't possibly be teaching or writing about politics from jail (yet), so this guy must be different. As you might imagine, I get quite a bit of confusion on Twitter, in particular, because I have the OG @michaelcohen username. During the 2016 campaign my famous doppelgänger went on CNN arguing that all polls showed Donald Trump winning the race for the presidency, which wasn't true at the time.

That was a tough night for my Twitter account and it still gets blown up hundreds with misdirected posts every now and then since @michaelcohen212 testified before Congress, went to jail, got released, and wrote a book about his Trump experience. I've been called out by none other than high-volume Twitter users Diamond and Silk, Geraldo Rivera, as well as the *Washington Examiner*, and many others. It makes for a complicated life on the platform. Bottom line: if your candidate has a common name, make sure there isn't a notorious double running around or change the name of the social media accounts. Taking a tip from Trump, adding "real" to the front of the name isn't a bad idea at all.

CAREERS

Digital is the hottest submarket in campaigns for jobs, and it is expected that if you are newly out of college, or even still taking classes, you are as qualified or more qualified than someone who is far more advanced in their political careers. The reason is simple: digital natives have been posting and consuming content on social media for much of their lives and have more real-world experience than their elders. This flips the experience scale on its head, where the younger you are the more qualified you are to help candidates on social media platforms than those who don't get it intuitively.

In addition, the digital director has become a pathway to becoming the campaign manager. In previous decades, the best way to the big job was through being a paid media consultant in charge of messaging. Now much of the messaging is running through social media. Again, Trump understands this far better than most elected officials far younger than he is, so the appointment of Brad Parscale, his 2016 digital director, to be his overall 2020 campaign manager was both groundbreaking and a natural promotion.

THE FUTURE

Social media has become highly professionalized, with candidates employing teams of content creators to leverage the platforms for fundraising, communications, and mobilization. The platforms themselves have become quite adept at selling themselves to the political market, although the rules governing those ads and who can place them have become curtailed due to foreign influence in the 2016 elections.

The technology behind these platforms varies what users see and will continue to do so. Those who are more politically active are more likely to get campaign content, but those decisions are left up to algorithms that track what you look at, how long you look at it, and whether or not you interact with it. It is unclear if what voters see on platforms will ultimately make it worth the time and money spent on creating the content, but for now it is relatively low cost compared with video, audio, and print alternatives.

While campaigns will take more time to create content directed at voters, what will not change is the speed at which this content can be released. Platforms cannot effectively preempt campaign posts, so there is no feasible editorial board that will slow down the process. However, with the increasing scrutiny of social media advertising, paid posts will likely take more time and resemble more traditional platforms in how long ads may take to be posted for users to algorithmically consume.

The future is bright for social media, but where we all congregate online will change often. For example, Vine was a platform for short-form videos limited to six seconds and became the go-to platform for wildly creative memes. The videos played in loops so if you missed the joke, you could see it again in the next round. While YouTube has no limits to video posts, the six-second rule made it easy for our short attention spans to snack on content and move on to something else. What killed Vine, ultimately, was its sale to Twitter, which bought it for $30 million in October 2012 and never got the joke. A version of Vine returned with Chinese ownership and was released worldwide in 2018. As of January 2020, TikTok has more than 1.5 billion downloads and has become far more popular than Vine.

While some social media platforms fail and get replaced, others' features find new homes in larger parent companies or in competing apps. Facebook is the master at this. Like Microsoft before them, when Facebook sees a popular feature it simply adds it to the platform, keeping users on it for longer periods of time and reinforcing lock-in. When Instagram, which is owned by Facebook, rolled out its stories feature, Facebook added it to its own platform, allowing Instagram users to post to both at the same time. Reportedly, YouTube will roll out short-form videos called "Shorts" within its mobile app and allow users to include licensed music and songs. Still, TikTok has a significant head start and it is unlikely that YouTube will replace the app that Generation Z loves to watch and share.

The splintering of social media platforms will continue, but there is a lot of user lock-in on the major ones—that's where most of your friends, families, and colleagues are—so the money will remain there for now. The dominant platform will remain Facebook, at least in the short term, because it has the most users and therefore the largest audience. Moreover, Facebook does an outstanding job of separating you from your advertising dollars through its Ads Manager, which remains best in class in its design as well as your ability to target people most likely to engage with your ad. While other platforms are catching up, the scale of Facebook makes it the best place for a campaign's paid media.

Attention of earned media on social platforms is much more difficult and will favor platforms that are shorter and more creative so they can break through the clutter. Shareability is key to driving viral content, and something that is six seconds is easier to get someone to watch than something that is thirty seconds or five minutes. While a mature platform like Facebook has the most users, the content there is fairly unoriginal—mostly personal updates, some clichéd memes, photos, and video. The really creative stuff is generated on other platforms and then shared to Facebook, so the future of some campaigns will, in part, go viral on platforms that we have not even seen yet. Don't worry—the content will wind up on Facebook and covered by mainstream media, eventually.

ASSIGNMENT

The hardest part of social media is being creative and launching content that goes viral. So let's do something easier: analyze greatness. After all, if you are going to be a digital director or campaign manager someday, you will not be producing the content yourself but will need to recognize and understand why something is great versus *just okay*. Choose the best short-form video you have ever seen for a political candidate on any platform and break it down into its components. Why did the campaign use that platform, what was the overall message of the post, why did it break through, and how did it go viral? Then choose the worst one you have ever seen and try to infer why it was posted on that platform, what the intended message was, why it failed, and how much damage it did to the candidate whose campaign created it. Finally, write down five things you have learned from the assignment and use them to evaluate content for your next campaign.

SOURCES AND ADDITIONAL READING

CBS News. "Facebook Changes Ad Policy after Bloomberg Hired Influencers." February 14, 2020. https://www.cbsnews.com/news/facebook-political-ad-policy-change-bloomberg-meme-instagram-influencers/.

Chandlee, Blake. "Understanding Our Policies around Paid Ads." TikTok, October 3, 2019. https://newsroom.tiktok.com/en-us/understanding-our-policies-around-paid-ads.

Constine, Josh. "Facebook and Instagram Launch US Political Ad Labeling and Archive." *TechCrunch*, May 24, 2018. https://techcrunch.com/2018/05/24/facebook-political-ad-archive/.

Facebook. "Ads about Social Issues, Elections, or Politics." Retrieved May 22, 2020, from https://www.facebook.com/business/help/597258763977273.

———. "Facebook for Government, Politics and Advocacy." Retrieved April 20, 2020, from https://www.facebook.com/gpa.

Feiner, Lauren, and Megan Graham. "Twitter Unveils Final Details for Political Ad Ban, but It's Still Looking Murky." CNBC, November 15, 2019. https://www.cnbc.com/2019/11/15/twitter-unveils-new-political-ad-policy.html.

Goodfellow, Jessica. "TikTok Bans Political Ads." *PR Week*, October 7, 2019. https://www.prweek.com/article/1661683/tiktok-bans-political-ads.

Kyung Kim, Eun. "Pinterest Gets Political with Bipartisan Boards." *Today*, October 5, 2012. https://www.today.com/news/pinterest-gets-political-bipartisan-boards-1C6299361.

Newton, Casey. "Why Vine Died." *Verge*, October 28, 2016. https://www.theverge.com/2016/10/28/13456208/why-vine-died-twitter-shutdown.

Leskin, Paige. "Inside the Rise of TikTok, the Viral Video-Sharing App Whose Ties to China Are Raising Concerns in the US." *Business Insider*, January 23, 2020. https://www.businessinsider.com/tiktok-app-online-website-video-sharing-2019-7.

Leskin, Paige. "YouTube Is Reportedly Planning to Launch an In-App Rival to Viral Video-Sharing App TikTok before the End of 2020." *Business Insider*, April 1, 2020. https://www.businessinsider.com/youtube-tiktok-rival-shorts-video-sharing-app-google-firework-2020-4.

MediaKix. "The Top 8 Reddit Statistics on Users, Demographics & More." December 28, 2018. https://mediakix.com/blog/reddit-statistics-users-demographics/.

Moses, Lucia. "Medium Gives Up on Ad Sales, Calling the System 'Broken.'" *Digiday*, January 5, 2017. https://digiday.com/media/medium-gives-ad-sales-calling-system-broken/.

O'Keefe, Ed, and Tim Perry. "Mike Bloomberg Doubles Ad Spending, Expands Staff after Iowa Caucuses." CBS News, February 4, 2020. https://www.cbsnews.com/news/bloomberg-doubles-ad-spending-expands-staff-after-iowa-caucus-debacle/.

Ruffini, Patrick. Interview with the author via Zoom. May 5, 2020.

Sehl, Katie. "28 Pinterest Statistics Marketers Should Know in 2020." Hootsuite. March 2, 2020, https://blog.hootsuite.com/pinterest-statistics-for-business/.

Snap. "Snap Political and Advocacy Ads Library." Retrieved May 22, 2020, from https://businesshelp.snapchat.com/en-US/article/political-ads-library.

———. "Snap Political & Advocacy Advertising Policies." Retrieved May 22, 2020, from https://businesshelp.snapchat.com/en-US/article/political-ads-library.

Spencer, Scott. "An Update on Our Political Ads Policy." Google, November 20, 2019. https://www.blog.google/technology/ads/update-our-political-ads-policy/.

Statista. "Number of Facebook Users in the United States from 2015 to 2023." Retrieved April 22, 2020, from https://www.statista.com/statistics/408971/number-of-us-facebook-users/.

———. "Number of Facebook Users Worldwide from 2015 to 2020." Retrieved April 22, 2020, from https://www.statista.com/statistics/490424/number-of-worldwide-facebook-users/.

———. "Number of Pinterest Users in the United States from 2017 to 2022." Retrieved April 22, 2020, https://www.statista.com/statistics/408974/number-of-us-pinterest-users/.

Timberg, Craig. "Critics Say Facebook's Powerful Ad Tools May Imperil Democracy. But Politicians Love Them." *Washington Post*, December 9, 2019. https://www.washingtonpost.com/technology/2019/12/09/critics-say-facebooks-powerful-ad-tools-may-imperil-democracy-politicians-love-them/.

Twitter. "Political Content." Retrieved May 22, 2020, from https://business.twitter.com/en/help/ads-policies/prohibited-content-policies/political-content.html.

ELEVEN
Field Operations

"I don't know how you do it without a platform that will force your campaign to be accountable. It makes a huge difference. I can tell you where a person is and if they knocked on a door."
—Sean Gagen, Democratic field operations consultant

Conversations are the essence of field operations. With all the technology discussed so far, it is easy to lose sight of the fact that politics remains a very human business. Whether it is organizing a team of volunteers to make calls or knock on doors or bring people together to maximize turnout on Election Day, people make campaigns move. Holding the field team accountable for voter contact is now a reasonable expectation at every level of modern political campaigns.

This chapter will discuss how to professionally organize field operations using the latest technologies and respond to changing conditions on the ground quickly to speed up the response in ways that motivate voters. When someone says it *always* comes down to turnout, they really mean that it comes down to people making decisions. Field leverages your best resource: people.

DEFINITION

Field operations include anything that fosters conversations with voters about the campaign, and the volunteer coordinator runs point on all of these efforts. The twin goals are to identify voters who are for or against the candidate and mobilize those who do to show up on Election Day. Recruiting, organizing, and motivating volunteers to these ends is the core of field operations, and all three have become more dependent on professionals, technology, and speed over the past thirty years. The field playbook has expanded from phone calls to and meeting in person with voters to e-mail, text, and remote video, which took off during the CO-VID-19 outbreak and will remain a staple of campaigns for years to come.

RECRUITING

All candidates believe they will win with grassroots support, but where this mission statement becomes a reality is in how many people can a campaign get to work for them for free. The answer, in the words of Obama campaign veterans David Axelrod and David Plouffe: "Organize, organize, organize." Recruiting begins with the people who know the candidate best: family, friends, and colleagues—anyone with a personal connection to the candidate.

Next, start talking with local, regional, and national groups that are in sync with the candidate's values and issues. These are great opportunities to find volunteers, and some groups will assign them to the campaign either part-time or full-time. If there is no primary, the political party may be in a position to identify local volunteers or pay for them, like they did for me in 2016. Beyond these groups, campaigns can leverage donors, local activists, and students.

From there, I agree with the excellent advice given by Johnny Alem's three rules for recruitment: strict accountability, rigid systemization, and creative informality. Volunteers need to be given guardrails and targets for field to work. This means asking for specific outcomes, like: "We need you to recruit ten people by Friday to help us make phone calls over the next month." Systems for accomplishing these asks, in modern campaigns, are easier to transmit. Volunteers need to be given step-by-step instructions on how to approach the task, move through it, and record results. Remember, volunteers are not pros, so they need direction.

Campaigns should stive to be what Democratic digital strategist Tyler Giles describes as "creatively informal," allowing individuals to make the campaign theirs by putting their own spin on voter contact with guidance from leadership. This can happen in a variety of ways, including letting volunteers modify call and canvassing scripts and giving volunteers digital tools they can customize to help organize. Giles told me a great story about how longtime Senator Ed Markey, a seventy-three-year-old incumbent, was outorganizing Representative Joe Kennedy III, who was just forty at the time of this writing and has the unique benefit of being Massachusetts royalty with his made-in-Camelot last name.

The septuagenarian was outorganizing the kid from Camelot online. Giles told me that the Markey campaign put together a set of tools directed at supporters, who could then build their own fan pages and connect with volunteers through social media. Markey's campaign field team had grown exponentially online largely due to Zoomers (great wordplay on Generation Z and Zoom, the videoconferencing platform of refuge), who were making this all happen for the older candidate from quarantine. As mentioned earlier, this was a huge success as Markey defeated his primary opponent Joe Kennedy, who was much younger and owns a magical political last name in Massachusetts.

ORGANIZING

Putting together the field operation begins with a professional, salaried coordinator who will identify local activists and supporters of the candidate, prepare projects and events, and manage them along the way. At their core, volunteer coordinators love people. They are outgoing, inspirational, and organized. For modern political campaigns, they need to be fluent with supportive technologies that keep everyone on track and motivated to return. They move fast, especially when volunteers need unexpected time off due to family or work commitments.

There are dozens of field operations platforms, but they all include a set of common functions that organize the campaign, including scheduling and tracking. While this used to be the "it's in my head" domain of the field organizer, or even tracked in a spreadsheet, modern campaigns are able to schedule volunteers for specific events, record their impressions of conversations with voters, and track this information so the team can provide feedback and offer rewards for a job well done.

MOTIVATING

Managing volunteers is a complex challenge. Understand that some volunteers will prefer to work the phones, while more outgoing volunteers might want to knock on doors. Specific, authentic appreciation from the leadership and the candidate can go a long way toward keeping volunteers motivated. I've seen quick notes from the campaign manager or candidate about something a volunteer did well become decades-long keepsakes among volunteers. Campaigns need to be sensitive to changes their volunteers' lives as well, in terms of flexible scheduling for parents with young kids or students managing their coursework. Overall, the important thing is to make it fun, and technologies are available that gamify the important grunt work of voter contact.

Field operations needs to be responsive to changing conditions on the ground. While polling is an essential tool for campaigns, the best information comes straight from voters in real time. An effective field operation captures and analyzes volunteer conversations with voters and can give instant feedback that challenges the assumptions of the campaign plan. The key is to make sure the field team is empowered to give bad news, because sometimes the data doesn't match the plan assumptions.

My former student Dan Bram told my class a couple of years ago that Hillary Clinton's field operation in Ohio was given a set of doors to knock that were supposed to be supportive, but many weren't. Bram's team fed the information back to the leadership in Brooklyn, but their reports were ignored. They were told that the modeling was sound and to keep knocking on the doors, which only ended up enraging voters the campaign mistook for Clinton supporters and more than likely turned them out for her opponent. Bram's team saw something real happening. In the end, Trump won Ohio by eight points.

In field, there is a difference between grassroots, which reflects the local community, and grasstops, which is a strategy of staffing door-to-door and voter contact by people who live elsewhere. On national campaigns, this is standard practice, and voters do get it. But authentic, local, grassroots support is always preferred to the imported variety. Voters are skeptical of volunteers with analog or digital pads, and hearing an accent that seems a bit off or a subtly local reference fumbled hurts the campaign more than if someone didn't knock on that door or make that call.

TOOLS

In 1996, I ran state house field operations using Campaign Manager, a desktop-only application that provided us with lists of voters by party but very little other information. After knocking on doors for the day—canvassing, in campaign jargon—volunteers then needed to type their notes into the software to keep track of who was contacted and how the conversation went. To be honest, we never used the data because it didn't categorize the feedback well, so it went underutilized. At the very least, however, we knew where we'd been.

Over the past three decades, there has been a merging of customer relationship management (CRM) software with voter files and field operations. Modern field software offers the ability to follow when a voter was contacted, by whom and when, and the content of the conversation as reported by the volunteer. While the programs I first used lived on a single campaign computer, voter relationship management (VRM) software now lives in the cloud, and a subset of the information is accessible by the team on their computers, tablets, and smartphones.

As with campaign consultants, technical platforms often work with and are endorsed by the Democratic or Republican Party, but not both. A left-leaning example of a platform specifically designed for field operations is Ecanvasser, which was created by a firm in Ireland but now supports campaigns worldwide. The app is a good example of bringing together volunteer conversations from canvassing, e-mail, phone, and social media outreach. It offers the ability to conduct outreach on mobile devices with preset scripts and questionnaires that are then uploaded to the campaign, where the volunteer coordinator can see stats in individual team members' activity so they can be rewarded and held accountable, and keep the larger team organized. It also integrates with other systems well, including NationBuilder's data (which also offers a field solution), MailChimp's e-mail platform, and Salesforce's CRM, which many larger campaigns use.

A right-leaning example is i360, which offers a data-centric field operations platform that allows volunteers ways to use their smartphones and tablets to help the campaign recruit volunteers, canvass, text, make calls, and follow up with voters. Their solutions offer real-time directions for canvassers, pre-interview overviews of voters before the door is knocked, and dynamic scripting so volunteers can have less-canned conversations. It is easy to get lost in the mountain of data a field operation produces, so i360 offers dashboards showing who was contacted, categorized by likely to vote for the candidate or the opponent as well as a host of demographics customized for the campaign. I360 also offers third-party software integrations.

The Democrats' NGP VAN and the Republicans' NationBuilder are widely respected field operations platforms and offer live support and a lot of self-serve content for maximizing their services. The first three letters of NGP VAN refer to its fund-raising and compliance tool, which includes paperless call time, a custom call sheet builder, and fund-raising dashboards that show progress toward goals. NGP now includes tools to handle digital and high-dollar fund-raising, such as integration of e-mail, online, and social outreach, and tracking long-term engagement with custom donor memos and donor ask plans. The VAN side of the business is for organizing and volunteer management.

NationBuilder offers a one-hour introductory course on using the platform, which includes everything from the "action website," which is a hub for organizing incoming voter contact, to "the heart of your nation," which enhances the voter file to include personal information, records interactions, and helps to manage volunteers. The communications side of the platform is e-mail and social-focused, which helps to track engagement with supporters.

Without a commitment to field operations, however, no technology can save a campaign. One postmortem of Marco Rubio's 2016 campaign blamed a lack of commitment to on-the-ground voter contact for not creating the kind of organic buzz the campaign needed to compete in Iowa. The counter was that Rubio could reach more voters through free and paid media than in person, trusting that the best surrogate for the candidate was himself. This floored former Cruz senior advisor Jeff Roe, who estimated that there was about "4.5% of the vote can be swung through field operations." Rubio finished third in Iowa, behind Ted Cruz and Donald Trump, but never found his footing. He left the race after a disappointing finish in his home state of Florida. Field was unlikely to be the reason he lost, but it was a symptom of a lack of grassroots support—what the postmortem called a "hollow campaign."

GET OUT THE VOTE

If you're reading this book and you know people who don't vote, it must drive you as crazy, as it does me, too. But remember, many people avoid politics and engage only when they feel that an election might impact them personally. There are lots of reasons why people don't vote, including that they don't think it will make a difference because they live in an area dominated by one party, they're busy and can't get away to make the trip to the ballot box, or they don't like the available candidates so they choose not to decide. Research has shown that nonvoters tend to be young and single, with lower levels of income and education. They also report higher levels of political alienation.

According to data of eligible voters compiled by Michael McDonald the percent who cast ballots in presidential years since 1980 has ranged from 52.8 percent in 1988 to 61.6 percent in 2008. Despite the pandemic and the competitiveness of the 2020 campaign, a remarkable 66.7 percent or about two-thirds of eligible voters cast ballots, a remarkable achievement. The expansion of mail-in voting as well as the intensity of support and opposition to a possible Trump second term were major factors in driving increased turnout.

The comparable set of midterm elections during this period began in 1982, where the overall turnout rate was 52 percent, steadily eroding through to 2014 to 42 percent, which was a seventy-year turnout low. While Black voter turnout was down in 2016, these voters returned in 2018, up 10 percent and fueling the Democrats' US House takeover with an overall 53 percent voter turnout rate, the highest since 1982. The percent of Latino voters nearly doubled as well, up from 7 percent in 2014 to 12 percent in the 2018 midterms.

While demographics certainly play a role in getting out the vote, campaigns have learned from a specific shift in political science, upending the traditional methodology of using surveys to ask voters about campaign contact exposure and then correlating that with turnout and voter preferences. Field experimentation returned to vogue, where households were assigned to receive a campaign mailing or not, and turnout effects were measured using postelection voter files, not self-reports. This is a bold step forward; ignoring the voters' recall and going directly to the data was a sea change in the field that was pioneered by Harold Gosnell in the 1930s and ignored because academics at the time were closed-minded to the change in approach.

It returned to vogue in the 2000s as a pair of academics, Alan Gerber and Donald Green, summarized the findings of nearly two hundred experimental field studies commissioned by campaigns. They found that while it is extremely difficult to increase turnout, it is possible at the margins and in close races that could change the outcome. The guidance is that personal contact matters. A canvasser who meets with a voter increases the likely turnout by four percent, but that goes down in the field because, on average, you reach one out of four doors when you knock on them. Volunteer phone calls can raise the turnout rate per voter by three percent. Nonpartisan mailings and commercial phone bank operations move less than one percent more voters to turnout. All of these potential upsides are mitigated by the type of election and the broader political environment. This is why GOTV is so hard.

Interestingly, one of the best ways to increase turnout is through sponsored mailings. The research shows four methods that pay off more than 1 percent. Here is a roundup of the approaches, with some of the upsides and cautionary tales:

- *Civic duty.* Calling on voters to "do their civic duty and vote" increases turnout rates by 1.8 percent. It is the least aggressive, an emotional appeal to our shared responsibility as Americans. It is unlikely to boomerang back on the campaign.
- *Hawthorne effect.* This is a creepier alternative where you explicitly tell voters that they are being studied and that their voting behavior will be examined by means of public records. Predictably, this boosts the turnout a bit more. The Hawthorne effect mailer increases turnout by 2.5 percent but, just as predictably, becomes a problem for the campaign due to privacy concerns.
- *Self-treatment.* The social pressure of being told who in the household voted in the past few elections increases turnout even more, to 4.8 percent. The mailer will either give voters a grade based on their voting behavior or show how often they've voted against those who live with them. It makes for some interesting conversations at the dinner table, and blowback is highly possible.
- *Neighbors.* The most aggressive is comparing voting patterns against voters' neighbors, which increases turnout by 8.1 percent, presumably because their reputation is now clearly on the line. If they are getting this, then so are their neighbors, who will now look at them differently if they choose not to vote this time. This is definitely the most invasive social tactic, but, again, it is completely legal because voting participation is public record.

Your mileage may vary, but the overall message is clear: Voters believe their ballot is secret and the vast majority think their voting patterns are also secret. This is why when Ted Cruz did this during the 2016 presidential campaign in Iowa, it backfired. Cruz's mailer looked too much like an official document, which made it all the more galling to many voters. Still, he won there using these techniques married with some truly remarkable data science targeting from my former team at WPA Intelligence, so it is worth considering whether it could work for your campaign. Without the targeting, it is likely to fail, so do not do this blindly.

Modern political campaigns are using social media to force some of this social pressure on nonvoters, but in a less aggressive manner. On Facebook, Twitter, and elsewhere, you can now post virtual "I Voted" badges to encourage your neighbors to vote. This melding of social networks and civic duty is perceived as less invasive as you are revealing you voted, not that you didn't vote. Still, those who don't post that they voted on Election Day, in some circles, subtly unmask themselves.

My view is that social pressure on these platforms is completely appropriate, and I look forward to the meta-analysis about the 2020 campaign by academics ten years from now. Early results from Facebook's field experiments show that people who saw the "I Voted" message were two percent more likely to click on it and share it, and just under a half-percent more likely to cast ballots. In the meantime, badges, tags, stickers, and all kinds of virtual social accoutrements can only help boost turnout on platforms, even those that don't allow political advertising.

During the pandemic, we all relied on our personal networks more than ever for support. Campaigns understood this and began to focus more on relational organizing, which focuses social pressure from people we respect to participate, give, and vote. Even as COVID-19 hopefully recedes, this insight into being prodded by people we know to engage in politics will continue to be an important part of how campaigns organize and get out the vote. Some of the voting rules in states are in flux, as some Republican-controlled legislatures seek to place additional restrictions on mail-in voting to ensure they're being cast by registered voters. But regardless of where these regulations ultimately land, campaigns will not only communicate directly with voters on the changes but through their personal networks, the relationships that matter in life and in politics.

CONSULTANT STORY

When it comes to organizing and turnout, sometimes the margins are extremely close. Sean Gagen, founder of the Democratic firm Grassroots SG, recalls a race his team did in Sarasota, Florida. It was an open seat, which was a significant opportunity because Republicans controlled the state legislature, giving them the power of gerrymandering, which protects incumbents. When I asked him for one great story about a campaign, he instead told me one about a loss: "We did, I think, an extraordinary job, spent $16 or 18 million, polled every week, got great data back, adjusted, changed, and it came down to Election Day. We were hitting all the metrics—we were doing really well here. And, unfortunately, we lost by 160 votes and the home precinct of our candidate, somehow the electronic machines broke."

"It was a really important lesson for me," he recalls. "What else have you checked in on? What things can you control? What things can't you?" He allows that he thought it was "right" that one of the lessons learned was to up your win totals, the vote targets set at the beginning of the campaign. "I didn't think about the *way* people vote. You may not be able to affect that," he says. But you have to account for it.

Highly competitive people and political consultants, including myself, always remember the losses more clearly than the wins, even years later. This campaign loss was in 2004. As Gagen puts it, "You learn more when you lose. Was it something you can control, something you did, or was it a wave? You get into wave elections and you just want to get in the jet stream and go with them if you're doing well, and if you're against it you have to figure out how to get out of it."

Sometimes all the great organizing and turnout plans get washed away in a wave. President George W. Bush's reelection in 2004 was not a blowout, as he defeated Senator John Kerry of Massachusetts by 2.4 percent, but it was a wave election in Florida, where Gagen experienced it firsthand. Kerry won only eleven of the sixty-seven counties in Florida, and Sarasota was not one of them. Kerry got waved there by 8.2 percent, almost quadrupling the national vote margin and certainly hurting candidates like Gagen's down ballot.

From that standpoint, looking at what Gagen's team did in that race was truly remarkable. The candidate came within a polling rounding error to almost win the seat, far outperforming what the top of the ticket earned on Election Day. And this is why this was a great story, even if Gagen didn't think it was. It shows what the power of a great organizing and GOTV effort can have even in the most difficult races, where the top of the ticket is a drag on your race and you have to struggle to make those human connections to get outside the jet stream. The campaign Gagen worked on almost made it there.

CAREERS

The best advice I've heard from a number of consultants is to find a candidate you are passionate about and intern on their campaign. Chances are, if you are "anywhere near competent," as several campaign managers told me off the record, you'll end up with a paid position rather quickly. Most campaign professionals start out in the field, like I did, and there is nothing more important than identifying the right race and candidate, because the hours can go long but if you are fighting for someone you believe in it makes that time well spent. At this point of your career, nurture it by choosing wisely so your experience will have a chance to catch up with your enthusiasm.

Once you're working in the field, network. Gagen suggests figuring out who the twenty people are on the campaign you want to meet and spending time with each of them one-on-one to "find out where the job leads are and go after them by getting introduced. In this business, mass résumés don't work. It's a referral business." For field operations, especially, politics is about who you know, because the jobs interact with voters directly and so the bar for making sure someone won't embarrass a campaign is justifiably high. A résumé alone cannot tell you how this person works, but referrals will.

Several field operations consultants told me they encourage higher-level operatives to be familiar with platforms like Ecanvasser, i360, and the digital clipboard app Republic VX, as well as the field packages in larger software platforms like Aristotle, NGP VAN, and NationBuilder. Fluency with what each platform offers, how they work, how much they cost, and how they integrate with other campaign components is crucial to keeping information flowing through the team so you don't end up missing voter land mines or opportunities. All this melding of data and technology fosters more personal, voter-centric conversations between volunteers and voters.

THE FUTURE

The future of field operations runs through the ability to organize, schedule, and integrate what the team learns in conversations with voters. Some of this technology exists in pieces, where a volunteer list is located on one platform, scheduling and voter data collection on others. This creates gaps in campaign management because it would be great to know how volunteers are performing. Some campaigns are using apps to corral their volunteers and gamify the experience around behaviors they're trying to drive, but for most campaigns this is not the case. As the technology improves, so will the speed at which campaigns can understand what is going on in an area and react accordingly.

In-person field operations ground to a halt when COVID-19 hit in 2020, but it created opportunities to leverage technologies that were once unnecessary. Several consultants reported using Zoom, GoToMeeting, FaceTime, and other platforms to connect with voters, either in groups or one-on-one. While nothing replaces meeting in person, this has helped to bring some more of the human element back to voter contact, which puts professionals and volunteers in a better position to read nonverbal cues to put into perspective what they're hearing from voters that a phone call or text cannot capture.

Sean Gagen is hopeful that field campaigning will return to form after a period of transition, but with the help of technology, initially: "Hopefully this comes back in phases. Perhaps it comes back with everyone in Phase 1 with having conversations on the phone or having conversations on Zoom. Figuring out a way how to deliver your message in a way that is not as intrusive as going up to them and shaking their hand. Phase Two might be when you're knocking on a door and you're six feet back." He adds that the data campaigns have will be helpful to avoid approaching houses with people over fifty years old, which is the guidance cutoff for being more vulnerable to the virus. As for when traditional field may return, it is impossible to estimate at this time, but what we do know is that technology will be a part of helping campaigns continue to reach out to voters wherever they are.

ASSIGNMENT

Choose a local race in your area and think about what kinds of GOTV mailers you would want your team to send, and what kinds you'd hope independent groups would send. Why would the various methods of increasing turnout work in your area, which voters might be most receptive, and could any of this backfire on your campaign? Do a cost-benefit analysis of each of the four options within the mix of door-to-door, phone calls, and other appeals.

SOURCES AND ADDITIONAL READING

Armadi, Fernand, Anthony Williams, Dave Feldman, Rick Hunter, Hannah Artman, Daniela Ferrera, and Maurizio Passariello. *The 100 Million Report: The Untold Story of American Non-Voters*. Miami: Knight Foundation, 2020. https://knightfoundation.org/wp-content/uploads/2020/02/The-100-Million-Project_KF_Report_2020.pdf.

Axelrod, David, and David Plouffe. "What Joe Biden Needs to Do to Beat Trump." *New York Times*, May 4, 2020. https://www.nytimes.com/2020/05/04/opinion/axelrod-plouffe-joe-biden.html.

Bram, Dan. Guest lecture at the University of California, District of Columbia. May 23, 2017.

Cook Political Report. "Vote by Mail Cheatsheet: Battleground States." Retrieved May 23, 2020, from https://cookpolitical.com/sites/default/files/2020-04/Vote By Mail.2.pdf.

File, Tom. "Voting in America: A Look at the 2016 Presidential Election." United States Census Bureau, May 10, 2017. https://www.census.gov/newsroom/blogs/random-samplings/2017/05/voting_in_america.html.

Gagen, Sean. Interview with the author via Zoom. April 29, 2020.

Gerber, Alan S., Donald P. Green, and Christopher W. Larimer. "Social Pressure and Voter Turnout: Evidence from a Large-Scale Field Experiment." *American Political Science Review* 102, no. 1 (2008). https://isps.yale.edu/sites/default/files/publication/2012/12/ISPS08-001.pdf.

Gerber, Alan S., and Gregory A. Huber. "Getting Out the Vote Is Tougher Than You Think." *Stanford Social Innovation Review*, March 7, 2016. https://ssir.org/articles/entry/getting_out_the_vote_is_tougher_than_you_think.

Green, Donald P., and Alan S. Gerber. *Get Out the Vote: How to Increase Voter Turnout.* Third Edition. Washington, DC: Brookings Institution Press, 2015.

Issenberg, Sasha. "Nudge the Vote." *New York Times*, October 29, 2010. https://www.nytimes.com/2010/10/31/magazine/31politics-t.html.

———. "The RNC Hopes This App Will Keep Campaigns from Going All in with the Koch Brothers." *Bloomberg*, August 4, 2015. https://www.bloomberg.com/news/articles/2015-08-04/the-rnc-hopes-this-app-will-keep-campaigns-from-going-all-in-with-the-koch-brothers.

———. *The Victory Lab*. New York: Random House, 2012.

Krogstad, Jens Manuel, and Mark Hugo Lopez. "Black Voter Turnout Fell in 2016, Even as a Record Number of Americans Cast Ballots." Pew Research Center, May 12, 2017. https://www.pewresearch.org/fact-tank/2017/05/12/black-voter-turnout-fell-in-2016-even-as-a-record-number-of-americans-cast-ballots/.

Krogstad, Jens Manuel, Luis Noe-Bustamante and Antonio Flores. "Historic Highs in 2018 Voter Turnout Extended Across Racial and Ethnic Groups." Pew Research Center, May 1, 2019. https://www.pewresearch.org/fact-tank/2019/05/01/historic-highs-in-2018-voter-turnout-extended-across-racial-and-ethnic-groups/.

Lee, Jolie. "Facebook 'I'm a Voter' App Nudges Voters to Polls." *USA Today*, November 4, 2014. https://www.usatoday.com/story/news/nation-now/2014/11/04/facebook-im-a-voter-app-election-day/18487479/.

McDonald, Michael. United States Elections Project. Visited February 16, 2021. http://www.electproject.org.

Misra, Jordan. "Voter Turnout Rates among All Voting Age and Major Racial and Ethnic Groups Were Higher Than in 2014." United States Census Bureau, April 23, 2019. https://www.census.gov/library/stories/2019/04/behind-2018-united-states-midterm-election-turnout.html.

NationBuilder. "Intro to NationBuilder." Retrieved May 21, 2020, from https://nationbuilder.com/course_intro_to_nationbuilder.

NGP VAN. "The Official VANual." Retrieved May 21, 2020, from https://cdn2.hubspot.net/hubfs/661521/Content Offer VANual Assets /NGP VAN VANual 2018.pdf.

No Labels, with polling conducted by Cohen Research Group. *No Labels Policy Playbook for America's Next President*. 2015. ftp://208.118.250.248/cohenadm/media/NoLabelsPolicyPlaybook.pdf.

Pew Research Center. "How Drop-Off Voters Differ from Consistent Voters and Non-voters." September 14, 2017. https://www.people-press.org/2017/09/14/how-drop-off-voters-differ-from-consistent-voters-and-non-voters/.

Rogers, Todd and Adan Acevedo. "In Iowa, Voting Science at Work." *New York Times*, February 5, 2016. https://www.nytimes.com/2016/02/07/opinion/campaign-stops/in-iowa-voting-science-at-work.html.

Sifry, Micah L. "Facebook Wants You to Vote on Tuesday: Here's How It Messed with Your Feed in 2012." *Mother Jones*, October 31, 2014. https://www.motherjones.com/politics/2014/10/can-voting-facebook-button-improve-voter-turnout/.

Stokols, Eli. "Inside Marco's Hollow Campaign." *Politico*, March 15, 2016. https://www.politico.com/magazine/story/2016/03/marco-rubio-2016-campaign-drop-out-213736.

Vogel, Kenneth P., and Darren Samuelsohn. "How Trump Let Himself Get Out-Organized." *Politico*, February 2, 2016. https://www.politico.com/story/2016/02/donald-trump-iowa-voter-data-218654.

Woodward, Colin. "Half of Americans Don't Vote. What Are They Thinking?" *Politico*, February 19, 2020. https://www.politico.com/news/magazine/2020/02/19/knight-nonvoter-study-decoding-2020-election-wild-card-115796.

TWELVE

The New Permanent Campaign

"It is my thesis [that] governing with public approval requires a continuing campaign."
— Pat Caddell, Pollster for President Jimmy Carter

This astute observation by Caddell in the early days of the Carter presidency may not have focused his client enough to win reelection, but he won the historical argument. Political campaigns have become ubiquitous and ongoing. There is no downtime between elections. Campaign managers continue to plan, fund-raisers stay in close touch with donors, and opposition researchers remain in the background to track potential opponents' every move. My business is a part of this, too. Pollsters and data scientists gather intelligence earlier than ever, ensuring that incumbents understand their standing and providing challengers more insight on how they can beat them. Earned, paid, and social political media reinforce all of this with highly targeted messaging appeals that feel modern and personal.

CAMPAIGN STRATEGY GETS PERSONAL

Political parties used to organize the marketplace of ideas and candidates. Bosses planned behind the scenes to win elections, keeping a thumb on the pulse of their constituent political and material needs and connecting with voters where they were. The strength of the relationship between voter and party was so strong that an entire science—political science—was built upon it. That was the first wave of what campaigns were to become: political broadcasting.

Candidate-centered campaigns were the second wave, moving voters to choose individuals over party. Diverse cities devolved into more cohesive suburbs, while consumer and media choices gave candidates direct lines to voters. But this narrowcasting of elections came at a price. Over time, voters became less satisfied with their prepackaged, almost too-perfect candidates. While attempting to reflect what the electorate wanted, candidates became less authentic, reinforcing our preexisting cynicism about politics. Campaigns didn't work when they were all about the candidate.

We are now in the third wave, a new permanent campaign. Our pro-style, tech-infused, always-on society now has the campaigns that best reflect our times. This is a revolution of politics putting us back at the center of elections, a small-*d* democratic shift that has wide-ranging consequences. Political professionals now have enough research, data, and media tools to give us the campaigns we want, based on what we say in focus groups, what we tell pollsters, and how we behave politically. Where campaigns were party-driven broadcasts before becoming candidate-focused narrowcasts, we have reached the natural conclusion of all of this: voter-centric targets.

One result of this has been a shift in strategy. Parties were built on a core strategy of base-plus: Winning elections requires base supporters plus voters who can be influenced. Candidate-centered campaign strategies were also base-plus, because of a belief that individual voters might form emotional connections that could transcend issue differences. Voter-centered campaigns are now built as base-dominant, because what we've learned about voter values and issue preferences is that the values and strongly held issue preferences, both of which can be divisive, is what moves them.

VOTER POLARIZATION INCREASES

In interviews with consultants of both parties, this surprised me. I thought they would at least pay some lip service to the notion that coalitions needed to be built. One reason is that the definition of who an independent voter is has become more refined over the past decade. Viewed broadly, there appears to be a plurality of independent voters, 36 percent according to polling by Gallup in mid-April 2020, with a virtual tie between Democrats at 31 percent and Republicans at 30 percent. Again, looking at the top line, the level of polarization had increased in just one year: In mid- to late April 2019, Gallup found that 40 percent identified as independents while Democrats and Republicans were split at 29 percent apiece.

The shift that has moved campaign strategy, however, was understanding that independents lean one way or another, and that there are very few truly independent voters. Combining party membership and voters leaning toward a party, in mid-April 2020 Gallup found 46 percent were Democrats and 46 percent were Republicans, leaving only 8 percent of voters who are unattached or party leaning, and who are less likely to vote. This adds up to a 54 percent voter target universe without having to contact voters from the other side or do the heavy lifting of persuasion. With homogenous communities and gerrymandered districts, there is little incentive to reach out beyond the dark or light reds and blues.

Another reason is demographics. With leaners included, younger voters are more likely to identify as Democrats, while voters in other generations are more closely contested. Millennials (born 1981 to 1996) are now the largest generation and the least likely to identify as Republicans. According to the Pew Research Center, 27 percent of Millennials said they were Republicans in 2002, compared with only 17 percent in 2017. That 10 percent seems to have moved to independents, from 34 percent to 44 percent, as Democratic identifiers inched up from 34 percent to 35 percent. With leaners, however, Millennials at 59 percent are most likely to be or lean toward the Democratic Party than any other voting population. The split among Generation X is 48 percent to 43 percent and the Baby Boomers 48 percent to 46 percent, both favoring the Democratic Party. The Silent Generation is the only one that favors the GOP, at 52 percent versus 43 percent.

The generational warning for Republicans raised by Kristen Solits Anderson in *The Selfie Vote* extends to other demographics as well. According to the Pew Research Center, the share of women who identify as Democrats or lean that way has increased from 48 percent in 1994 to 56 percent in 2019, while the share of men during that time period increased from 39 to 42 percent. Women comprise a greater share of the electorate, so this makes it harder on the GOP to win elections on party identification alone. Among white registered voters, 53 percent identify as Republicans while 83 percent of Black and 63 percent of Hispanic voters identify as Democrats. A base-dominant strategy may work for both parties in certain areas now, but at some point, soon this is going to stop making sense for the Republican Party. The nation is getting younger and more diverse, and that does not paint a bright red future. In 2020, the Trump campaign and Republican candidates saw this and made inroads through policy and outreach but there is a long way to go.

TACTICS GO DIGITAL

The strategy of identifying and activating targeted voter groups rests on the ability to deploy technology. As David Perell notes, we are all living in a Hawthorne effect simulation: The internet is always tracking what we do online for advertisers, and it has changed our behavior. Political conversations that used to happen at community functions, around dinner tables, and at the door with volunteers are now held online for public consumption. Political messages voters might have once seen or heard are now there for everyone to interact with, tracked by search engines and social media platforms. Pausing on an ad registers interest, reacting with a suggested emoji indicates soft support. A click, a sign-up, a donation, and you have become an extended member of the campaign, whether that was your intent or not. Technology has moved tactics that were once analog to digital.

Voter contact points and reactions are recorded, combined, and analyzed. Political campaign plans have become dashboards of moving data targets, where managers can refine tactics daily and distribute assignments more efficiently. Fund-raisers know exactly who has been contacted, what was given and where, and the progress on different donor targets. Opposition researchers now see their work integrated into the daily lives of campaigns, well beyond the initial messaging choices made. They now have living dossiers available to them when the race shifts. Data scientists can identify voter patterns that would have never seen the light of day not too many years ago. Pollsters are able to turn results around extremely fast to better understand changes in the dynamic and the opportunities they present. Media teams field test messages with clearly identified audiences, seeing what works and what needs to be shelved. Volunteers are able to ensure that no interaction with a voter gets lost.

The more touchpoints, the better the profile, and this data lives on within the ecosystem of the new permanent campaign. What is shared is combined with other information. What is learned is never unlearned; it is passed along to future campaigns. All the data we provide to free platforms is monetized, commercially and politically. Parties have sold themselves as brands. Candidates have sold themselves as products to voters, their political customers. Now voters are the products—and parties, groups, and candidates are the customers of our data.

The marketplace for votes is only going to increase over time as the tools used by campaigns will reach generations growing up online, willingly giving intelligence in exchange for free platforms. Radio and television were founded on these principles: In exchange for content, you gave your time to advertisers. The tactics once used by campaigns almost exclusively in media planning are no longer paid services but are blended with advertising.

Their data is better, too; they know what we are watching, and that information is shared with political advertisers. The internet has blown this wide open with the ability to track our interests, create profiles, and sell them. Targeting individuals is now possible and will only increase. No one wants to pay for a Google search in exchange for the right to be forgotten. No one wants a paid Facebook, Instagram, Twitter, or Snapchat.

THE PARTIES INVEST

Both parties are doubling down on their investments, serving as high-tech political incubators and extending new permanent campaign ecosystem of tactical political technology. In 2018, $5.7 billion was spent by political parties, candidates, committees, and independent groups, a 50 percent increase in overall spending from the previous midterms in 2014. While most of this was spent on television and digital advertising, a lot of it was spent directly on campaign technology. Both parties now invest heavily in campaign technology. While tech investment has skewed Democratic, in 2019 Republicans launched Startup Caucus, which is serving to provide seed money for conservative tech firms. This is a direct answer to Higher Ground Labs, which was founded by former Obama campaign aides. Both groups are working hard to serve not only the top of the ticket but down ballot races.

The pivot point in party investment began with Howard Dean's race for the presidency in 2004. Dean was the first candidate to focus on internet donations and signing up volunteers online. He outraised the eventual nominee, Senator John Kerry, by close to $5 million, which vaulted him to first in the race. He peaked too early and came in third in Iowa, prompting the Vermont governor to list all the places he'd win with an emphatic "Yeeeeeeaaaaaahhhh!" that was captured live and replayed endlessly online. The internet bit back, and the Dean Scream became the first political meme.

But, again, what was learned could not be unlearned. In 2008 the Obama campaign integrated e-mail, cell phones and websites, empowering supporters to create their own networks of support. The Obama team tried to deploy an app called Houdini on Election Day, but it failed the morning of the election. By 2012, Obama had hired a team of technologists who deployed Narwhal, a proprietary data platform, and other products that unified everything the campaign knew in real time about its volunteers and the voters they were attempting to win. On top of this was a grassroots app called NGP VAN, covered earlier in this book, which continues to dominate the market today on the Democratic side. Blue State Digital was another key tech partner that continues to be relevant today. It all worked so well that as president, Obama was the first to have a chief technology officer in the White House.

The Romney campaign's app, Orca, failed on Election Day in 2012, prompting the GOP to pull the nurturing of technology in-house. The failure of the app to work may have left some votes on the table, but they were not going to radically change the electorate because of the lack of underlying data science, which the Obama team nailed. In my interview with Matt Knee, he said this prompted GOP leaders like Reince Priebus to fund in-house data scientists and strategic vendors to close the gap, which they ultimately did. Once the field of data was leveled, each party could help fund investments in team-facing tech.

The platforms helped. As reported widely, Facebook, Twitter, and Google offered "embeds" to each presidential candidate in 2016, and the understaffed Trump team took them up on it. They taught digital director Brad Parscale's team how to place advertising and best communicate using their tools. According to *Bloomberg News*, the Clinton campaign tested sixty-six thousand separate Facebook ads, while Trump's campaign tested a total of 5.9 million. If losing is the best teacher, success is a close second. The 2016 experience prompted both parties to work more closely with internet platforms.

CAMPAIGNS BETWEEN ELECTIONS

The new permanent campaign goes well beyond preparing for elections. It now includes a well-funded industry of mini campaigns focused on issues and public affairs. This began during the first full year of Bill Clinton's presidency, after the passage of his economic recovery package. The campaign for healthcare reform began with a flourish, the appointment of First Lady Hillary Rodham Clinton to lead a task force to make recommendations to Congress.

What Clinton did not anticipate was that interest groups might try to compete for attention as well. As recounted in chapter 9, a relatively small investment of advertising in key states helped undermine the effort, delaying Senate action and eroding public support. Clinton didn't realize that while television and his voice remained dominant, others could grab attention as well, to his detriment. Clinton lost the first permanent campaign ad war, but it would not be the last. Today, every major legislative or regulatory effort has a public advertising component. Clinton's healthcare reform, ironically, is patient zero in the growth of public affairs public outreach.

Advertising is just one component of campaigns that now look very familiar. For example, pharmaceutical companies hire opposition research firms now to help them understand their vulnerabilities as well as those of groups trying to block FDA approvals. Social media companies, vendors to campaigns, now hire their own lobbyists and public affairs communications teams. Polling firms help pretest public affairs messaging by credit card companies before the press releases are written and earned media events are scheduled. Data on members of independent groups and corporate customers is shared to create voter contact campaigns. Grassroots campaigns are waged on issues ranging from pipeline builds to pro sports stadium construction. All of these activities offer political campaigning professionals work in between elections to move public policy.

There is an underlying sense of burnout in campaigns, but working with the private sector and nonprofits by applying techniques learned during elections keeps these teams firmly in the arena. In dozens of conversations with campaigners over the years, I have found that it has become work that most firms grow into and appreciate not only for the business but because for many of these professionals, this is what drew them into politics in the first place: to make a difference. Modern political campaigns never end; they just continue to leverage all of the professionalism, technology, and speed honed in the crucible of elections to help move public policy outcomes.

THE FUTURE OF MODERN POLITICAL CAMPAIGNS

The devolution of campaigns from parties to candidates and now to voters has flipped the Founders' expectations of our system of government. The intent was to provide a system where the public will could be checked through elections, but representatives would then take the baton to city councils, to state capitols, and to Washington to make decisions in the public interest. The permanent campaign and all we've covered in this book has broken the republican system and brought us to a more democratic baseline of governing. I know it is good business for political campaign professionals, but I'm not sure this is good for us as a country.

Collective decision making has become more contentious over the past three decades. It seems that the more we know about voters, the easier it is to separate them into winnable groups. Not enough work is being done on the persuasion side of campaigns, and I am bothered by the notion that because it is difficult, it is not worth the time or money. Voters are now mobilized, but not led. Leaders represent, but do not bring us together. There is no going back to a time where campaigns are less professional, where technology becomes less a part of our lives, and where speed is less valued in favor of patient, collegial, deliberation. I get that.

But I remain encouraged by my work with No Labels, a nonpartisan group dedicated to solving our nation's problems together. My firm conducted national surveys of Americans on big goals, such as creating new jobs, securing the social safety net, balancing the budget, and energy independence. The *Policy Playbook for America's Next President* included dozens of proposals that 60 percent of Americans agreed with, including majorities of Democrats, Republicans, and independents.

The COVID-19 pandemic drove home to many Americans that they want more from their leaders. The roadmap exists. Permanent campaigns do not have to mean perpetual paralysis, as my No Labels colleague William Galston once wrote. Modern political campaigns have the fundraising, research, communications, and grassroots tools to move us toward greater unity and progress. I am a part of this ecosystem in the fields of education, research, and mobile technology and commit to doing everything I can to help us get closer to that ideal.

SOURCES AND ADDITIONAL READING

Anderson, Kristen Soltis. *The Selfie Vote*. New York: HarperCollins, 2015.

Blumenthal, Sidney. *The Permanent Campaign*. Boston: Beacon Press, 1980.

Doherty, Carroll, Jocelyn Kiley, and Olivia O'Hea. "Wide Gender Gap, Growing Divide in Voters' Party Identification." Pew Research Center, March 20, 2018. https://www.people-press.org/wp-content/uploads/sites/4/2018/03/03-20-18-Party-Identification-CORRECTED.pdf.

Frier, Sarah. "Trump's Campaign Said It Was Better at Facebook. Facebook Agrees." *Bloomberg*, April 3, 2018. https://www.bloomberg.com/news/articles/2018-04-03/trump-s-campaign-said-it-was-better-at-facebook-facebook-agrees.

Friess, Steve. "The Father of All Web Campaigns." *Politico*, September 30, 2012. https://www.politico.com/story/2012/09/how-deans-wh-bid-gave-birth-to-web-campaigning-081834.

Fry, Richard. "Millennials Overtake Baby Boomers as America's Largest Generation." Pew Research Center, April 28, 2020. https://www.pewresearch.org/fact-tank/2020/04/28/millennials-overtake-baby-boomers-as-americas-largest-generation/.

Galston, William. "The "Permanent Campaign" = Perpetual Paralysis." *Wall Street Journal*, October 28, 2014. https://www.wsj.com/articles/william-galston-the-permanent-campaign-perpetual-paralysis-1414539559.

Gallup. "Party Affiliation." Retrieved May 25, 2020, from https://news.gallup.com/poll/15370/party-affiliation.aspx.

Gross, Grant. "Election 2004: Howard Dean Profits from Web Campaign." CIO, January 15, 2004. https://www.cio.com/article/2439855/election-2004--howard-dean-profits-from-web-campaign.html.

Howard, Alex. "US Election Campaign Technology from 2008 to 2018, and Beyond." *Technology Review*, August 22, 2018. https://www.technologyreview.com/2018/08/22/140643/us-election-campaign-technology-from-2008-to-2018-and-beyond/.

Isenstadt, Alex. "Republicans Launching Innovation Fund to Match Democrats." *Politico*, August 13, 2019. https://www.politico.com/story/2019/08/13/republicans-innovation-fund-digital-startups-1459814.

Knee, Matt. Interview with the author. May 18, 2020.

Madrigal, Alexis C. "When the Nerds Go Marching In." *Atlantic*, November 16, 2012. https://www.theatlantic.com/technology/archive/2012/11/when-the-nerds-go-marching-in/265325/.

Newton, Casey. "How Facebook's Crisis PR Firm Triggered a PR Crisis." *Verge*, November 17, 2018. https://www.theverge.com/2018/11/17/18099065/facebook-definers-nyt-pr-crisis.

OpenSerects.org. "Most Expensive Midterm Ever: Cost of 2018 Election Surpasses $5.7 Billion." Center for Responsive Politics, February 6, 2019. https://www.opensecrets.org/news/2019/02/cost-of-2018-election-5pnt7bil/.

Ornstein, Norman J., and Thomas E. Mann, es. *The Permanent Campaign and Its Future*. Washington, DC: AEI Press, 2000.

Perell, David. "The Social Media Trap." *Monday Musings Newsletter*. Retrieved May 25, 2020, from https://www.perell.com/blog/social-media-trap.

Pew Research Center. "In Changing U.S. Electorate, Race and Education Remain Stark Dividing Lines." June 2, 2020. https://www.pewresearch.org/politics/2020/06/02/in-changing-u-s-electorate-race-and-education-remain-stark-dividing-lines/

Stahl, Leslie. "Facebook 'Embeds,' Russia and the Trump Campaign's Secret Weapon." *60 Minutes*, October 8, 2017. https://www.cbsnews.com/news/facebook-embeds-russia-and-the-trump-campaigns-secret-weapon/.

Afterword

"It's a very sad moment. To me this is a very sad moment, and we will win this. And as far as I'm concerned, we already have won it."
— Donald J. Trump, Election Eve Speech, November 3, 2020

The end of the 2020 cycle was a lot to digest, mainly because it did not quite end and for some Americans, will never land the way they wanted it. Politics has always been a tough business, especially when your team loses. But the professionalism of campaigns paired with advances in political technology, and the always-on speed of our communications makes it even more difficult to unwind a campaign, even if it isn't successful.

THE DARKEST TIME LINE

This is not to say that Trump got caught up in the maelstrom of 2020, but his post-election efforts are examples of how modern political campaigns can go awry. Trump saw opportunities to continue to fight with willing political professionals who had little incentives to give up the fight. In conjunction with surrogates and outside groups, Trump reframed his loss on social media fraudulent, to the point that most Republicans in public polling said they believed it.

Trump's efforts to wage a continuing campaign, and maybe even a permanent one, were funded with the technologies of our age including texting and email. The speed at which all of this happened was striking. Within a few short weeks, it was reported that Trump had raised over $170 million, which cowered elected Republicans in Washington to privately hope this would all end soon. It didn't after states certified ballots, courts by the dozens dismissed claims, and even after the Electoral College certified the victory for Joe Biden. Then it got worse, and deadly.

As more of the story behind the rally-turned-insurrection on January 6, 2021, comes out it becomes apparent that the tools of modern campaigning were literally weaponized. The rally was staged by an outside group supporting Trump, paid for by wealthy and low-dollar donors, headlined by Trump and his family, as well as other high-profile supporters, and then filmed by those who rallied, rioted, and disrupted the ministerial counting of ballots in Congress. It was ugly, violent, and deadly. Insurrectionists not only called for the hanging of Vice President Mike Pence and brought a noose with them. It was the darkest timeline of the age of our modern political campaigns.

Social media companies immediately took action after Donald Trump's pre-taped entreaty to those on Capitol Hill to "go home" and that he loved them. Instead of labeling the post, the account was locked. Within short order most major social media and other technology companies either froze or banned Trump entirely from their platforms, bringing another word to the lexicon: deplatforming. Even the far-right social media platform Parler was shut down through a combination of actions by Apple and Google as well as Amazon Web Services. We are not far enough along in that story to know where it will end but I am sure there will be lawsuits and hearings in Congress about how to modify the statues governing technology companies to ensure fairness. The result of all of this was to shutter Trump's ability to communicate rapidly.

THE SYSTEM HOLDS AND THE ELECTORATE EXPANDS

Despite all of the forces tearing at the nation after the election, democracy survived. Not a single court case overturned any state's slate of electors. No counties or state legislatures voted to dismiss the voice of the people. Trump did his best to find a way through the system to overturn the results anywhere and everywhere, but it didn't happen. Even Kelly Loeffler, who lost her Georgia Senate election but wouldn't initially concede, eventually did. Trump didn't, but he recognized that a new administration would take over on January 20, 2021, and he did leave town. What will become of the insurrection is yet to be seen. While Trump was acquitted at his second impeachment trial, many of the insurrectionists faced significant legal consequences for their actions, and some will find the inside of a jail cell their new home.

What got lost in this post-election period is the fact that more Americans voted in 2020 than at any time in our nation's history. Trump's 74 million votes was the most any one has ever earned in a campaign for president—in a loss. Biden's vote count was about 81 million and the margin about seven million over Trump. This is an amazing thing considering the barriers to voting during the pandemic. While Republicans continued to knock on doors, Democrats stayed away, limiting the potential electorate. While Biden won, Republicans gained in the U.S. House of Representatives and won more races downballot than Democrats did.

Voters had every reason to turn away from an extremely negative campaign, and one that could actually kill you if you contracted the virus at a polling place. While the presidential campaign was hostile, remember that negative campaigns can, and in this case did, charge people up to find a way to vote. To counter the virus, several states improved drop-off and mail-in balloting processes, enabling voters who didn't' feel comfortable to vote in-person do so remotely. Moreover, most of the ballots were counted quickly enough to have a result projected late Election Eve, even though most predictions said it might be days or weeks before we got a definitive winner. Virtually all downballot elections were called without being contested.

AN OPPORTUNITY FOR DEMOCRACY

The past, present, and future of democracy has always rested on good people doing the right thing, even when it was not in their political interest. While 2020 will be remembered for what went wrong, or what could have gone wrong, it is important to remember that the system works and that campaigns are getting better, not worse. The tools of the trade discussed in this book will continue to evolve over time but there is no going back. The future of campaigning will continue to become more professional, more technologically driven, and like our lives, will not slow down.

The opportunity to continue to expand and engage the electorate will remain a challenging one. My hope is that campaigns will focus more on how we bring more voters to our side than simply activating those who are already there. The further integration of data science will help, but it will also take creativity at all levels of organization, communication, and activation to make this a reality. That's the next big leap forward and I am excited about it. The more reasons we can find to persuade beyond supporter identification, creating better voter-centric appeals, the better our campaigns will be and the more unifying our governance can be.

SOURCES AND ADDITIONAL READING

Associated Press. "Two Fox News Political Executives Out After Arizona Call." January 19, 2021. https://apnews.com/article/joe-biden-donald-trump-arizona-elections-a11f8112a58eb45854be59f64d47e1dc
Baker, Peter, Haberman, Maggie, and Anni Karni. "Pence Reached His Limit with Trump. It Wasn't Pretty." *New York Times.* January 13. 2021. https://www.nytimes.com/2021/01/12/us/politics/mike-pence-trump.html
Ballotpedia. "State and Legislative Elections, 2020." Retrieved on February 2, 2021. https://ballotpedia.org/State_legislative_elections,_2020
Best, Robin E. and Steve B. Lem. "Republicans Didn't Lose Big in 2020—They Held onto Statehouses and the Power to Influence Future Elections." The Conversation. November 24, 2020. https://theconversation.com/republicans-didnt-lose-big-in-2020-they-held-onto-statehouses-and-the-power-to-influence-future-elections-150237
Caldera, Camille. "Fact Check: Biden Won the Most Total Votes—and the Fewest Total Counties—of Any President-Elect." *USA Today.* December 9, 2020. https://

www.usatoday.com/story/news/factcheck/2020/12/09/fact-check-joe-biden-won-most-votes-ever-and-fewest-counties/3865097001/

Dawsey, Josh, and Michelle Ye Hee Lee. "Trump Raises More than $170 Million Appealing on False Election Claims." December 1, 2020. https://www.washingtonpost.com/politics/trump-raises-more-than-150-million-appealing-to-false-election-claims/2020/11/30/82e922e6-3347-11eb-afe6-e4dbee9689f8_story.html

Fisher, Sara. "All the Platforms That Have Banned or Restricted Trump So Far." January 11, 2021. https://www.axios.com/platforms-social-media-ban-restrict-trump-d9e44f3c-8366-4ba9-a8a1-7f3114f920f1.html

Karni, Annie, and Maggie Haberman. "Fox's Arizona Cal for Biden Flipped the Mood at Trump Headquarters." *New York Times.* November 16, 2020. https://www.nytimes.com/2020/11/04/us/politics/trump-fox-news-arizona.html

Nobles, Ryan. "Loeffler Concedes Georgia Senate Runoff to Warnock." CNN. January 8, 2021. https://www.cnn.com/2021/01/07/politics/georgia-senate-runoff-loeffler-warnock/index.html

Scanlan, Quinn. "Here's How States Have Changed the Rules Around Voting Amid the Coronavirus Pandemic." ABC News. September 22, 2020. https://abcnews.go.com/Politics/states-changed-rules-voting-amid-coronavirus-pandemic/story?id=72309089

Swan, Jonathan and Zachary Basu. "Off the Rails: Episode Library." Series begins on January 16 and goes through February 2, 2021. https://www.axios.com/off-the-rails-episodes-cf6da824-83ac-45a6-a33c-ed8b00094e39.html

Trump, Donald J. Election Night Speech. Retrieved November 4, 2020. https://www.rev.com/blog/transcripts/donald-trump-2020-election-night-speech-transcript

Wikipedia. "Post-Election Lawsuits Related to the 2020 United States Presidential Election." Accessed on February 2, 2021. https://en.wikipedia.org/wiki/Post-election_lawsuits_related_to_the_2020_United_States_presidential_election

Zillinsky Jan, Nagler, Jonathan, and Joshua Tucker. "Which Republicans are Most Likely to Think the Election was Stolen? Those Who Dislike Democrats and Don't Mind White Nationalists." *The Washington Post.* January 19, 2021. https://www.washingtonpost.com/politics/2021/01/19/which-republicans-think-election-was-stolen-those-who-hate-democrats-dont-mind-white-nationalists/

Acknowledgments

First, I'd like to note that this book is late, at least sixteen years late. As I wrote in the preface, there are several good reasons for this, but it would have been understandable if my publisher eventually just took a pass. To the extraordinarily patient folks at Rowman & Littlefield, led by Jon Sisk, Benjamin Knepp, and Brennan Knight, I am not only grateful that you honored the deal when I handed in the book for review but hopeful it was worth the wait.

My informal team of editors was led by Dr. Tevi Troy, who unwittingly got me back on this project after we reconnected at the American Israel Political Action Committee (AIPAC) policy conference this year. His experience in writing books is unique among my core group of friends and colleagues, and his perspectives and suggestions were invaluable. Every time I picked up his book *Fight House*, I was inspired to keep writing mine.

To all of the incredible political professionals who contributed their stories to my course and to this book, you have my eternal gratitude. As I once told a colleague after I was fired from a job that I should have left months earlier, Washington is a town where it is relatively easy to find high-talent people, but matching that with high integrity is a challenge. The pros in this book, Republican and Democrat, are high on both measures, and I'm honored to be their friends.

Thank you to my mentors, including Tony Fabrizio, Mark Penn, and Celinda Lake; brilliant contemporaries of mine such as Lisa Spies, Jeff Berkowitz, Sean Gagen, Terry Sullivan, Mark Putnam, Patrick Ruffini, Alan Rosenblatt, Mark Blumenthal, and Bryon Allen; next-gen superstars, including Rory McShane, Zac Moffatt, Alex Finland, Sue Zoldak, Erik Dyskant, Dan Porter, and Matt Knee; and former star students such as Dan Bram, Tyler Giles, and Arden Dressner Levy, who brought context and stories from the front lines.

I'd like to thank Dr. Helen Shapiro, executive director of the Washington Program for the University of California system (UCDC). She took a chance on me to create the course that, seven years later, became this book. The freedom and support Dr. Shapiro has given me throughout my time at UCDC has been unique in my academic career. Her commitment to providing students all over the state of California a launching pad in DC is evidenced by how many return after graduation.

In addition, I'd like to thank others I've worked with and learned from in academia including Dr. Taylor Hahn of Johns Hopkins University; Dr. Dora Kingsley Vertenten at the University of Southern California; Drs. Lara Brown, Michael Cornfield, and Steve Billet at George Washington University; and Dr. Steven Malter at Washington University in St. Louis, who gave me my first shot at teaching college courses.

Thank you to my close group of friends who have supported me over the years, as well as challenged some of my political assumptions along the way. My own political history begins on the campus at the University of Florida where all of us studied practical politics under the guidance of everyone's mentor Myra Morgan. Those of us who are "Sons and Daughters of Spurrier" remain close to her and to each other.

To my local DMV friends and extended family, thank you for your decade-plus indulgence and encouragement of this project. All of the personal experiences and political stories we've shared over the years were with me as I was writing this during the pandemic. Many of us lost someone during this period, and our family lost David Specland, who has supported me over a lifetime and would have truly enjoyed this book.

To my kids, Jessica and Ryan: I am so proud of the both of you and hope you know that delaying this book to be a fully engaged dad when you were young is something I'd never take back. Books can wait; childhood waits for no parent.

Finally, I'd like to thank my wife of close to twenty-five years, Lisa Michelle Cohen. There were many times where I all but gave up on this project, but she kept supporting me throughout my writer's block and the years where I didn't have enough time because we were building a family and I was building a business. There were so many things ahead of this, but she always knew I'd return to it. I can't thank her enough for her confidence in me and faith that I would see this through.

Appendix

The following is a list of national political resources I recommend my students join, read, or subscribe to within the campaigning field. Some of these were discussed in the preceding chapters, but you can use this as an easy reference in case you skipped chapters irrelevant to your interests or campaign. This list will continue to develop over time, so make sure you visit http://modernpoliticalcampaigns.com every so often for an update. If you have one that I missed here, please contact me on the site or DM me on Twitter at @MPCampaigns. If it's great, national, and nonpartisan, it's in the next online and printed updates, with my thanks.

ORGANIZATIONS

There are very few national professional campaign organizations worth joining at this point, but over time I expect one to be founded specifically for digital political strategists. The professionalization of politics still has a long way to go. In the meantime, there is one main organization that most people belong to, if they belong to one at all, and two role-specific ones I can recommend:

- The American Association of Political Consultants (AAPC; http://theaapc.org/) is the umbrella organization for political professionals and the one group you must join. It's excellent for networking and awards the field's highest honors.
- For pollsters and qualitative researchers, the American Association of Public Opinion Research (AAPOR; https://www.aapor.org/) is more of an academic organization, but it has a strong professional network of professionals as well. The part of AAPOR I use the most is its old-school Listserv, where you can post questions and get well-informed answers or be directed to vendors and resources.
- National Association of Political Fundraisers (NAPF; https://www.napf.us/) is the national group for those interested in being professional fund-raisers, either in digital or working with high-dollar donors. It provides learning and networking opportunities as well as a way for clients to find you.

SUBSCRIPTIONS

Years ago, the best political content was found in print, in either daily newspapers or weekly magazines. Now, the best political daily news has moved to e-mail, online content, or podcasts. All of the following are free to subscribe, access, or download. While there are some excellent content sources on the left and the right, this list includes only those that are at least attempting to be bi- or nonpartisan.

- *Axios* AM/PM (https://www.axios.com/newsletters) by Mike Allen. Washington's most indispensable chronicler's newsletter is a very fast read that gets to the point and allows you to go deeper for more content. It also rounds up some of the brand's best reporting twice daily, so you don't have to subscribe to everything.
- *Axios* Sneak Peek (https://www.axios.com/newsletters) by Jonathan Swan. Written with the same smart brevity ethos, this is a way to get out ahead of the week politically, the newsletter covers both the White House and Congress. Weekly e-mail sent on Sundays.
- *Campaigns & Elections* (https://www.campaignsandelections.com/) began as a magazine but has become a multiplatform professional resource. The content is written by professionals in the field who do an excellent job of providing webinars and events. If the AAPC's Pollies are the formal Oscars, the AAPC's Reeds are the rowdier Golden Globe awards. Both provide excellent networking opportunities.
- *Politico* Playbook (https://www.politico.com/subscribe/playbook) by Tara Palmeri, Eugene Daniels, Ryan Lizza, and Rachel Bade. The franchise Mike Allen has grown over the years and now features four outstanding reporters. A deeper dive into national politics and sharable content. Daily e-mail.
- The Daily 202 (https://subscribe.washingtonpost.com/newsletters/?itid=nb_front_newsletters#/newsletters) by James Hohmann. The longest daily political e-mail I get every day; recently reformatted, it remains too dense to read every word. The best part of it is Hohmann's front piece, which focuses on the most important story of the day. The rest is skimmable, as main points are in bold. But in a pinch, I skip it.
- Lunchtime Politics (http://www.lunchtimepolitics.com/) by Ron Faucheux. An excellent polling update e-mailed by an industry veteran who has had a unique career as an elected official, adjunct professor, author, and pollster. During campaign season it is published daily. It's very quick and readable, and Faucheux adds his point of view in a "comment" under each set of polls. He cites who did the polls at the bottom under "Sources."

- Real Clear Politics (https://www.realclearpolitics.com/) by John McIntyre and Tom Bevan rounds up the best national political stories and has the best polling aggregator anywhere. You can subscribe to the newsletter (http://us7.campaign-archive1.com/?u=61572bb8acf7b8704903af7b8&id=e0d756898e), download the iPad app (https://apps.apple.com/us/app/real-clear-politics-for-ipad/id485836226), or just visit the website directly, like many political professionals do several times a day. This is the rare case where the website is better than the app.
- Hacks on Tap (https://www.hacksontap.com/) with Democrat David Axelrod and Republican Mike Murphy is an interesting weekly podcast between two industry veterans who competed at the highest levels. Their insight into political strategy is extremely well informed, but note that both are enthusiastically Never-Trump, so if you are a supporter this is the wrong pod for you.
- The Pollsters (http://www.thepollsters.com/) with Democrat Margie Omero and Republican Kristen Soltis Anderson is an outstanding podcast that breaks down political polling in an easy-to-understand manner. Their show notes are very detailed, so you can take a self-guided deep dive on any of the topics they cover on their show.
- FiveThirtyEight Politics (https://fivethirtyeight.com/tag/politics-podcast/) is a nerdier podcast focusing on data, modeling, statistical analysis of polls, and other information available in the political environment. While there is quite a bit of debate in the professional realm about Nate Silver and his methods (prediction is hard!), I credit his team for their transparency and determination to be nonpartisan.
- *Punchbowl News* (https://punchbowl.news/?rh_ref=6d217fcc) from two of the former authors of *Politico* Playbook, Anna Palmer and Jake Sherman, as well as their mentor and colleague John Bresnahan. The content is written primarily for a Capitol Hill policy audience, but it includes insider campaign information as well. Daily free e-mail in the morning; there is a paid subscription option that includes midday and evening editions as well as special events.

Index

About the Author

Michael D. Cohen, PhD, is CEO of Cohen Research Group, a political, public affairs, and corporate research firm. He publishes the award-winning Congress in Your Pocket suite of mobile apps and teaches college courses on political campaigns, research, digital strategy, and public policy in Washington, DC. He began his career leading political campaigns in Florida and then joined The Gallup Organization, where he served as Senior Research Director. Other career highlights include serving as Vice President of Public Affairs for Fabrizio, McLaughlin & Associates, Polling Team Lead for Microsoft, and Chief Strategy Officer for WPA Intelligence. Dr. Cohen served as assistant professor and the interim director of the political management program at The George Washington University, as well as an adjunct professor for the Johns Hopkins University graduate communications program, the University of Southern California's Price School of Public Policy, and the University of California's DC program.

He is the coauthor of "Campaigns 2016: Hashtagged Phrases and the Clinton-Trump Message War" published in *Campaigning for President 2016: Strategy and Tactics*, 3rd ed. He has appeared on various media, including CNN, Fox News, CNBC, Bloomberg, NPR, and VICE, as well as in the *New York Times*, *Washington Post*, *Campaigns & Elections* magazine, and *Politico*. Dr. Cohen is a three-time graduate and member of the Hall of Fame at the University of Florida, earning BS and MA degrees in mass communications and political campaigning and a PhD in political science. He lives in northern Virginia with his wife, Lisa, and their two children.

Connect with Dr. Cohen on LinkedIn at http: //linkedin.com/in/michaeldavidcohen

Follow Dr. Cohen on Twitter at http: //twitter.com/michaelcohen

Visit Dr. Cohen's official website at http: //michaelcohen.us

Additional book and course materials are available at http: //modern-politicalcampaigns.com

Follow *Modern Political Campaigns* on Facebook, Twitter, and Instagram @MPCampaigns.